Media Education

Media Education

*Literacy, Learning and
Contemporary Culture*

David Buckingham

polity

First published in 2003 by Polity Press in association with Blackwell Publishing Ltd

Reprinted 2004, 2005 (twice), 2006 (twice), 2007, 2008, 2009

Polity Press
65 Bridge Street
Cambridge CB2 1UR, UK

Polity Press
350 Main Street
Malden, MA 02148, USA

Library of Congress Cataloging-in-Publication Data
Buckingham, David, 1954–
Media education: literacy, learning, and contemporary culture
/ David Buckingham.
    p. cm.
Includes bibliographical references and index.
ISBN 978-0-7456-2829-5—ISBN 978-0-7456-2830-1 (pbk.)
    1. Mass media in education.   2. Media literacy.   I. Title.
LB1043 .B77 2003
371.33′5—dc21

                                          2002155222

Typeset in 10.5 on 12 pt Palatino
by Graphicraft Limited, Hong Kong

For further information on Polity, visit our website: www.polity.co.uk

Contents

Preface and Acknowledgements   ix

Part I   Rationales

1 Why Teach the Media?   3
   What are media?   3
   What is media education?   4
   Why media education?   5
   The evolution of media education in the UK   6
   Democratization and defensiveness   9
   Towards a new paradigm   12
   Moving ahead: teaching and learning   14
   Moving ahead: a bigger picture   15
   A continuing story   17

2 New Media Childhoods   18
   Childhood and the media   19
   Changing childhoods   21
   Technologies   23
   Economics   25
   Texts   27
   Audiences   29
   Implications for education   32

3 Media Literacies   35
    Defining literacy   36
    A social theory of literacies   38
    Mapping media literacies   39
    Beyond the magic window   42
    Reality problems   44
    The limits of assessment   47
    Why literacy?   49

Part II   The State of the Art

4 Defining the Field   53
    Production   54
    Language   55
    Representation   57
    Audiences   59
    Key concepts in practice   61
    Conclusion: some general principles   67

5 Classroom Strategies   70
    Textual analysis   71
    Contextual analysis   73
    Case studies   75
    Translations   77
    Simulations   79
    Production   82
    Conclusion   84

6 Locating Media Education   86
    A separate academic subject: Media Studies   87
    Media education across the curriculum   89
    Media education in language and literature teaching   93
    Media education and ICTs   95
    Vocational media education   98
    Media education beyond the classroom   99
    Conclusion   101

Part III   Media Learning

7   Becoming Critical   107
    The social functions of 'criticism'   109
    Critical language games   111
    Approaching 'ideology'   114
    Learning critical discourse   119
    Beyond criticism?   120

8   Getting Creative   123
    Changing practices   125
    The limits of 'creativity'   127
    The social worlds of production   128
    Writing media   131
    Using genres   134
    Conclusion   137

9   Defining Pedagogy   139
    Understanding conceptual learning   140
    Towards a dynamic model   143
    Researching audiences: the social self   146
    Self-evaluation: from practice to theory   149
    Beyond the model   153

Part IV   New Directions

10   Politics, Pleasure and Play   157
    Postmodern identities?   158
    Playful pedagogies   162
    The politics of parody   165
    Working through pleasure?   169
    Conclusion   171

11   Digital Literacies   173
    Towards digital literacies   175
    Models of digital production   179
    The meanings of 'access'   181
    Processes and products   183
    Technology and pedagogy   186

12 New Sites of Learning   189
    Media education beyond the classroom   191
    Media and youth work   194
    Media and 'informal' learning   196
    Evaluation   199
    Towards deschooling?   201

References   204
Index   216

Preface and Acknowledgements

When I started work on this book, I was alarmed to discover that I had been involved in media education – as a teacher, teacher trainer and researcher – for almost a quarter of a century. In some ways, this is a book I could probably have attempted to write several years ago. Indeed, to some extent, it represents a summation of a body of work that I have been engaged in over the past two decades; although it is also a book that looks forward, to respond to the new challenges that currently face media educators. I have set out to provide a clear and comprehensive overview of the field, drawing on my own and others' research, and on what is now a well-established body of educational practice; but I have also sought to raise further questions, and to lay the ground for future developments.

My immediate motivation for writing the book, however, arises from a sense of frustration. This has at least three dimensions. Firstly, like many advocates of media education, I am frustrated by the lack of progress we seem to have made among educational policy-makers in recent years. Where students are free to choose it – and teachers free to offer it – media education continues to expand at a quite alarming rate. Yet in the core of the school curriculum – at least in the UK – there is still little more than a token recognition of its importance. This is not to say that the case has not been made, merely that it has not been listened to. It is still common for popular commentators on education, and some media professionals, to dismiss media education on the basis of prejudice and ignorance; and despite occasional signs of commitment to the field, policy-makers still appear to be ill-informed about its basic aims and methods. It is quite extraordinary that the majority of young people should go through their school careers with so little opportunity to study and engage with the most significant contemporary forms of culture and communication. Clearly, there is an argument here that still needs to be made.

Secondly, I am frustrated by some of the strategies that have been adopted by supporters of media education in recent years. Among academics, there has been a flourishing of esoteric political rhetoric and an increasing taste for utopian fantasies about educational change. While these tendencies may reflect an understandable rejection of the 'fundamentalism' of contemporary educational policy, the general enthusiasm for wholesale change can lead to a neglect of the value of what is already happening in the field. Meanwhile, I have also been dismayed by the haste with which some advocates of media education have sought to reposition it in line with passing trends in educational policy. Re-branding media education in order to align it with the latest emphasis on 'creativity' – or, in particular, with the push to implement new technologies in schools – is, in my view, quite short-sighted. Some of these issues will be taken up in the chapters that follow, although my primary intention here is not to 'settle scores' or to engage in the kind of in-fighting that has become rather too common in our field. Here again, my aim is to emphasize what I regard as fundamental, shared principles; and to identify a coherent basis for real educational practices.

Thirdly, I am frustrated by the fact that teachers of media education still seem to be insufficiently recognized and supported. Despite the generally inhospitable climate, there is a great deal of excellent work being done in the field by highly dedicated teachers and committed students. Media education generates a degree of enthusiasm and enjoyment that is all too rare in contemporary schooling; and it offers a form of educational practice that is not just engaging for students, but also intellectually rigorous, challenging and relevant to their everyday lives. Without being at all uncritical of what goes on, I believe this is something we should affirm and celebrate.

This book is therefore partly a restatement of the case for media education – albeit one that tries to take account of changing times. It sets out a rationale for media teaching that reflects the changing nature of contemporary culture, and of young people's experiences. It outlines a conceptual framework, a set of pedagogic principles and a role for media education in a range of curriculum locations. While recognizing some of the difficulties and contradictions of teaching and learning in this field, it points towards a model of 'media pedagogy' that is both theoretically coherent and practically possible. And it also seeks to provide a measured response to some of the new developments and challenges that currently face media educators. My main focus is on media education in schools, and particularly secondary schools. While the book inevitably draws primarily on the situation in the UK, it has been consciously written for an international readership.

This is not a 'how-to-do-it' book. It does not provide detailed suggestions for classroom activities, or teaching materials that can be adapted for use in lessons or projects. Nor is it a potted summary of the current state of academic research on the media, which teachers might then be expected to transmit to their students. Many other books and resources of this kind already exist; and in any case, teaching materials need to be specific to students' and teachers' needs, in ways that a book of this kind cannot hope to be. In my view, the best teaching happens when teachers have really thought through what they are doing, and are therefore committed to students' learning. It does not happen when teachers simply implement the available plans or 'deliver' curriculum resources, however good they may be. Good teaching also depends upon teachers taking account of their students' own cultures and perspectives, and paying close attention to how they learn. These things depend upon having a clear set of aims, a coherent conceptual framework, and an understanding of the dynamics and complexities of teaching and learning. These are what this book sets out to provide.

The book is in four parts. Part I addresses the fundamental aims of media education. It looks at how the field has developed historically; at the changing nature of the modern media; and at the forms of 'literacy' they now require of young people. Part II defines the 'state of the art' of media education today. It outlines the conceptual basis of the field; the range of teaching and learning strategies that are used; and the place of media education within and beyond the school curriculum. Part III considers the nature of teaching and learning in media education in more detail. It looks at the complementary practices of critical analysis and creative production in media classrooms; and outlines a model of 'media pedagogy' that relates the different aspects of the field. Part IV discusses the challenges and opportunities currently facing media education. It focuses specifically on the changing nature of 'identity politics'; the impact of new media technologies; and the potential for using and learning about the media beyond the school classroom.

I have drawn here, both directly and indirectly, on the guidance and inspiration of a great many people. Among them, I would count my current and former colleagues Bob Ferguson, Ken Jones, Chris Richards and Andrew Burn; the members of various Media Teachers' Research Groups, past and present; colleagues at the British Film Institute, particularly Cary Bazalgette; current and past doctoral students who have worked on aspects of media education – Sara Bragg, Rebekah Willett, Hyeon-Seon Jeong, Chris Richards, Julian Sefton-Green, Steve Archer, Issy Harvey, Liesbeth de Block, Keith Perera, Elizabeth Funge, Shaku Banaji and Seon-Jeong Ki; and the numerous classroom teachers from whom I have learned over the years, including Pete Fraser, Netia Mayman, Peter Male and Celia Greenwood. I am particularly grateful to Julian Sefton-Green, with whom much of the empirical research reported in Part III of this book was undertaken. And I owe an enormous debt to the person who has done more than anyone else to define and support good practice in media education in Britain: Jenny Grahame of the English and Media Centre.

While some of the material presented here has been published previously, it has been extensively re-worked and rewritten for this book. Where relevant, original sources are cited in the text.

Part I

Rationales

Why should we teach and study the media? Part I explores the changing arguments for media education, and the assumptions on which they are based. Chapter 1 considers the history of the field, and its fundamental aims and principles. Chapter 2 looks at children's changing media environment, and its implications for media educators. Chapter 3 addresses the notion of 'media literacy' and its uses and limitations in media teaching. Taken together, these three chapters set out to provide a comprehensive, contemporary rationale for media education.

1

Why Teach the Media?

What are media?

My dictionary defines a 'medium' as 'an intervening means, instrument or agency': it is a substance or a channel through which effects or information can be carried or transmitted. A medium is something we use when we want to communicate with people *indirectly*, rather than in person or by face-to-face contact. This dictionary definition tells us something fundamental about the media, which forms the basis of the media education curriculum. The media do not offer a transparent window on the world. They provide channels through which representations and images of the world can be communicated *indirectly*. The media *intervene*: they provide us ← *Bias?* with selective versions of the world, rather than direct access to it.

As I will use it in this book, the term 'media' includes the whole range of modern communications media: television, the cinema, video, radio, photography, advertising, newspapers and magazines, recorded music, computer games and the internet. Media *texts* are the programmes, films, images, web sites (and so on) that are carried by these different forms of communication. Many of these are often called 'mass' media, which implies that they reach large audiences; although of course some media are intended to reach only quite small or specialized audiences. And there is no reason why more traditional forms such as books cannot also be seen as 'media', since they too provide us with mediated versions or representations of the world.

In principle, the questions and approaches outlined in this book can be applied to the whole range of media – from big-budget blockbuster movies to the snapshot photographs that people take in their daily lives; and from the latest pop video or computer game to the best-known 'classic' films or literature. All these media are equally worthy of study, and there is no logical reason why they should be considered separately. The claim that we should study 'literature' in isolation from other kinds of printed texts, or films in isolation from other kinds of moving image media, clearly reflects broader social judgements about the *value* of these different forms – and while these judgements may be institutionalized within the curriculum, they are nevertheless increasingly questionable.

What is media education?

Media texts often combine several 'languages' or forms of communication – visual images (still or moving), audio (sound, music or speech) and written language. Media education therefore aims to develop a broad-based competence, not just in relation to print, but also in these other symbolic systems of images and sounds. This competence is frequently described as a form of *literacy*; and it is argued that, in the modern world, 'media literacy' is just as important for young people as the more traditional literacy of print.

Media *education*, then, is the process of teaching and learning about media; media *literacy* is the outcome – the knowledge and skills learners acquire. As I shall argue in more detail in chapter 3, media literacy necessarily involves 'reading' and 'writing' media. Media education therefore aims to develop *both* critical understanding *and* active participation. It enables young people to interpret and make informed judgements as consumers of media; but it also enables them to become producers of media in their own right. Media education is about developing young people's critical *and* creative abilities.

Media education, therefore, is concerned with teaching and learning *about* the media. This should not be confused with teaching *through* or *with* the media – for example, the use of television or computers as means of teaching science or history. Of course, these educational media also provide versions or representations of the world; and, for that reason, media educators have often sought to challenge the instrumental use of media as 'teaching aids'. This emphasis is particularly important in relation to the contemporary enthusiasm for new technologies in education, where media are frequently seen as neutral means of delivering 'information'. Yet while it can have a fruitful critical dialogue with these areas, media education should not be confused with educational technology or with educational media.

Why media education?

education

Media is important because young people spend most of their time interacting w/media.

Why should we be teaching young people about the media? Most rationales for media education tend to begin by documenting the statistical significance of the media in contemporary children's lives. Surveys repeatedly show that, in most industrialized countries, children now spend more time watching television than they do in school, or indeed on any other activity apart from sleeping (e.g. Livingstone and Bovill, 2001; Rideout et al., 1999). If we add to this the time they devote to films, magazines, computer games and popular music, it is clear that the media constitute by far their most significant leisure-time pursuit.

These points often lead on to broader assertions about the economic, social and cultural importance of the media in modern societies. The media are major industries, generating profit and employment; they provide us with most of our information about the political process; and they offer us ideas, images and representations (both factual and fictional) that inevitably shape our view of reality. The media are undoubtedly the major contemporary means of cultural expression and communication: to become an active participant in public life necessarily involves making use of the modern media. The media, it is often argued, have now taken the place of the family, the church and the school as the major socializing influence in contemporary society.

Of course, this is not to imply that the media are all-powerful, or that they necessarily promote a singular and consistent view of the world. Yet it is to suggest that they are now ubiquitous and unavoidable. The media are embedded in the textures and routines of everyday life, and they provide many of the 'symbolic resources' we use to conduct and interpret our relationships and to define our identities. As Roger Silverstone (1999) has argued, the media are now 'at the core of experience, at the heart of our capacity or incapacity to make sense of the world in which we live'. And, as he suggests, it is for this reason that we should study them.

In these terms, therefore, the argument for media education is essentially an argument for making the curriculum *relevant* to children's lives outside school, and to the wider society. In practice, however, many rationales for media education adopt a much less neutral approach. Media education is typically regarded as a solution to a problem; and children's relationship with the media is seen, not so much as a fact of modern life, but as a harmful and damaging phenomenon that educators must seek to confront. As we shall see, the reasons why that relationship is seen to represent a problem – and hence the nature of the solutions which are offered – are quite variable. For some, the central concern is about the media's apparent lack of *cultural value*, as compared with the 'classics' of great art or literature; while for others, the problem is to do with the undesirable *attitudes* or *forms of behaviour* which they are seen to promote.

Like any other field of education, then, media education has been characterized by an ongoing debate about its fundamental aims and methods. Few teachers are initially trained in media education; and they therefore tend to approach it from diverse disciplinary backgrounds, and with diverse motivations. One way of tracing these different rationales and motivations is through a historical perspective. In the following sections, I will offer a brief account of the historical evolution of approaches to media education, specifically in the UK, although the broad lines of this development have been replicated elsewhere.

The evolution of media education in the UK

Recovering the history of educational change is not an easy undertaking. While it is possible to rely on published sources – for example, on 'handbooks' for teachers, on teaching materials and curriculum documents, and on professional journals – these can give only a limited insight into the realities of classroom practice. Yet on this basis at least, it is possible to divide the early history of media education in the UK into three broad phases (for more extensive accounts, see Alvarado and Boyd-Barrett, 1992; Alvarado, Gutch and Wollen, 1987; Masterman, 1985).

Discrimination

The most commonly quoted starting point in this history can be found in the work of the literary critic F. R. Leavis and his student Denys Thompson. Their book *Culture and Environment: The Training of Critical Awareness* (1933) represented the first systematic set of proposals for teaching about the mass media in schools. The book, which was revised and reprinted a number of times over the

Leavis wanted students to resist media

following two decades, contains a series of classroom exercises using extracts from journalism, popular fiction and advertisements. This approach was subsequently promoted through journals like the *Use of English*, which Thompson edited, and found its way into several official reports on education.

The central mission for Leavis and his associates was the preservation of the literary heritage, and the language, the values and the health of the nation it was seen to embody and to represent. The media were seen here as a corrupting influence, offering superficial pleasures in place of the authentic values of great art and literature. The aim of teaching about popular culture, therefore, was to encourage students to 'discriminate and resist' – to arm themselves against the commercial manipulation of the mass media and hence to recognize the self-evident merits of 'high' culture.

This process of training students in 'discrimination' and 'critical awareness' has been described by subsequent critics as a form of 'inoculation' – in other words, as a means of protection against disease (Halloran and Jones, 1968; Masterman, 1980). What remains notable about it in educational terms is its extraordinary self-confidence. Leavis and Thompson sought to enable teachers to expose what they saw as the crude exploitation and the cheap emotional falsity of popular culture; and they took for granted that, once exposed, it would be recognized and condemned.

Cultural studies and the popular arts

The next phase in this brief history brings us forward to the late 1950s and early 1960s, and to the founding moment of 'British Cultural Studies'. Most explicitly in the work of Raymond Williams (1958, 1961) and Richard Hoggart (1959), this approach offered a challenge to the Leavisite notion of 'culture'. Culture was no longer seen here as a fixed set of privileged artefacts – an approved 'canon' of literary texts, for example – but as 'a whole way of life'; and cultural expression was seen to take a whole range of forms, from the exalted to the everyday. This more inclusive approach thus began to challenge the distinctions between high culture and popular culture, and ultimately between art and lived experience.

The key text which sought to disseminate this approach to teachers in schools was *The Popular Arts* (1964) by Stuart Hall and Paddy Whannel, which offered an extensive range of suggestions for teaching about the media, and particularly about the cinema. This less obviously 'inoculative' approach to studying the media was also reflected in teaching materials and in official reports of the time. Graham Murdock and Guy Phelps (1973), in a research study of secondary schools, found that the Leavisite approach was steadily losing ground as younger teachers sought to recognize and to build upon their students' everyday cultural experiences.

Nevertheless, this approach still sought to preserve fundamental cultural distinctions. Hoggart (1959), for example, clearly distinguished between the 'living' culture of the industrial working classes and the 'processed' culture which derived from Hollywood – striking a characteristically anti-American tone which was also apparent in the work of Leavis. Likewise, in Hall and Whannel (1964) and in the Newsom Report on English teaching which was published in the previous year (Department of Education and Science, 1963), distinctions between high culture and popular culture were not so much abolished as shifted. Thus, while teachers were now encouraged to consider films in the classroom – although preferably European or British films – the increasingly dominant medium of television remained quite beyond the pale.

Screen Education and demystification

In the 1970s, we can identify another paradigm shift, again deriving initially from the academy. The key development here was that of 'Screen theory', as expounded in the pages of the journals *Screen* and *Screen Education*. *Screen* was the most significant vehicle for new developments in semiotics, structuralism, psychoanalytic theory, post-structuralism, and Marxist theories of ideology. The difficult role of *Screen Education* was to suggest how these academic approaches might be applied to classrooms in schools – although this was a task that it addressed only intermittently (see Alvarado, Collins and Donald, 1993).

The most influential exponent of this approach was undoubtedly Len Masterman (1980, 1985). In fact, Masterman was highly critical of what he regarded as the academic elitism of *Screen* theory; yet his books *Teaching about Television* (1980) and *Teaching the Media* (1985) shared the central concerns of that theory with questions of language, ideology and representation. The fundamental aim here was to reveal the constructed nature of media texts, and thereby to show how media representations reinforced the ideologies of dominant groups within society.

Masterman strongly rejected what he saw as the middle-class, evaluative approach of Leavis and his inheritors – an approach which he suggested remained prevalent among teachers of English. By contrast, he promoted analytical methods drawn from semiology, which were seen to offer the promise of objectivity and analytical rigour. (These methods will be considered more fully in chapters 5 and 7.) These forms of analysis were to be combined with the detailed study of the economics of the media industries (Masterman, 1985). Students were urged to put aside their subjective responses and pleasures, and to engage in systematic forms of analysis which would expose the 'hidden' ideologies of the media – and thereby 'liberate' themselves from their influence. *Discrimination* on the grounds of cultural value was thus effectively replaced by a form of political or ideological *demystification*.

Democratization and defensiveness

This brief history inevitably neglects some of the complexities of these various positions, and the historical contexts in which they were formed. A fuller analysis of the evolution of media education would need to locate these approaches within the changing social and cultural climate of their times; and in particular to relate them to the ongoing struggles for control over educational policy-making.

With these qualifications in mind, however, it is possible to read this history in terms of two contradictory tendencies. On the one hand, the development of media education is part of a wider move towards *democratization* – a process whereby students' out-of-school cultures are gradually recognized as valid and worthy of consideration in the school curriculum. In these terms, media education could be seen as one dimension of the 'progressive' educational strategies that began to gain widespread acceptance in the 1960s and 1970s. For example, students of English were increasingly encouraged to write about their everyday experiences; to discuss the poetry of popular songs; and to debate contemporary social issues. Such strategies attempted to 'validate' students' cultures, and to build connections between the cultures of the school and those of the home and the peer group.

This move reflected the growing recognition that the traditional academic curriculum was inadequate for the large majority of students, and particularly for working-class students. Even in the work of Leavis and Thompson, one can detect an acknowledgement that teachers had to begin by working with the cultures that students brought with them into the classroom, rather than seeking merely to impose the values of 'high' culture. In more recent years, this democratization of the curriculum should also be seen as part of a wider political move, which is apparent in different ways in the work of Williams and in the project of *Screen Education*. The attempt to include popular culture within the curriculum represented a direct challenge to the elitism of established literary culture; and in this respect, it was implicitly informed by a wider class politics.

On the other hand, however, this history is also one of *defensiveness*. It reflects a long-standing suspicion of the media and popular culture that might be seen as a defining characteristic of modern education systems (Lusted, 1985). Despite the growing inclusiveness of the curriculum, all these approaches seek in different ways to inoculate or protect students against what are assumed to be the negative effects of the media. Such an approach is implicitly premised on a notion of the media as an enormously powerful (and almost entirely negative) influence, and of children as particularly vulnerable to manipulation. Teaching children about the media – enabling them to analyse how media texts are constructed, and to understand the economic functions of the media industries – is seen as a way of 'empowering' them to resist such influences. In the process, it is argued, children will become rational consumers, able to view the media in a 'critical' and distanced way.

This defensiveness may have several motivations, which take on a different significance at different times and in different national and cultural contexts. Particularly in the work of Leavis and his followers, there is a powerful form of *cultural* defensiveness – that is, an attempt to protect children from the media on the grounds of their apparent lack of cultural value, and thereby to lead the children on to superior forms of art and literature. While they are now distinctly unfashionable in some circles, such motivations nevertheless often underlie more apparently 'objective' or 'political' concerns. As in the case of Leavis and Hoggart, they are often reinforced by a resistance to what is seen as American cultural imperialism – which (for obvious reasons) is particularly prominent in English-speaking countries, and to some degree in Latin America.

More recently, it is possible to identify a form of *political* defensiveness, which is most apparent in the third perspective outlined above. Here the aim is to use media education, and particularly media analysis, as a means of disabusing students of false beliefs and ideologies. This remains a major motivation for media educators in many countries, although since the 1970s the range of concerns addressed here has increasingly encompassed wider forms of 'identity politics', particularly around issues of gender and ethnicity. From this perspective, it is the media that are seen to be primarily responsible for making students sexist or racist; and it is through media analysis that such ideologies will be displaced or overcome.

Less apparent in the UK, but a powerful motivation for media educators elsewhere, is what might be termed a *moral* defensiveness. In the United States, for example, media education is strongly motivated by anxieties about the effects of sex and violence in the media, and to some extent about the media's role in promoting consumerism or materialism. Here again, the media are seen to be primarily responsible for inculcating these false beliefs or behaviours – for encouraging children to believe that all their problems can be solved through violence, or through the acquisition of material goods. And it is through a rigorous training in media analysis that such dangers can be prevented or overcome (Anderson, 1980).

In each case, therefore, media education is proposed as a way of dealing with some very wide and complex social problems – and if the media are routinely identified as the overriding cause of these problems, media education frequently seems to be seen as the solution. In the process, the need to consider any of the more intractable causes of such problems – or any more thoroughgoing and potentially unpalatable ways of dealing with them – is neatly side-stepped. For example, if we can blame the media for the rise in violence, media education becomes a sensible alternative to gun control, or to addressing poverty or racism. Media education therefore comes to be seen, not just as an alternative form of media regulation – a liberal alternative to censorship, perhaps – but as a means of modifying more general attitudes and behaviours (see Bragg, 2001).

As in media research, these arguments tend to recur as new media enter the scene. For instance, the advent of the internet has seen a resurgence of many of these protectionist arguments for media education. Much public debate about children's uses of the internet has focused on the dangers of pornography, on paedophiles lurking in chat rooms and on the seductions of online marketing. Here, media education is yet again perceived by some as a kind of inoculation – a means of preventing contamination, if not of keeping children away from the media entirely. In this scenario, the potential benefits and pleasures of the media are neglected in favour of an exclusive – and in some instances, highly exaggerated – emphasis on the harm they are assumed to cause.

Yet however diverse these concerns may be, the positions that students and teachers appear to occupy here remain remarkably consistent. By and large, students are seen to be particularly at risk from the negative influence of the media, and as seemingly unable to resist their power; while teachers are somehow assumed to be able to stand outside this process, providing students with the tools of critical analysis which will 'liberate' them. In each case, media education is regarded as a means of counteracting children's apparent fascination and pleasure in the media – and hence (it would seem) their belief in the values the media are seen to promote. Media education will, it is assumed, automatically lead children on to an appreciation of high culture, to more morally healthy forms of behaviour, or to more rational, politically correct beliefs. It is seen to offer nothing less than a means of salvation.

Towards a new paradigm

To some degree, all the approaches outlined above have remained influential. Yet in the last decade, media education in the UK and in many other countries has begun to move into a further new phase. While protectionist views have been far from superseded, there has been a gradual evolution towards a less defensive approach. In general, the countries with the most 'mature' forms of practice in media education – that is, those which have the longest history, and the most consistent pattern of development – have moved well beyond protectionism. (For accounts of the evolution of media education internationally, see Bazalgette, Bévort and Saviano, 1992; Buckingham and Domaille, 2001; Hart, 1998; Kubey, 1997; and Von Feilitzen and Carlsson, 1999.)

There have been several reasons for this shift. To some degree, it reflects changing views of young people's relationships with the media, both in academic research and in public debate more generally. The notion of the media as bearers of a singular set of ideologies and beliefs – or indeed as uniformly harmful or lacking in cultural value – is no longer so easy to sustain. Of course, there are still significant limits in the diversity of views and cultural forms represented in the mainstream media; but the development of modern communication has resulted in a more heterogeneous, even fragmented, environment, in which the boundaries between high culture and popular culture have become extremely blurred. Likewise, the notion that the media are an all-powerful 'consciousness industry' – that they can single-handedly impose false values on passive audiences – has also come into question. Contemporary research suggests that children are a much more autonomous and critical audience than they are conventionally assumed to be; and this is increasingly recognized by the media industries themselves.

To some extent, this shift is also part of a broader development in thinking about the regulation of the media. Technological changes are making it increasingly difficult to prevent children gaining access to material that is deemed harmful or unsuitable; and regulation of this kind can restrict their opportunities for active participation. Among media regulators themselves, the emphasis is now moving away from censorship, and towards 'consumer advice' – of which media education is often seen as one dimension (Buckingham and Sefton-Green, 1997). Meanwhile, there has also been a growing recognition among educators that the protectionist approach does not actually work in practice. Especially when it comes to the areas with which media education is so centrally concerned – with what students see as their own cultures and their own pleasures – they may well be inclined to resist or reject what teachers tell them.

To some extent, these developments could also be seen as the result of a generational shift. There is evidence that younger teachers today, who have grown up with electronic media, are more relaxed in their attitudes: they are less likely to see themselves as missionaries denouncing the influence of the media, and are more enthusiastic about young people using media as forms of cultural expression (Morgan, 1998a; Richards, 1998a). For this generation, a merely defensive approach to media education would be at odds with their own experience as media consumers, and would place them in a false, paternalistic position as teachers.

Taken together, these developments are leading to the emergence of a new paradigm for media education. Media education is now no longer so automatically opposed to students' experiences of the media. It does not begin from the view that the media are necessarily and inevitably harmful, or that young people are simply passive victims of media influence. On the contrary, it adopts a more student-centred perspective, which begins from young people's existing knowledge and experience of media, rather than from the instructional imperatives of the teacher. It does not aim to shield young people from the influence of the media, and thereby to lead them on to 'better things', but to enable them to make informed decisions on their own behalf. Media education is seen here not as a form of *protection*, but as a form of *preparation*.

In some respects, this rationale appears rather more 'neutral' than those described above. In broad terms, it aims to develop young people's *understanding* of, and *participation* in, the media culture that surrounds them (Bazalgette, 1989). Advocates of this approach emphasize the importance of media education as part of a more general form of 'democratic citizenship', although they also recognize the importance of students' enjoyment and pleasure in the media.

Broadly speaking, therefore, this new approach seeks to begin with what students *already* know, and with their existing tastes and pleasures in the media, rather than assuming that these are merely invalid or 'ideological'. This approach does not seek to replace 'subjective' responses with 'objective' ones, or to neutralize the pleasures of the media through rational analysis. On the contrary, it aims to develop a more reflexive style of teaching and learning, in which students can reflect on their own activity both as 'readers' and as 'writers' of media texts, and understand the broader social and economic factors that are in play. Critical analysis is seen here as a process of dialogue, rather than a matter of arriving at an agreed or predetermined position.

From this perspective, media production by students also assumes a much greater significance. Of course, the primary aim of media education is not to train the television producers and journalists of the future: this is a task for higher education, and for the media industries themselves. Nevertheless, the participatory potential of new technologies – and particularly of the internet – has made it much more possible for young people to undertake creative media production, and for teachers to do so with their students. By emphasizing the development of young people's creativity, and their participation in media production, media educators are enabling their voices to be heard; and in the longer term, they are also providing the basis for more democratic and inclusive forms of media production in the future.

Moving ahead: teaching and learning

One major aim of this book is to define, explain and illustrate this more contemporary approach to media education. In particular, part II offers a systematic and detailed account of the conceptual framework of media education, of its characteristic teaching strategies, and of the possibilities for media education in a range of curriculum areas.

However, the book also seeks to explore a series of unresolved questions and problems in the field; and to address some new challenges. To some extent, these questions reflect a general 'coming of age' of media education. In the past ten years, media educators have increasingly begun to reflect on their own practice, and to cast a more self-critical eye on the effectiveness of their work. There has been a new attention to questions about students' *learning* in media education. To some extent, these questions relate to broader theoretical debates in academic studies of the media – debates, for example, about the relationship between pleasure and ideology, and about the place of 'rational' analysis. Yet there are also specific pedagogical issues here. How are we to identify what students already know about the media? How do they *acquire* 'critical' or conceptual understandings? How do they learn to use the media to express themselves and to communicate with others? How do they relate the academic discourse of the subject to their own experiences as media users? How can we evaluate evidence of their learning? And how can we be sure that media education actually makes a difference?

In addressing these and related questions in part III of the book, I will be drawing on the insights of classroom-based research conducted by myself and my colleagues over the past ten years. This research questions many of the grandiose claims of previous approaches to media education; and in many respects, it reflects a broader challenge to 'modernist' conceptions of education as a means of developing forms of 'critical consciousness' or rationality. Indeed, to some extent, it emerges from a more widespread rethinking of some of the earlier assumptions of 'progressive' educational practice (Buckingham, 1998). However, the aim here is not merely to deconstruct the certainties of previous generations of purportedly radical educators; it is also to provide the basis for a more coherent and inclusive conception of what *counts* as learning.

Moving ahead: a bigger picture

In addition to these more 'internal' questions, there has also been a range of broader developments that have complex implications for media educators. To some degree, they make the case for media education all the more urgent; yet they also suggest that it needs to be extended – and perhaps rethought.

The proliferation of media technologies, the commercialization and globalization of media markets, the fragmentation of mass audiences and the rise of 'interactivity' are all fundamentally transforming young people's everyday experiences of media. In this new environment, children have increasingly come to be seen as a valuable target market for the media industries. Children today can and do gain access to 'adult' media, via cable TV or video or the internet, much more readily than their parents ever could; but they also have their own 'media spheres', which adults may find increasingly difficult to penetrate or understand. Digital media

– and particularly the internet – significantly increase the potential for active participation; yet for the large majority of children who do not yet have access to these opportunities, there is a growing danger of exclusion and disenfranchisement.

These developments, and their implications for young people, will be considered in more detail in chapter 2; yet it is important to stress that they are not simply confined to the domain of the media. On the contrary, they reflect much broader tendencies in the contemporary world, which have been widely discussed and debated by a range of social theorists. At least in Western countries, the shift towards a 'post-industrial' consumer society is seen to have destabilized existing patterns of employment, settlement and social life. Established social institutions, the rules of conduct of civil society and traditional conceptions of citizenship are increasingly being called into question. Meanwhile, economic and cultural globalization has precipitated a crisis in the legitimacy of the nation state, and begun to reconfigure the relations between the local and the global.

Many social commentators agree that the contemporary world is characterized by a growing sense of fragmentation and individualization. Long-standing systems of belief and ways of life are being eroded, and familiar hierarchies overthrown. Social and geographical mobility is undermining traditional social bonds, such as those of family and community; and the majority of young people today are growing up in increasingly heterogeneous, multicultural societies, in which very different conceptions of morality and very different cultural traditions exist side-by-side. In this context, identity comes to be seen as a matter of individual choice, rather than birthright or destiny; and in the process, it is argued, individuals have also become more diverse – and to some extent more autonomous – in their uses and interpretations of cultural goods. Yet despite appearances, these new societies are also more unequal and more polarized than those they appear to be replacing.

These developments are also seen to have unsettling implications for education (Usher and Edwards, 1994). Educators, it is argued, can no longer see themselves as 'legislators', imposing the values and norms of official culture. The best they can hope for is to act as 'interpreters', making available 'multiple realities' and diverse forms of perception and knowledge. Meanwhile, the missionary rhetoric of public schooling – its claim to 'emancipate' students from power, and transform them into autonomous social agents – has been condemned as merely another illusion of capitalist modernity.

The nature and extent of these developments is certainly very debatable, although there is little doubt about the central role of the media – and of consumer culture more broadly – in the continuing transformation of modern societies. On one level, this would seem to reinforce the need for media education; yet it also raises some significant questions about its characteristic forms and practices. The 'identity politics' of contemporary media education, with their emphasis on rationality and 'realist' conceptions of representation, need to be questioned, as does the rhetoric of 'democratic citizenship' on which they are often based. Technological developments challenge conventional distinctions between critical analysis and creative production, and may create opportunities for very different – and much more 'playful' – forms of pedagogic practice. And as the legitimacy of the school as a social institution itself comes into question, we need to assess the potential contribution of media education to new forms of learning, beyond the classroom. All these are issues that will be taken up in more detail in part IV of this book.

A continuing story

This introductory chapter has sought to provide an overview of some of the key issues and arguments that will be explored in more detail in the remainder of the book. It has offered a brief outline of the history of media education, and suggested some of the factors at stake in its continuing development. However, it has sought to avoid the temptations of a teleological account – as though the bad old ideas of the past had simply been thrown out in favour of the good new ideas of the present. While this book will seek to explain and to justify the current 'state of the art' in media education, it will also question it and point beyond it. Like any form of educational practice, media education needs a clear model of the curriculum and a coherent theory of learning. Yet if they are to remain alive to changing circumstances, and to students' changing needs and experiences, media teachers also need to reflect on their own practice, and to be ready to respond to new challenges. As this book will make clear, the evolving story of media education is thankfully very far from concluded.

2

New Media Childhoods

Our approach to media education is bound to depend upon the assumptions we make about the relationships between media and their audiences. To what extent do the media simply impose 'negative' messages on passive minds, as many media educators have tended to suppose? To what extent do audiences have the power to create their own meanings and pleasures? And in what ways can *children* be seen as a 'special' audience, with distinctive characteristics and needs? Clearly, these are questions that cannot be answered in the abstract. As I indicated in chapter 1, contemporary social and cultural changes are having a significant impact on the nature of children's experiences of the media – and these are changes that media educators cannot afford to ignore. If we intend to start – as I have suggested we should – with what children *already* know about the media, we need to situate that knowledge and experience within a broader social and historical context.

Public debates about these issues typically overstate the negative and (less frequently) the positive influences of media in children's lives. In this chapter, I present a more complex analysis of the changing nature of children's media environment, which builds on the account contained in my book *After the Death of Childhood* (2000a). I suggest that we need to understand the role of the media as a dynamic and multi-faceted process, a matter of the interaction between *technologies, economics, texts* and *audiences*. A discussion of these four elements forms the core of this chapter; and in the final section, I consider some of the general implications of these arguments for the aims and practices of media education.

Childhood and the media

It is possible to identify two contrasting views of the relationship between children and media, both of which have been influential in popular and academic debate. On the one hand, there is the idea that childhood as we know it is dying or disappearing, and that the media are primarily to blame for this. On the other, there is the idea that the media are now a force of liberation for children – that they are creating a new 'electronic generation' that is more open, more democratic, more socially aware than their parents' generation. In some ways, these two views are diametrically opposed, not least in their underlying assumptions about childhood; yet there are also some striking similarities between them.

The notion that the media are destroying childhood is most popularly associated with the American critic Neil Postman's book *The Disappearance of Childhood* (1983). Essentially, Postman argues that our modern conception of childhood was a creation of the print media; and that new media, particularly television, are destroying it. According to him, this is primarily to do with children's access to information. Whereas acquiring print literacy took a long period of apprenticeship, we don't have to learn to read or interpret television. Television is, he argues, a 'total disclosure medium': through television, children are increasingly learning about the 'secrets' of adult life – sex, drugs, violence – that would previously have been hidden in the specialized code of print. As a result, they are increasingly coming to behave like adults, and to demand access to adult privileges.

One can certainly challenge Postman on the grounds of his evidence, both about the incidence of the phenomena he is describing and about his explanation of the causes (see Buckingham, 2000a). But his argument also rests on a set of assumptions about childhood and about the media that are highly questionable. Ultimately, Postman's position is that of a technological determinist: technology is seen to produce social (and indeed psychological) change, irrespective of how it is used, or the representations it makes available. While he distances himself from the so-called Moral Majority, Postman clearly wants to return to an imaginary Golden Age of traditional moral values – and thereby to reinforce adult authority and control. Significantly, he is also directly opposed to the use of television in education: for him, the school is the last bastion in the defence of print culture.

More recently, we have seen the emergence of an argument that is in some respects a mirror image of Postman's. Perhaps the most distinctive expression of this is by the American journalist and media consultant Don Tapscott (1998), in his book *Growing Up Digital*. In some ways, Tapscott seems to support Postman's diagnosis, although he interprets it in a very different way. He agrees that the boundaries between childhood and adulthood are blurring; and he agrees that media technology – particularly digital technology – is primarily responsible for this. But rather than regretting this development, he sees it as a form of liberation or 'empowerment' for young people.

The argument here is partly based on the contrast between 'new' and 'old' technologies. Tapscott in fact sets up a direct opposition between television and the internet. Television is seen as passive, while the net is active; television 'dumbs down' its users, while the net raises their intelligence; television broadcasts a singular view of the world, while the net is democratic and interactive; television isolates, while the net builds communities; and so on. Just as television is the antithesis of the net, so the 'television generation' is the antithesis of the 'net generation'. Like the technology they now control, the values of the television generation are increasingly conservative, 'hierarchical, inflexible and centralized'. By contrast, the members of the 'net generation' are 'hungry for expression, discovery and their own self-development': they are savvy, self-reliant, analytical, creative, inquisitive, accepting of diversity, socially conscious, globally oriented – all, it would seem, because of their intuitive relationship with technology.

Here again, it is possible to challenge Tapscott on the grounds of his evidence – or lack of it (Buckingham, 2000a) – although it is his underlying assumptions that are particularly dubious. As with the 'death of childhood' thesis, this argument reflects a form of 'media determinism', albeit of a very different kind. Postman sees children as vulnerable and in need of protection from the corrupting influence of media technology; while Tapscott sees them as naturally wise, and as having an innate thirst for knowledge which media technology can satisfy. Where Postman wants to return to a situation in which children knew their place, Tapscott argues that adults should try to 'catch up' with their children. Where Postman places his faith in adult authority, Tapscott looks to technology alone as the solution to social problems. In some respects, therefore, these apparently contrasting arguments could be seen as two sides of the same coin. Both have an undeniable appeal: they tell simple stories that speak directly to our hopes and fears about children's futures.

Yet ultimately, they are based on highly questionable – and, indeed, unduly generalized – views of childhood and of media technology, and of the relationships between them.

Changing childhoods

In some respects, both these arguments could be seen as symptomatic of a sense of crisis that has been brought about by wider social changes. While my primary focus in this chapter is on the role of the media, it is important to locate this briefly within a broader account of the changing social position of children. Generalizations about such changes are obviously risky. We cannot talk about children as a homogeneous category: what childhood means, and how it is experienced, obviously depends upon other social factors, such as gender, 'race' or ethnicity, social class, geographical location, and so on. Nevertheless, it is possible to identify a number of general ways in which children's lives have changed over the past century, and specifically in the past three or four decades (for more detail, see Buckingham, 2000a).

Thus, we have seen a gradual shift away from extended families to nuclear families; and then increasingly to non-traditional family structures of various kinds – most notably single-parent families. At least in the UK, research suggests that children are now much more likely to be confined to their homes, and much less independently mobile, than they were twenty years ago; and while parents now spend much less time with their children, they are attempting to compensate for this by devoting increasing economic resources to child-rearing. Meanwhile, there has been a steady extension of the years of compulsory schooling, and of the proportion of young people continuing in post-compulsory education. Increasing numbers of children are also now in pre-school education of some kind. On the other hand, youth unemployment is rising, and in some countries state benefits for young people have been withdrawn; and as a result, young people are now becoming increasingly dependent upon their parents. There have also been significant changes in peer group culture. Young people are now having sex earlier than in previous decades; and they are maturing physically at an ever-earlier age. Drugs have become an almost taken-for-granted aspect of young people's recreational experiences; and despite the 'war on drugs', drug use is now at higher levels than ever before. There is also increasing anxiety about the incidence of child crime, although statistically children are much more likely to be victims of crime than other age groups.

As a result of these developments, there have been changes in children's status as a distinctive social group. On the one hand, there is growing concern about the need to protect children, particularly from forms of abuse; on the other, there have been increasingly punitive attempts to deal with a perceived breakdown in discipline. At the same time, the issue of children's rights has become much more significant in recent years. Following the UN Convention on the Rights of the Child, many countries have passed new legislation to protect children's rights, both in the family and in their dealings with state agencies. However, this concern for children's rights goes along with a new emphasis on children as a potential market. If capitalism can be said to have created 'the teenager' in the 1950s, children are now increasingly addressed directly as a consumer market in their own right, rather than simply as a means of reaching parents. Nevertheless, over the past two decades, many Western countries have seen an increasing polarization between rich and poor, and the creation of a growing underclass, in which children are disproportionately represented.

These changes clearly do not tell a simple story; and they will obviously affect different children in different ways. Indeed, in some respects they point to a growing polarization among children – not only between rich and poor, but also between those who are living 'modern' and 'traditional' childhoods. In general, however, it is clear that relations of authority and power between adults and children are changing. While there are some who wish to reassert traditional relationships, and to return to an era in which children were 'seen but not heard', there are others who welcome these changes as an extension of democracy and of the rights of citizenship to children. At the same time, we might well argue that children have gained power, not merely as citizens but also as *consumers*; and indeed that the two may have become impossible to separate.

These changes both reinforce, and are reinforced by, changes in children's relationships with the media. In the following sections of this chapter, I review recent developments in this field, looking in turn at technologies, economics, texts and audiences. As I shall argue, these changes have ambivalent consequences for our views of childhood: on the one hand, the boundaries between children and adults appear to be blurring, while on the other, they appear to be being reinforced. Children are being 'empowered' and yet simultaneously denied the opportunity to exercise control.

Technologies

As we have seen, discussions of young people's relationships with the media often attribute a determining power to technology. Such arguments are problematic for several reasons. Technologies do not produce social change irrespective of how they are used; nor are the inherent differences between technologies as absolute as is often supposed. In this case, we need to consider how technological changes are related both to economic developments and to changes in the behaviour of audiences.

Recent developments in media technologies can be understood, firstly, as a matter of *proliferation*. Since the advent of television, the domestic TV screen has become the delivery point for an ever-broader range of media. The number of channels has grown, both on terrestrial television and (more spectacularly) with the advent of cable, satellite and digital TV; while the screen is also being used for video in various forms, as well as for the ever-broadening range of digital media, from computer games and CD-ROMs to the internet.

Secondly, there has been a *convergence* between information and communications technologies. Over the coming decade, the advent of digital TV, internet set-top boxes, online shopping, video-on-demand and other developments will increasingly blur the distinctions between linear broadcast media such as television and 'narrowcast', interactive media such as the internet. Like the other developments identified here, this has been commercially driven; but it has also been made possible by digitization.

These developments have implications, thirdly, in terms of *access*. Hitherto expensive aspects of media production, and a whole range of new media forms and options, have been brought within reach of the domestic consumer. The price of video camcorders, digital cameras and multimedia PCs has steadily fallen as their capabilities have increased; and at least in principle, the internet represents a means of communication that cannot be exclusively controlled by a small elite. In the process, it is argued, the boundaries between production and consumption, and between mass communication and interpersonal communication, are beginning to break down.

These changes have several specific implications for children. Children and parents are among the most significant markets for these new technologies. Cable and satellite television, for example, have been strongly targeted towards the younger audience, while much of the advertising and promotion for home computers trades in a popular mystique about children's natural affinity with technology (Nixon, 1998). In the UK, for instance, the take-up of satellite and cable television, video, camcorders and home computers has been much higher in households with children. Technology is also being used in more individualized ways. Thus, a majority of children in the UK have televisions in their bedrooms, and a significant proportion have VCRs. These tendencies are encouraged by the general democratization of relationships within the family, although collective uses of media – 'family viewing' – are far from disappearing (Livingstone and Bovill, 2001).

Similarly, many of the new cultural forms made possible by these technologies are primarily identified with the young. Computer games, for example, are predominantly addressed to the children's and youth market, while popular music is increasingly generated by digital technology, via sampling, editing and other software. The increasing accessibility of this technology is also enabling some young people to play a more active role as cultural producers. More and more teenagers have home computers in their bedrooms that can be used to create music, to manipulate images or to edit video to a relatively professional standard. Nevertheless, we should not exaggerate the scale of these developments. Levels of access to technology will increase significantly in the coming years, as prices fall; yet there is also a polarization between the 'technology rich' and the 'technology poor', both within societies and in global terms (Van der Voort et al., 1998; Wartella et al., 1990).

Children's growing access to media is generating increasing concern about their exposure to material hitherto largely confined to adults – most obviously to 'sex and violence' (both of which are often very loosely defined). When compared with older technologies such as the cinema or broadcast television, media such as video and cable/satellite television significantly undermine the potential for centralized control by national governments. Video, for example, has made it possible to copy and circulate material to a much greater extent than has ever been the case with moving images. It also makes it possible to view it, not in a public space to which access can be controlled, but in the private space of the home; and to do so at a time chosen by the viewer, not by a centralized scheduler working with ideas about what is appropriate for children to watch. A large majority of children have seen material on video which they should not legally have been able to obtain (Buckingham, 1996a).

This anxiety about control is accentuated by the advent of digital technology. It is now possible, not only for material to be easily copied and circulated, but also for it to be sent across national boundaries on the telephone line. At present, the internet is a relatively decentralized medium: anyone with access to the technology can 'publish' anything they like, and anyone else can get access to it. Via the internet, children can communicate much more easily with each other and with adults, without even having to identify themselves as children. And, of course, the privacy and anonymity afforded by the internet particularly lends itself to the easy dissemination and sale of pornography. This situation has led to growing calls for stricter regulation and censorship; and to the search for a 'technological fix' in the form of the V-chip or so-called 'blocking software' that will prevent children from gaining access to material that is deemed undesirable. Yet evidence of the effectiveness of such devices is decidedly limited (Waltermann and Machill, 2000).

Economics

These technological developments have helped to reinforce – and been reinforced by – fundamental institutional and economic changes in the media industries. The past two decades have been characterized by growing *privatization*. The media have been inextricably caught up in the broader commercialization of contemporary culture, in which fields such as politics, sport, health care – and indeed education itself – have increasingly been 'invaded' by commercial forces. Meanwhile, public sector provision – for example in broadcasting – has gradually been commercialized from within; and regulation concerned with the social and cultural functions of the media is being abandoned in favour of a narrower concern with morality.

One inevitable consequence of this development has been the *integration* and *globalization* of the media industries. The media market is now dominated by a small number of multinational conglomerates; and global brands now provide an international language or 'common culture', particularly among young people. For nationally based companies, success in the international market is increasingly necessary for survival. Significantly, most of these global corporations are cross-media empires: they integrate broadcasting, publishing, media and digital technology, and in many cases have interests in both hardware and software. Yet integration does not necessarily mean homogenization: growing competition has also resulted in the fragmentation of audiences, and the rise of 'niche marketing'. Media are increasingly targeted towards specialized fractions of the mass audience, albeit on a global scale; and new technologies also permit more decentralized communications, and the creation of 'communities' that transcend national boundaries.

These developments affect children in quite ambiguous ways. Children have effectively been 'discovered' as a new target market only in the past few decades. In the case of commercial television, for example, children were not initially seen as an especially valuable audience. In the early decades of the US commercial system, programmes would be provided for children only at minimum cost, and at times when other audiences were not available to view (Melody, 1973); and even in the UK, where the public service tradition has been very strong, children's television has been comparatively underfunded. In the contemporary era of niche marketing, children have suddenly become much more valuable: they are seen to have significant influence on parents' purchasing decisions, as well as substantial disposable income of their own. At least within the media industries, the vulnerable child in need of protection has increasingly given way to the child as 'sovereign consumer'. The formation and development of 'youth culture' – and, more recently, of a global 'children's culture' – are now inextricable from the commercial operations of the modern media. As a result, today's children may have more in common with children in other cultures than they do with their own parents (Ohmae, 1995).

Of course, we should be wary of economic determinism here. It is far too easy to fall back on traditional notions of children as vulnerable to commercial exploitation or to the seductions of media imperialism. A large proportion of commercial products aimed at children simply fail to generate a profit: the market is highly competitive and uncertain. To this extent, there is some justification in producers' recurrent claim that children are a volatile, complex market, which cannot easily be known and controlled.

Nevertheless, the fact remains that children's leisure activities are becoming steadily more privatized and commercialized. More of their time is spent in the home or in supervised activity of some kind, while the cultural goods and services they consume increasingly have to be paid for in hard cash. The public spaces of childhood – both the physical spaces of play and the virtual spaces of broadcasting – have increasingly fallen into decline or been overcome by the commercial market. One inevitable consequence of this is that children's social and media worlds are becoming increasingly unequal. The polarization between rich and poor is positively reinforced by the commercialization of the media, and the decline in public sector provision. In the case of computers, just as in the early days of television, those with greater disposable income are the 'early adopters': they have newer and more powerful equipment, and more opportunities to develop the skills that are needed to use it. Poorer children simply have less access to cultural goods and services: they live, not just in different social worlds, but in different media worlds as well.

Texts

Perhaps the most obvious manifestation of these technological and economic developments is in the changing characteristics of media texts – that is, the television programmes, movies, games and other artefacts children are engaging with. On one level, this can be seen as a further consequence of technological and economic *convergence*. More and more media texts are somehow 'spin-offs' or advertisements for other texts or commodities; and the media have become much more closely bound up with the merchandising of a whole range of other products.

As a result, *intertextuality* has become a dominant characteristic of contemporary media: texts are constantly referring to and drawing upon other texts, often in ironic ways. Many contemporary cartoons, for example, self-consciously draw upon other media in the form of pastiche, homage, or parody; they juxtapose incongruous elements from different historical periods, genres or cultural contexts; and they play with established conventions of form and representation. In the process, they implicitly address their readers or viewers as knowing, 'media literate' consumers.

Finally, many of these new media forms are characterized by types of *interactivity*. As we have seen, some of the more utopian advocates of interactive multimedia (such as Tapscott) have seen it as a means of liberation from the constraints of more traditional 'linear' media such as film and television. Hypertext, CD-ROMs and computer games have been seen to abolish the distinction between 'reader' and 'writer': the reader (or player) is no longer passively manipulated by the text – and indeed the only text is the one the reader chooses to 'write'. In consequence, at least some of these new media appear to exercise a much stronger fascination for their users than the 'older' media with which they are now competing.

Many of these developments are dictated by a primarily economic logic. As media have become increasingly commodified, producers need to exploit successes across a wider range of media within a shorter time scale, and are bound to use the same material in different forms. Meanwhile, 'irony' has become a useful marketing device, enabling media corporations to secure additional profit by recycling existing properties; and 'interactivity' is often little more than a form of packaging.

Nevertheless, many of these characteristics apply with particular force to media texts that are aimed at children and young people (see Bazalgette and Buckingham, 1995; Buckingham, 2002a; Kinder, 1991, 2000). As children's access to technology increases, they no longer have to watch or read what their parents choose. As the 'niche market' of children grows in importance, they are increasingly able to confine themselves to media that are produced specifically for them. Indeed, the new 'postmodern' cultural forms that characterize children's and youth culture often exclude adults: they depend upon particular cultural competencies and on a prior knowledge of specific media texts (in other words, on a form of 'media literacy') that are accessible only to the young.

Thus, many of the most popular cartoons and TV magazine programmes for children – from *The Simpsons* to *SMTV Live* – are permeated with references to other texts and genres, sometimes in the form of direct quotation or 'sampling'. They raid existing cultural resources – both from high culture and from the popular culture of the past and present – in a fragmentary and often apparently parodic manner. Comparing current animation series with those of thirty years ago, one is struck not just by their rapid pace, but also by their irony and intertextuality, and their complex play with reality and fantasy (Wells, 2002).

Yet TV programmes are not just TV programmes: they are also films, records, comics, computer games and toys – not to mention T-shirts, posters, lunchboxes, drinks, sticker albums, food, and a myriad of other products. Children's media culture increasingly crosses the boundaries between texts and between traditional media forms – most obviously in the case of phenomena such as *Teenage Mutant Ninja Turtles*, *Mighty Morphin' Power Rangers* and, most spectacularly, *Pokémon*. In this process, the identity of the 'original' text is far from clear: these commodities are packaged and marketed as integrated phenomena, rather than the text coming first and the merchandising following on. And this development is not confined to the work of exclusively 'commercial' corporations – as is illustrated by the success of public service productions such as *Sesame Street* and the BBC's *Teletubbies*.

Disney is of course the classic example of this phenomenon. Right from the early days of the Mickey Mouse clubs, merchandising and subsequently theme parks have been a key dimension of the enterprise – and in fact it is these aspects which have guaranteed its continuing profitability (Gomery, 1994). However, this horizontal integration is now moving to a different scale. Once you have seen the latest Disney movie, you can catch the spin-off episodes on the Disney Channel, or meet the characters at the theme park; you can visit the Disney store at your local mall and stock up on the video, the posters, the T-shirts, and other merchandise; you can collect the 'free gifts' of character toys in cereal packets and fast-food restaurants; and you can buy the animated storybook on CD-ROM, play the computer game, visit the web site, and so on. Children are very much in the vanguard of what Marsha Kinder (1991) calls 'trans-media intertextuality' – and, as she argues, the logic of this development is primarily driven by profit.

It is also important to recognize changes at the level of *content* – which, as in the case of Postman (1983), are often those that cause most alarm among adult critics. At least in the UK, children's television has steadily changed over the past twenty years to incorporate topics such as sex, drugs and family breakdown that would previously have been considered taboo. Likewise, magazines and books aimed at the early teenage market have attracted widespread criticism for their frank and explicit treatment of such issues (see Jones and Davies, 2002; Rosen, 1997).

Indeed, it could be argued that the age at which childhood *ends* – at least as far as the media industries are concerned – seems to be steadily reducing. Children, it is argued, are 'getting older younger'. Children's television producers, for example, now acknowledge that the bulk of older children's viewing is given over to 'adult' programmes; and the content and style of programmes aimed at them clearly reflects this. The social issues addressed in children's dramas have much in common with those in adult soaps; while the visual style and pace of kids' magazine shows have clearly influenced the approach of 'adult' programmes. While some critics have always complained about the precocity of children's programmes, others are beginning to bemoan what they see as the infantilization of 'adult' television. Yet either way, it would seem that 'childishness' – like 'youth' before it – has become a valuable commodity for sale in the media market (Davies, Buckingham and Kelley, 2000).

Audiences

As the media have evolved, they have come to assume quite different kinds of competence and knowledge – and to encourage very different forms of 'activity' – on the part of audiences. Contemporary media are increasingly addressing children as highly 'media literate' consumers. Whether they actually *are* more media literate, and what we might mean by that, is a rather more complex question, however, as we shall see in the following chapter.

As I have noted, advocates of the 'communications revolution' have argued that audiences are increasingly 'empowered' by these new media – although critics have suggested that they are simply more open to manipulation and commercial exploitation. Thus, some claim that there is now much greater *choice* for consumers, while others argue that such choice is merely spurious. For example, the proliferation of television channels has led to a significant increase in the quantity of television available for children, even taking account of the fact that much of it is frequently repeated. Whether this increase will be sustained over the longer term is more debatable, however: the amount of new product cannot keep pace with the increase in outlets for it – not least because the audience for each channel is decreasing as more become available, and hence the funding for new production will decline. In practice, therefore, what viewers are more likely to be offered is ever-increasing opportunities to watch the same things (Buckingham et al., 1999).

These issues are to some extent compounded by *interactivity*. Leaving aside the question of whether surfing the web actually is more 'active' than surfing TV channels or browsing through a magazine (for example), there are significant questions about whether audiences actually *want* greater 'activity'. Even for regular users, there is room for scepticism about the 'empowerment' that is apparently offered here. The web clearly allows users much greater control over the selection of content and the pace at which it is 'read'. Yet in the process it also permits much more detailed surveillance of consumer behaviour: it is now very easy to track users' movements between and within particular web sites, and thereby to build up consumer profiles which can subsequently become the basis for electronic advertising. Children have become key targets in this respect (Center for Media Education, 1997).

Finally, there are questions about the growing *fragmentation* of audiences, as texts are increasingly targeted at specialized groups of consumers. Multi-channel television, for example, may bring about the decline of broadcasting (and the 'common culture' it makes possible) in favour of 'narrowcasting', while the internet is the medium *par excellence* for those with specialist or minority interests. Yet in the longer term, it remains to be seen how far consumers actually *want* to pursue wholly individualized or 'customized' uses of media, or whether they want a more shared experience – at least to the extent of being able to talk about what they have seen the following day. Here too, the idea that new media necessarily offer a form of 'empowerment' is open to question.

Nevertheless, these changes have specific implications for our views of the child audience. At least in the English-speaking world, sensational stories about the harm the media allegedly inflict on children have increasingly come to dominate the headlines. There is a clear acknowledgement that children are no longer restricted to material that is designed for them – although research suggests that in fact they have always preferred 'adult' media, at least insofar as they could gain access to them (Abrams, 1956). Yet if public debates about children and the media have become more and more preoccupied with defending children from harm, the views of those who work within the media industries seem to be moving in a rather different direction (Del Vecchio, 1997). Here, children are no longer predominantly seen as innocent and vulnerable to influence. On the contrary, they are increasingly regarded as sophisticated, demanding, 'media-wise' consumers. This shift is certainly apparent in the recent history of children's television (Buckingham et al., 1999). The broadly 'child-centred' ethos that flourished in Britain during the 1960s and 1970s is increasingly losing ground to an essentially consumerist approach. The child viewer is no longer seen as the developing consciousness of the psychological imagination, but as a sophisticated, discriminating, critical consumer. Children have become 'kids'; and kids, we are told, are 'smart', 'savvy' and 'streetwise'. Kids are hard to please; they see through attempts at deception and manipulation; and they refuse to be patronized.

This discourse is in turn often connected with arguments about *children's rights*. Internationally, the most successful exponent of this approach has been the dedicated children's channel Nickelodeon (owned by the US media giant Viacom). What we find here is a rhetoric of empowerment – a notion of the channel as a 'kid-only' zone, giving voice to kids, taking the kids' point of view, as the friend of kids (Laybourne, 1993). This is reinforced in the channel's publicity and on-screen continuity material. Significantly, children seem to be defined here primarily in terms of being *not adults*. Adults are boring; kids are fun. Adults are conservative; kids are fresh and innovative. Adults will never understand; kids intuitively *know*. Yet despite its emphasis on 'children's rights', this discourse does not define children as independent social or political actors, let alone offer them democratic control or accountability: it is a discourse of consumer sovereignty masquerading as a discourse of cultural rights. As Nickelodeon's company slogan puts it, 'what's good for kids is good for business'.

Implications for education

In several respects, recent developments in the media could be seen to reinforce – and to be reinforced by – changes in childhood, of the kind identified earlier in this chapter. Both are characterized by a growing sense of instability and insecurity: established distinctions and hierarchies are breaking down, as new cultural forms and new identities emerge. In relation to the media, as in many other areas of social life, previously distinct boundaries between children and adults are disappearing. And yet, as I have suggested, such boundaries are simultaneously being reinforced or redrawn. The separation between children's and adults' media worlds is becoming more apparent, although the terms of that separation are changing. Older children can no longer be so easily 'protected' from experiences that are seen to be morally damaging or unsuitable. The walls that surround the garden of childhood have become much easier to climb. And yet children – particularly younger children – are increasingly participating in cultural and social worlds that are inaccessible, even incomprehensible, to their parents.

So what are the implications of this situation for education? Most obviously, it would seem to reinforce the urgent need for systematic programmes of teaching and learning about the media. The account I have presented here points to the central role of the media in children's lives, and their significance in defining the meanings and experiences of contemporary childhood. It also illustrates the increasing degree of convergence between media – to the point where studying a single medium in isolation would seem positively reactionary. And it points to the growing opportunities for media production by young people themselves – opportunities which must surely be seized by media educators.

Ultimately, my analysis suggests that there is a widening gap between children's worlds outside school and the emphases of many education systems. While the social and cultural experiences of children have been dramatically transformed over the past fifty years, schools have signally failed to keep pace with change. The classrooms of today would be easily recognizable to the pioneers of public education of the mid-nineteenth century: the ways in which teaching and learning are organized, the kinds of skills and knowledge that are valued in assessment, and a good deal of the actual curriculum content, have changed only superficially since that time. Indeed, some have argued that schooling is now heading determinedly backwards, retreating from the uncertainty of contemporary social change towards the apparently comforting stability of a new 'educational fundamentalism', in which traditional relationships of authority between adults and children can be restored (Kenway and Bullen, 2001).

Of course, this is not to posit an absolute opposition between 'school culture' and 'children's culture'. The school is inevitably a site for negotiation (and often for struggle) between competing conceptions of knowledge and cultural value. Nevertheless, there is now an extraordinary contrast between the high levels of activity and enthusiasm that characterize children's consumer cultures and the passivity that increasingly suffuses their schooling. Of course, teachers have perennially complained about children's weakening 'attention span'; although in fact the levels of intense concentration and energy that characterize children's playground engagements with phenomena like Pokémon are quite at odds with the deadening influence of mechanical teaching and testing that currently prevail in many classrooms (Buckingham and Sefton-Green, 2003). Indeed, as Jane Kenway and Elizabeth Bullen (2001) point out, the 'knowledge politics' of children's consumer culture often explicitly oppose those of formal schooling, presenting teachers as dull and earnest, worthy not of emulation but of well-justified rebellion and rejection. Like a Rabelaisian 'carnival', children's media culture has increasingly become an arena in which authoritarian values of seriousness and conformity are subverted and undermined.

In this context, it is hardly surprising if children perceive schooling as marginal to their identities and concerns – or at best, as a kind of functional chore. Yet if schools are to engage with children's media cultures, it is clearly vital that, in doing so, they do not simply attempt to re-inscribe traditional notions of what counts as valid knowledge. To a much greater extent than in conventional academic subjects, teacherly attempts at imposing cultural, moral or political authority over the media that children experience in their daily lives are very unlikely to be taken seriously. If, as in many cases, they are based on a paternalistic contempt for children's tastes and pleasures, they certainly deserve to be rejected. It is for these reasons that protectionist approaches to media education – whether cultural, moral or political in nature – are at least redundant, if not positively counter-productive.

However, this is not to suggest that media education should abandon the project of cultural criticism, or that it should merely celebrate the activity and energy of children's relationships with the media. If it were to exist, such an approach would at best be merely superficial; and at worst, it could be seen to represent a form of complicity with the assertions of children's 'consumer sovereignty' that are so enthusiastically promoted by the media industries. As I have indicated in this chapter, there are significant constraints on children's autonomy as users of media, and on the diversity of their experiences. The media are inextricably tied up in broader networks of social, economic and institutional power; and it is vital that young people should understand the complex and sometimes contradictory ways in which these operate. Indeed, as I shall argue in the following chapter, this kind of understanding is central to any contemporary definition of literacy. Yet if media education is to help bridge the widening gap between the school and the world of children's out-of-school experience, it must surely begin with the knowledge that children already possess.

3

Media Literacies

Advocates of media education have frequently invoked the notion of 'literacy' in attempting to define and justify their work. The use of the term in this context dates back at least to the 1970s, where a range of mostly short-lived 'television literacy' curricula were introduced in the United States (Anderson, 1980). In North America generally, the term 'media literacy' is still often used in preference to 'media education'. The reference to literacy came onto the agenda in the UK in the late 1980s, partly as a result of attempts to integrate media education within the teaching of English (e.g. Bazalgette, 1988; Buckingham, 1993b). More recently, educators whose primary interest is in the teaching of language and literature have come (perhaps belatedly) to recognize the importance of dealing with a wider range of media (e.g. Marsh and Millard, 2000; Watts Pailliotet and Mosenthal, 2000). This more recent emphasis has also led to the emergence of the term 'multiliteracies' (Tyner, 1998; Cope and Kalantzis, 2000).

Such authors typically claim that the 'new' literacies required by the modern media are just as important as the 'old' literacies demanded by print. Of course, communication almost always involves a combination of different modes, visual as well as verbal; but the development of new communications media has decisively undermined the dominance of the printed word – and indeed, is fundamentally reshaping how we use language. Literacy today, it is argued, is inevitably and necessarily *multimedia* literacy; and to this extent, traditional forms of literacy teaching are no longer adequate.

To some extent, therefore, this use of the term 'media literacy' could be seen as a polemical claim – and in this respect, it has much in common with the fashionable use of the term in contexts such as 'computer literacy', 'economic literacy' and even 'emotional literacy'. It is based on an analogy between the competencies which apply in relatively new or controversial or low-status areas (in this case, media) and those which apply in the established, uncontroversial, high-status area of reading and writing. The analogy is used to bolster claims for the importance – and indeed the respectability – of the new area of study. On the other hand, of course, it may also give hostages to fortune, not least because it implicitly acknowledges the primacy of written language. Because writing is seen as the only 'real' mode of communication, it appears that all the others have to be described as forms of literacy (Kress, 1997).

Defining literacy

The term 'media literacy' refers to the knowledge, skills and competencies that are required in order to use and interpret media. Yet defining media literacy is far from straightforward. To talk about 'literacy' in this context would seem to imply that the media can in some sense be seen to employ forms of language – and that we can study and teach visual and audio-visual 'languages' in a similar way to written language. The linguist Ferdinand de Saussure is generally credited with proposing this kind of extension of linguistic methods to the study of other forms of communication – a field that has subsequently been termed semiotics or semiology (that is, the study of signs). Media educators have frequently employed semiotic methods or principles for analysing media texts (see chapter 5).

Yet for some, the analogy with written language – and hence the term 'media literacy' – is simply too imprecise, if not positively misleading. Some scholars of literacy, for example, caution against this rather loose and metaphorical use of the term, arguing that it blurs necessary distinctions between written language and other modes of communication (e.g. Barton, 1994; Kress, 1997). Meanwhile, some media analysts reject the idea that our understanding of visual communication is based on a mastery of cultural conventions like those that apply in language. On the contrary, they suggest that we understand visual and audio-visual representations using the same skills that we use to interpret the everyday world around us (Messaris, 1994).

Ultimately, the value of the literacy analogy depends on the level at which we decide to locate it. As Paul Messaris (1994) suggests, the basic conventions of 'film language' do have to be learned; but they are learned comparatively easily and quickly, not least because they mimic familiar processes of perception and comprehension. Interpreting a zoom or a dissolve, for example, is relatively straightforward if one takes account of contextual information (the other shots in the film, or the development of the storyline). In fact, attempts to develop a theory of 'film language' have been fraught with difficulty: it is very hard to find analogies between the 'small elements' of film (shots or camera movements, for example) and the equivalent elements in verbal language (the word or the phoneme), let alone aspects such as tenses or negatives. Several analysts conclude that film does not in fact possess a syntax, which would enable us to distinguish between 'grammatical' and 'ungrammatical' statements (see Buckingham, 1993a).

Likewise, psychologists' attempts to identify the component skills that make up 'television literacy' have been fraught with difficulty. At least in principle, it should be possible to break down what a competent viewer needs to do in order to 'understand' a piece of television; yet this does not necessarily correspond to the ways in which meanings are actually produced. Particular formal features of television do not carry fixed meanings which can be objectively defined. A camera zoom, for example, may 'mean' different things at different times; and it may on certain occasions 'mean' the same thing as a tracking shot or a cut to close-up. Such apparently basic elements of media language cannot be said to be processed automatically. However momentarily, viewers have to make active choices about their meaning (for a fuller discussion, see Buckingham, 1993a: ch. 2).

Nevertheless, it is important to distinguish here between interpretation at this 'micro' level and the 'macro' level of textual meaning. How we interpret a film, for example, does not depend only on how we 'read' particular shots or sequences. It also depends on how the text as a whole is organized and structured, for example via narrative; on how it relates to other texts we may have seen (intertextuality), or genres with which we are familiar; on how the text refers to, and makes claims about, aspects of reality with which we are more or less familiar (representation); and on the expectations we bring to it, for example as a result of the ways in which it has been publicized and distributed. Understanding these different elements might also be seen as forms of 'literacy', in the sense that they involve the production of meaning and pleasure from a range of textual signs.

Thus, the 'literacy' that is generally referred to in the case of 'media literacy' is clearly more than simply a *functional* literacy

– the ability to make sense of a TV programme, for example, or to operate a camera. Literacy is not seen here merely as a kind of cognitive 'tool kit' that enables people to understand and use media. And media education is thus rather more than a kind of training course or proficiency test in media-related skills. For want of a better term, media literacy is a form of *critical* literacy. It involves analysis, evaluation and critical reflection. It entails the acquisition of a 'metalanguage' – that is, a means of describing the forms and structures of different modes of communication; and it involves a broader understanding of the social, economic and institutional contexts of communication, and how these affect people's experiences and practices (Luke, 2000). Media literacy certainly includes the ability to use and interpret media; but it also involves a much broader analytical understanding.

A social theory of literacies

For the advocates of 'multiliteracies' (Cope and Kalantzis, 2000), and for others in this field (Buckingham, 1993a; Spencer, 1986), this emphasis on the plurality of literacies is not just about multiple modes (or media) of communication. It is also to do with the inherently *social* nature of literacy – and hence with the diverse forms that literacy takes in different cultures, and indeed within the increasingly multicultural societies in which we live. Research on print literacy clearly shows that different social groups define, acquire and use literacy in very different ways; and that the consequences of literacy depend upon the social contexts and social purposes for which it is used (e.g. Heath, 1983; Scribner and Cole, 1981; Street, 1984). It is for this reason that such researchers tend to refer to 'literacy practices' or 'literacy events' rather than merely to 'literacy' *per se*: in other words, they regard reading and writing as social activities, rather than as manifestations of a set of disembodied cognitive skills.

From this perspective, therefore, literacy cannot be considered separately from the social and institutional structures in which it is situated. This is a *social* theory, which effectively dispenses with a singular notion of literacy and replaces it with a notion of plural litera*cies*, that are defined by the meanings they produce and the social interests they serve. It implies that individuals do not create meanings in isolation, but through their involvement in social networks, or 'interpretive communities', which promote and value particular forms of literacy. The study of literacy should thus necessarily address questions about the economic and institutional contexts of communication – for example, how different social groups have different kinds of access to literacy, and how access and distribution are related to broader inequalities within society (Luke, 2000). This approach also implies that acquiring literacy (in whatever form) makes possible particular forms of social action. It enables people to *do* things, whether in their occupations, in their private lives or in civil society; and the forms it takes depend on what it is that is being done. Social action is inevitably related to the operation of power within society; and so we might say that literacy is about the production of symbolic meanings, which in turn embody and enact particular relationships of power.

In the case of 'media literacy', therefore, this approach suggests that we cannot regard – or indeed, teach – literacy as a set of cognitive abilities which individuals somehow come to 'possess' once and for all. We would need to begin by acknowledging that the media are an integral part of the texture of children's daily lives, and that they are embedded within their social relationships. We would need to recognize that the competencies that are involved in making sense of the media are socially distributed, and that different social groups have different orientations towards the media, and will use them in diverse ways. In this sense, we should expect that children will have different 'media literacies' – or different modalities of literacy – that are required by the different social situations they encounter, and that will in turn have different social functions and consequences. And we should acknowledge that individuals have 'histories' of media experiences that may be activated in particular ways in particular social contexts, or by particular 'literacy events'.

At this point, let us step back from this rather abstract discussion and consider what 'media literacy' might actually mean in practice. How might we define media literacy in such a way that we could actually teach it? Is it possible to specify the constituent parts of media literacy, and to identify how young people might be expected to acquire them? In the following section, I consider one practical attempt to address these questions.

Mapping media literacies

There have been various attempts to define the components of 'media literacy', and to prescribe how these might be taught to children at different ages (see e.g. Bazalgette, 1989; Brown, 1991; Tyner,

1998; Worsnop, 1996). The British Film Institute's model of 'cineliteracy', first proposed in the Report *Making Movies Matter* (Film Education Working Group, 1999), is one recent example. The BFI's model refers specifically to moving images, although most of the aspects identified can also apply to other media, including print; and there is no compelling logic for considering moving images in isolation.

The BFI model breaks down the field into three 'conceptual areas': 'the language of moving images', 'producers and audiences' and 'messages and values'. (These areas are effectively the same as those I will be describing in detail in the following chapter, although I will be separating 'producers and audiences' into two distinct categories.) The document seeks to provide a model of 'learning progression' that will inform teaching about the moving image at different ages and stages of children's school careers. In addition to defining the 'experiences and activities' students should be able to engage in at each stage, it also defines the 'outcomes' that are to be expected, and the 'key words' that suggest 'the areas and types of knowledge that each stage might involve'.

Box 3.1 provides an example of the outcomes that are specified in one of the three areas, 'messages and values'. According to the text, this area is broadly concerned with questions about the 'effects' of the media on 'ideas, values and beliefs'; and it focuses particularly on the relationship between moving image texts and reality. (This area corresponds to that of 'representation', discussed in detail in chapter 4.) It is important to note that this model is defined in terms of *stages*, rather than *ages*; although it is no coincidence that the UK National Curriculum is also currently divided into five 'key stages', which *are* defined by age. (Thus, Key Stage 1 is ages 5–7; Key Stage 2, ages 7–11; Key Stage 3, ages 11–14; Key Stage 4, ages 14–16; and Key Stage 5, ages 16–18.)

Box 3.1 'Cineliteracy': messages and values

At Stage 1, learners should be able to:

- Identify and talk about different levels of 'realism', e.g. naturalistic drama vs. cartoon animation.
- Refer to elements of film language when explaining personal responses and preferences (e.g. shot, cut, zoom, close-up, focus).

- Identify devices such as flashback, dream sequences, exaggeration; and discuss why they are needed and how they are conveyed.

At Stage 2, learners should be able to:

- Identify ways in which film, video and television can show things that have not 'really' happened, such as violence or magic.
- Explore reasons for and against censorship, age classification and the broadcasting 'watershed'.

At Stage 3, learners should be able to:

- Explain how social groups, events and ideas are represented in film, video and television, using terms such as 'stereotype', 'authentic' and 'representation'.
- Explain and justify aesthetic judgements and personal responses.
- Argue for alternative ways of representing a group, event, or idea.

At Stage 4, learners should be able to:

- Discuss and evaluate film, video and television texts with strong social or ideological messages, using terms such as 'propaganda' and 'ideology'.

At Stage 5, learners should be able to:

- Discuss and evaluate ideological messages in mainstream film, video and television texts, using terms such as 'hegemony' and 'diegesis'.
- Describe and account for different levels of realism in film, video and television texts.
- Explain relationships between aesthetic style and social/ political meaning.

Source: Slightly adapted from *Moving Images in the Classroom*, British Film Institute, 2000: 52–6.

While there are some 'functional' elements at Stage 1 here, this is very clearly a model of 'critical' literacy, in the terms identified above. This is characteristic, not just of the area of 'messages and values', but of the approach as a whole. While this critical element is perhaps less apparent in the area of 'language', it is quite strongly emphasized in that of 'producers and audiences'. Thus, under 'language', learners are expected to cover the different elements of film language, the interaction of image and sound, narrative structure, the role of technology and the evolution of 'film style'. Under 'producers and audiences', they develop an understanding of the production, economic organization, marketing and distribution of moving image texts, and of the ways in which audiences respond to them. These are all key areas of media education, which will be considered in detail in chapter 4.

Models of this kind are almost certainly necessary, but they also raise several problems, both in detail and in principle. The BFI document does not refer to any research in this area – indeed, it describes the model as 'hypothetical', and suggests that research has yet to be undertaken. However, there is in fact a substantial body of research on these issues, within a range of academic disciplines. In order to illustrate some of the difficulties raised by this kind of 'mapping' of media literacy, the following sections of the chapter discuss the broad outlines of this research and the different ways in which it can be interpreted. My focus here is on one particular aspect of the field, and on one medium – namely, on how children understand the relationship between television and the real world. This discussion therefore provides a *case study* of some of the broader issues at stake in attempting to define media literacy. We begin with a 'classical' developmental account.

Beyond the magic window

For babies, television must appear as simply a random selection of shapes, colours and sounds. However, as they develop the ability to identify three-dimensional shapes, and come to understand the functions of language, children begin to develop hypotheses about the relationship between television and the real world. To begin with, television may be perceived as a kind of 'magic window', or alternatively as a magic box in which tiny people are living. Yet by the time they are about two, children seem to have understood that television is a *medium* that represents events which are taking place (or have taken place) elsewhere. Through the experience of video, they also come to understand that television can be recorded and replayed, and that it is not necessarily 'live'.

From the age of two, children are also developing an understanding of the 'language' of television. They learn that it follows rules or conventions which are different from those of real life (Messaris, 1994). Thus, they learn that a zoom in to close-up does not mean that an object has got bigger, and that a cutaway to another object does not mean that the first object has disappeared (Salomon, 1979). They learn to 'fill the gaps' which have been left in editing, for example when a character leaves a room and is next seen walking down the street (Smith, Anderson and Fisher, 1985). They learn to recognize the beginnings and endings of programmes, and to perceive the differences between programmes and advertisements (Jaglom and Gardner, 1981).

Between the ages of three and five, the distinction between television and real life gradually becomes more flexible. While very young children appear to believe that all television is real, slightly older children may express precisely the opposite view; yet by around the age of five, children generally give more considered responses, suggesting that television is sometimes real, sometimes not (Messaris, 1986). Between about five and seven, they also begin to distinguish between different kinds of programmes according to how realistic they are perceived to be. For example, they are likely to distinguish between cartoons, puppet animation and live action, and may well find events portrayed in live action drama or news much more frightening than similar events shown in cartoons (Chandler, 1997; Dorr, 1983; Hawkins, 1977). These relationships are often worked through in their television-related play, where children are actively experimenting with the differences between 'real life' and 'just pretend'.

By middle childhood (age eight to nine), children are becoming more aware of the possible motivations of television producers – and indeed often quite cynical about them. For example, they will discuss how the narrative of a soap opera is organized in an attempt to keep us watching, or how advertisements attempt to persuade us to buy (Buckingham, 1993a). They are also keenly interested in how programmes are produced, and (by the age of ten or eleven) are offering increasingly 'critical' judgements about the quality of the acting or the realism of the décor (Davies, 1997; Dorr, 1983; Hodge and Tripp, 1986). In both respects, they are much more likely to regard television as an artefact, and much less likely to see it as simply a 'slice of life'.

Between middle childhood and early adolescence (between nine and twelve), children are also increasingly bringing more general social understandings to bear in their judgement of television, noting what is absent as well as questioning what is present (Hawkins, 1977). They may compare their own experience of family life, for example, with the representations provided on television, judging them to be less realistic as a result. Yet they may also acknowledge that in many cases, and for many reasons, television may not seek to be realistic in the first place, and that the need for plausibility has to be balanced against the need to amuse or entertain. Similarly, while a particular scene may be perceived as unrealistic on an empirical level – for example, in genres like science fiction or melodrama – it may also be seen to express an 'emotional realism' which children may recognize and find moving (Buckingham, 1996a).

Finally, from the age of about eleven or twelve upwards, children may begin to speculate about the ideological impact of television, and the potential effects of 'positive' or 'negative' images of particular groups on audiences, even hypothetical ones. They begin to become aware of the process of 'stereotyping', both in real life and in the media. They may also come to perceive the differences between different styles of 'realism', and develop an aesthetic appreciation of the various ways in which the illusion of reality is created by television (Buckingham, 1996a).

Reality problems

To some degree, this account describes an inherently *educational* process. Explicitly or implicitly, television as a medium teaches the competencies that are required to make sense of it, just as books teach children how to read, and what reading means (Meek, 1988). A good deal of children's television, for example, is concerned to 'demystify' the medium, by demonstrating how programmes are produced, and by playing with the distinctions between television and real life – even if its attempts to do this are sometimes contradictory. Furthermore, parents and peers are also informally teaching children as they watch television together. By confirming or questioning the accuracy of television representations, explaining and supplementing what is shown, and offering advice about whether television should be taken as a model of real-life behaviour, they are helping children to develop a more complex and nuanced understanding of the relationships between the medium and the real world (Alexander, Ryan and Munoz, 1984; Messaris and Sarrett, 1981).

Nevertheless, there are several problems that might be raised with such an account, and with psychological research of this kind more broadly. The sequence identified here can easily be mapped on to a Piagetian model of cognitive development (see Dorr, 1986); and as such, it runs the risk of being reduced to a mechanical sequence of 'ages and stages'. Critics of psychological research also suggest that it tends to adopt a rationalistic notion of child development as a steady progression towards adult maturity and rationality. In the case of work on children and the media, this developmentalist approach inevitably privileges certain kinds of judgements (particularly rational, 'critical' judgements) at the expense of others. Thus, a distanced critique of the implausibility of television is taken as a sign of 'maturity'; and in the process, any expression of pleasure or enjoyment may come to appear positively naïve.

Perhaps more significantly, this kind of account runs the risk of neglecting the *social* dimensions of children's engagements with television. Rather than seeing judgements about the reality of television simply as cognitive phenomena, my research suggests that they can also serve a variety of interpersonal functions (Buckingham, 1993a). In the context of group discussion, condemning programmes as 'unrealistic' provides a powerful means of defining one's own tastes, and thus of claiming a particular social identity. For example, girls' frequent complaints about the 'unrealistic' storylines or events in action-adventure cartoons often reflect a desire to distance themselves from what are seen as boys' 'childish' tastes, and thereby to proclaim their own (gendered) maturity. On the other hand, boys' rejection of the 'unrealistic' muscle-bound men in a programme like *Baywatch* may reflect anxieties about the fragility of their own masculine identity. Boys' rejection of melodrama or girls' rejection of violent action movies can thus be seen as rather more than the mechanical application of fixed judgements of taste: on the contrary, they represent an active *claim* to a particular social position – a claim which is sometimes tentative and uncertain, and in many cases open to challenge by others.

There is undoubtedly a considerable pleasure in this kind of critical talk: mocking the 'unrealistic' nature of television, speculating about 'how it's done', and playing with the relationship between television and reality would seem to be important aspects of most viewers' everyday interaction with the medium. Yet this kind of talk clearly does rely to some extent on disavowing one's own pleasure – or indeed displeasure – at the moment of viewing.

Drawing attention to the special effects in horror movies, or laughing at the over-acting in soap operas, seems to offer a sense of power and control over experiences that might have been frightening or moving at the time, and thus provides a pleasurable sense of security (Buckingham, 1996a).

However, it is important to stress that this kind of critical talk also serves particular functions in the context of *dialogue* with others. The context of research itself is clearly crucial here. Any adult asking children questions about television – particularly in a school context, as has generally been the case in my research – is likely to invite these critical responses. Most children know that many adults disapprove of them watching 'too much' television, and they are familiar with at least some of the arguments about its negative effects upon them. In some instances, these arguments are addressed directly, although children are generally keen to exempt themselves from such charges: while their younger siblings might copy what they watch, such accusations certainly do not apply to *them*. Just as adults appear to displace the 'effects' of television onto children – thereby implying that they themselves are not at risk – so children tend to suggest that these arguments apply only to those much younger than themselves.

In a sense, judgements about the 'unreality' of television could be seen to serve a similar function, albeit in a more indirect way. They enable the speaker to present himself or herself as a sophisticated viewer, who is able to 'see through' the illusions television provides. In effect, they represent a claim for social status – and, particularly in this context, a claim to be 'adult'. While these claims may be at least partly directed towards the interviewer and towards other children in the group, they often seem to rely on distinguishing the speaker from an invisible 'other' – from those viewers who are immature or stupid enough to believe that what they watch is real.

Significantly, there are often clear distinctions here in terms of social class. Broadly speaking, the middle-class children in my research have been more likely to perceive the interview context in 'educational' terms, and to frame their responses accordingly. By contrast, many of the working-class children have tended to use the invitation to talk about television as an opportunity to stake out their own tastes and to celebrate their own pleasures for the benefit of the peer group. While the middle-class children direct much of their talk towards the interviewer, and tend to defer to the interviewer's power, this is much less true of the working-class children, for whom the interviewer occasionally appears to be little more than an irrelevance. Thus, judgements about the reality of television are much more of a preoccupation for middle-class children. Both quantitatively and qualitatively, their judgements appear more complex and sophisticated than those of the majority of their working-class counterparts. Yet these arguments should not be seen to support any simplistic conclusions about the levels of 'media literacy' in different social classes. Rather, it would seem that these critical discourses serve particular social functions for these children, which are at least partly to do with defining their own class position. They provide a powerful means whereby middle-class children can demonstrate their own critical authority, and thereby distinguish themselves from those invisible 'others' – the 'mass' audience – who are, by implication, more at risk of suffering the harmful effects of television. Some further implications of this use of 'critical' discourse will be considered in more detail in chapter 7.

The limits of assessment

This detour into research about children and television illustrates several broader issues that are directly relevant to media education. On one level, it suggests that a social scientific concept such as 'representation' is not some kind of alien academic imposition on students. On the contrary, it shows how children's understanding of this issue derives (at least initially) from their everyday attempts to make sense of the medium, which begin in early childhood. However, it also suggests that judgements about representation or realism are frequently very complex. Children use a range of different types of knowledge in making such judgements, which include their developing knowledge about the processes of media production, their knowledge of the 'language' of media, and their knowledge of the real world. As this implies, judgements of reality are almost bound to be a focus of tension and debate. Some people (such as teachers in classrooms) may assume the power to impose particular definitions or versions of reality; and, as Hodge and Tripp (1986) suggest, 'reality' is often seen here as a matter of what children *ought* to think, rather than how things are. For this reason, these definitions are very likely to be resisted. This should at least caution us against the difficulties of attempting to enlighten children about the 'inaccuracies' and 'distortions' of the media – an approach which still informs many media education curricula (Bragg, 2001).

The key point here, however, is that children's judgements about the reality of what they watch on television cannot be seen as a purely cognitive or intellectual process, or as a merely individual one. On the contrary, it is through making 'critical' judgements of this kind that children seek to define their social identities, both in relation to their peers and in relation to adults. Likewise, assertions about the 'effects' of the media – whether explicit or implicit – inevitably reflect broader claims about one's own position. What we believe to be 'real' also depends to a large extent on what we *want* to be real, and hence on the pleasures that particular representations may offer us. Debating these kinds of issues in the classroom is undoubtedly a central aspect of media education; but for the reasons I have implied, it is also likely to be fraught with difficulty. The classroom is not a neutral space of dispassionate scientific enquiry, in which objective 'truth' can be easily established. On the contrary, it is a social arena in which students and teachers engage in an ongoing struggle over the right to define meaning and identity.

This account therefore illustrates the importance of what I have termed a *social* theory of media literacy. It suggests that making sense of the media is not simply a matter of what goes on inside children's heads: it is an interpersonal phenomenon, in which social interests and identities are unavoidably at stake. In this sense, a model like the British Film Institute's map of 'cineliteracy' is inevitably very reductive. It encourages us to assess 'outcomes' against normative statements of particular stages – defined, at least partly, through students' ability to employ particular 'key words' (from 'zoom' through 'stereotype' to 'hegemony'). It does not particularly help us to know how we might intervene in order to move particular students onwards in their understanding; nor does it acknowledge the social dynamics of learning in the classroom. Ultimately, it is not so much a model of 'learning progression' as a model of *assessment*.

In the following three chapters, I will be considering the different components of media literacy in more detail, and describing a range of relevant teaching strategies. In part III of the book, however, I will revisit some of these more awkward questions about learning, in the light of classroom-based research. Without denying the potential value of a developmental model, I will be arguing that we need a more dynamic – and more *social* – understanding of learning, that goes beyond the mechanical specification of 'ages and stages'. In concluding this chapter, however, I would like to

summarize what I see as the most significant emphases and benefits of this focus on 'literacy'.

Why literacy?

As I have suggested, the notion of 'media literacy' is far from
unproblematic. Yet it firmly situates the study of media within a
broader analysis of communication; and in doing so, it implicitly
questions the continuing dominance of print culture within education. As I shall indicate in more detail in chapter 6, media education
directly challenges many of the assumptions and practices that
characterize the teaching of language and literature in schools. It
represents a call for a more inclusive and relevant – but also more
coherent and rigorous – approach to teaching about culture and
communication.

In particular, the social theory of literacy outlined here implicitly
challenges the *textual* emphasis of much literature teaching – and
indeed, a good deal of media education as well (Morgan, 1998b).
Media literacy necessarily entails a systematic understanding of
the formal strategies and conventions of communication – and
media education is thus bound to entail close textual analysis.
Yet texts are only part of the picture. As Roger Silverstone (1999)
argues, media literacy obviously entails 'a capacity to decipher,
appreciate, criticise and compose'; but it also requires a broader
understanding of the social, economic and historical contexts in
which texts are produced, distributed and used by audiences. This
broader, multi-faceted approach is certainly apparent in the model
of assessment outlined above; and it is reflected both in the conceptual framework of media education outlined in chapter 4 and in
the range of teaching strategies described in chapter 5.

At the same time, the emphasis on literacy reminds us of an
element that is often neglected in media education. For literacy
clearly involves both reading *and* writing; and so media literacy
must necessarily entail both the interpretation and the production of media. As I shall indicate in more detail in part III of this
book, media teaching has historically been dominated by 'critical
analysis' – and indeed, by a relatively narrow form of *textual* analysis, which is primarily designed to expose the 'hidden ideologies'
of media texts. By contrast, media production has been regarded
with considerable unease and suspicion. Even where teachers
have given students opportunities to engage in their own creative

production – making their own videotapes or magazines or photographs, for example – they have often failed to integrate the two
elements. The model of 'media learning' I will be outlining in
chapter 9 attempts to provide a more dynamic, reflexive approach,
which combines critical analysis and creative production. In this
sense, I would argue that it represents a more comprehensive form
of media literacy than has been promoted in the past.

Part II

The State of the Art

What does media education look like in practice? Part II outlines the current 'state of the art' in media education, drawing on a range of published teaching materials and curriculum documents. Chapter 4 looks at the conceptual basis of media teaching, and how this is applied in specific classroom activities. Chapter 5 discusses a range of practical teaching and learning strategies. Chapter 6 considers the place of media education within and beyond the school curriculum.

4

Defining the Field

There are many ways in which we might choose to define a given subject or discipline within education. It could be defined in terms of a *body of knowledge* – a collection of facts or content to be learned. Alternatively, it could be defined in terms of a set of *skills* – a series of competencies to be performed and mastered. In general, however, media education has come to be defined in terms of *conceptual understandings*. This definition is often rendered in terms of a set of 'key concepts' or 'key aspects'. This approach has several clear advantages. It does not specify particular objects of study (a 'canon' of prescribed texts, for example); and this enables media education to remain responsive to students' interests and enthusiasms. Neither does it specify a given body of knowledge – which in a field such as media education would quickly become out-of-date.

There are various versions of the 'key concepts', several of which are embodied in curriculum documents around the world (see e.g. Bazalgette, 1989; Buckingham and Domaille, 2001; Grahame, 1991a; Hart, 1998; Ministry of Education, Ontario, 1989). In practice, however, there is a considerable degree of overlap between them. In this book, I use four key concepts: Production, Language, Representation and Audience. These concepts provide a theoretical framework which can be applied to the whole range of contemporary media, and indeed to 'older' media as well. In the following sections, I introduce these concepts in turn. My aim here – and in the two subsequent chapters in this part of the book – is to provide a straightforward, and indeed relatively schematic, summary of the current 'state of the art' in media education.

Production

At its most basic, 'production' involves the recognition that media texts are consciously manufactured. Although some media texts are made by individuals working alone, just for themselves or their family and friends, most are produced and distributed by groups of people, often for commercial profit. This means recognizing the economic interests that are at stake in media production, and the ways in which profits are generated – not least by 'exploiting' a given property or brand across a range of media. It also means acknowledging the increasingly global scale of the media industries, and the changing balance between global and local (or indigenous) media. More confident students should be able to debate the implications of these developments in terms of national and cultural identities, and in terms of the range of social groups that are able to gain access to media.

Studying media *production* means looking at:

- *Technologies*. What technologies are used to produce and distribute media texts? What difference do they make to the product?
- *Professional practices*. Who makes media texts? Who does what, and how do they work together?
- *The industry*. Who owns the companies that buy and sell media? How do they make a profit?
- *Connections between media*. How do companies sell the same products across different media?
- *Regulation*. Who controls the production and distribution of media? Are there laws about this, and how effective are they?
- *Circulation and distribution*. How do texts reach their audiences? How much choice and control do audiences have?
- *Access and participation*. Whose voices are heard in the media? Whose are excluded, and why?

In analysing production, students might focus on case studies of specific media institutions or companies. These should obviously include companies that operate on a global scale, with interests in a range of media, like Rupert Murdoch's News Corporation or the BBC. Here the focus would be on discovering how the different aspects of the business inter-connect and reinforce each other. An alternative approach here would be to investigate the international sale and distribution of television formats, such as *Big Brother* and *Who Wants to be a Millionaire?* Here, the focus would be on the global trade in media, and the ways in which formats are used and reinterpreted in specific national contexts. However, it is important that students are also aware of other models of media production. Thus, they might focus on public service broadcasters, or on smaller organizations such as non-profit 'alternative' media groups or minority publications, and compare their working practices and ideologies with those of major corporations. They should also be aware of the work of regulatory bodies.

Studying production is often best achieved through research-based tasks. Thus, students might identify the companies that own their favourite magazines, and the other titles or companies they own; or investigate the patterns of cross-ownership in their national television industry. Another possibility here would be to analyse how different audiences are targeted by a particular medium: for example, the ways in which different TV channels create 'brand identity' or the ways in which women's magazines address different sections of the audience, as defined in terms of age or social class.

Finally, it is important to emphasize that these kinds of questions can also be applied to students' own experiences of media production. In making their own magazines or videos, for example, students will have to make choices about their working methods and the technologies they will use, and about how they will identify and target their audience; and they will also have to confront all sorts of limitations in terms of the production and distribution of their finished product. Reflecting systematically on these experiences can help them to develop a more first-hand understanding of how media industries work.

Language

As I have noted, every medium has its own combination of languages that it uses to communicate meaning. Television, for example, uses verbal and written language as well as the 'languages' of moving images and sound. These things can be seen as languages in the sense that they use familiar codes and conventions that are generally understood. For example, particular kinds of music or camera angles may be used to evoke particular emotions; and a page of a newspaper or a sequence of shots in a film will be put together according to certain established rules. As in the case of verbal language, making meaningful statements in 'media languages' involves *paradigmatic* choices – that is, selecting from a range of possible elements – and *syntagmatic* combinations – that is, putting the elements together in sequences or combinations. To some extent, there are linguistic 'rules' here, which can be broken; and there are familiar idioms or genres that use particular combinations of linguistic tropes and devices. By analysing these languages, we can come to a better understanding of how meanings are created.

Studying media *languages* means looking at:

- *Meanings*. How do media use different forms of language to convey ideas or meanings?
- *Conventions*. How do these uses of language become familiar and generally accepted?
- *Codes*. How are the grammatical 'rules' of media established? What happens when they are broken?
- *Genres*. How do these conventions and codes operate in different types of media texts – such as news or horror?
- *Choices*. What are the effects of choosing certain forms of language – such as a particular type of camera shot?
- *Combinations*. How is meaning conveyed through the combination or sequencing of images, sounds or words?
- *Technologies*. How do technologies affect the meanings that can be created?

Studying media language should involve close observation and analysis. For instance, many media teachers use a broadly semiotic approach to analysing still images, such as those in advertising. Here, students might be encouraged to look systematically at elements such as framing and composition, the use of colour, typefaces and graphics, special effects, and so on, in order to assess how a particular 'product image' is created. Similarly, students might look at the rules and conventions of news broadcasts, noting the 'mise-en-scène' of the studio, the use of lighting, the newsreader's dress and body language, and the sequencing of items within a bulletin.

The 'syntagmatic' aspects of media language are often difficult to identify, precisely because they have become so naturalized and widely accepted. Drawing attention to this may require students to look at texts that consciously set out to 'break the rules': for example, students might compare the use of continuity editing in a mainstream Hollywood movie with the editing in an art movie or some 'alternative' pop videos.

As this implies, studying media language often involves close analysis of particular texts. It involves 'making the familiar strange' by looking in detail at how texts are composed and put together. For example, this might involve producing a storyboard from a television advertisement, or physically 'deconstructing' an image by breaking it down into its component parts. Another useful way of analysing media language is by means of comparison. Comparing several instances of a particular genre – for instance, advertisements for a particular type of product, or fashion photographs – can provide a good basis for identifying shared conventions, as well as patterns of variation across the genre.

However, understanding of media language is not only achieved through analysis. Here again, the experience of producing one's own media texts – and systematically experimenting with the 'rules' of media language – can offer new insights, and in a more direct way. Taking a photograph, for example, involves a whole series of 'linguistic' choices, to do with the composition of the objects in the shot, the framing and camera angle, the lighting, the focus and so on. Combining one's photograph with written text or with other images (for example in a layout or photomontage) involves further choices to do with how the meaning of the photograph is to be defined. These choices may be made unthinkingly; and one of the aims of media education is to encourage students to reflect on the choices they have made, and to consider their consequences.

Representation

The notion of 'representation' is one of the founding principles of media education. As I noted at the very start of this book, the media do not offer us a transparent 'window on the world', but a mediated *version* of the world. They don't just present reality, they re-present it. Even when it is concerned with real life events (as in news and documentary), media production involves selecting and combining incidents, making events into stories, and creating characters. Media representations therefore inevitably invite us to see the world in some particular ways and not others. They are bound to be 'biased' rather than 'objective'. However, this is not to imply that they are therefore deceiving audiences into mistaking representations for reality: as I have indicated, audiences also compare media with their own experiences, and make judgements about how 'realistic' they are, and hence how far they can be trusted. Furthermore, media representations can be seen as real in some ways but not in others: we may know that something is fantasy, yet recognize that it can still tell us about reality.

Studying media *representations* means looking at:

- *Realism.* Is this text intended to be realistic? Why do some texts seem more realistic than others?
- *Telling the truth.* How do media claim to tell the truth about the world? How do they try to seem authentic?
- *Presence and absence.* What is included and excluded from the media world? Who speaks, and who is silenced?
- *Bias and objectivity.* Do media texts support particular views about the world? Do they put across moral or political values?
- *Stereotyping.* How do media represent particular social groups? Are those representations accurate?
- *Interpretations.* Why do audiences accept some media representations as true, or reject others as false?
- *Influences.* Do media representations affect our views of particular social groups or issues?

Studying media representation therefore inevitably raises difficult questions about ideologies and values. In some instances, these values are quite overt. For instance, students should find it fairly easy to identify the political 'line' of a given newspaper, at least as this is expressed in the editorial section; however, they might find it more challenging to identify how that line is manifested in the selection and treatment of particular news stories, both in words and in images. Here again, comparison between different newspapers is a useful technique. Another aspect of representation that older students will be familiar with is *stereotyping*. They will be familiar with the argument that the media ignore minority or less powerful groups, or show them in a negative light. However, it is important that they should consider the functions of stereotypes,

both for producers and for audiences; and avoid the facile conclusion that stereotypes can simply be replaced with 'accurate'
representations.

As we have seen, students are frequently keen to assess media
representations in terms of their 'realism', but they should be encouraged to reflect on these judgements and the different criteria
that are used in making them. In this respect, it is important
to consider texts that are clearly marked as 'fantasy', or that
play with the distinction between fantasy and reality, as well as
documentary-style texts. More confident students will be able
to debate the implications of these different kinds and levels of
'realism' in terms of the potential influence of the media.

Here again, important insights into these issues can be gained
from the experience of media production. Students can explore
questions about accuracy and bias by being asked to produce
contrasting representations of an institution or an area that they
are familiar with, perhaps aiming at different audiences. The complexity of debates about stereotyping – and about 'positive images'
and 'negative images' – can often be explored more productively
by encouraging students to produce their own representations
of social issues, and to reflect on the ways in which audiences
respond to them.

Audiences

As I have noted, media education itself has often been informed
by simplistic assumptions about media audiences. The 'mass
audience' is often seen as gullible and easily influenced – and this
is particularly the case when that audience is children and young
people. Yet research has shown that audiences are much more
sophisticated and diverse than this would suggest. As the media
have proliferated, they increasingly have to compete for people's
attention and interest. Finding and keeping an audience is not easy:
producers might imagine they know what different groups of
people will want, but it is often hard to explain why some things
become popular and others do not. Studying audiences means
looking at how audiences are targeted and measured, and how
media are circulated and distributed; and at the different ways in
which individuals and social groups use, interpret and respond to
media. Debating these views about audiences, and attempting
to understand and reflect on our own and others' uses of media, is
therefore an indispensable element of media education.

Studying media *audiences* means looking at:

- *Targeting*. How are media aimed at particular audiences? How do they try to appeal to them?
- *Address*. How do the media speak to audiences? What assumptions do media producers make about audiences?
- *Circulation*. How do media reach audiences? How do audiences know what is available?
- *Uses*. How do audiences use media in their daily lives? What are their habits and patterns of use?
- *Making sense*. How do audiences interpret media? What meanings do they make?
- *Pleasures*. What pleasures do audiences gain from the media? What do they like or dislike?
- *Social differences*. What is the role of gender, social class, age and ethnic background in audience behaviour?

Like studying production, studying media audiences is therefore partly a matter of finding out about how the media industries operate. For example, students might look at how television audiences or newspaper readerships are measured, and how this information is then used, say, to set advertising rates. They might also consider how particular social groups or 'niche' audiences are targeted, for example by comparing the layout and cover design of different magazines; or the assumptions about audiences which are made by media regulators. There may also be an element of first-hand research here, for example looking at how 'fans' are cultivated by the media industries and how they organize and communicate among themselves (for example, on the internet).

As with representation, there is also likely to be a strong element of debate here. For example, students will be aware of public debates about issues such as media violence and censorship, and should be encouraged to consider the different motivations of the participants in such debates. Students need to analyse the kinds of assumptions that are typically made about different sections of the media audience, and the evidence on which these assumptions are based.

Studying audiences should also involve an element of self-reflection and first-hand research. For instance, students might be encouraged to keep 'media diaries', and collate and compare their findings with peers; or to observe the uses of media within their household. In the process, students should be encouraged to consider the merits and disadvantages of different research methods, and the validity and reliability of the information they generate. Such investigations often raise questions about the social differences in media use, and the extent to which it is possible to generalize about them; and about the different 'interpretive communities' of which media audiences are composed. Here again, the experience of production – for example, attempting to target a particular audience, and then taking account of their responses – can also offer important insights.

Key concepts in practice

The key concepts seem to offer a comprehensive and systematic approach to media education that can be applied to a range of media. However, they are not intended as a blueprint for a media education curriculum, or a list of contents that should be 'delivered' to students. They are not hierarchically organized, nor are they intended to be addressed in isolation from each other – as though one would spend one semester on language, followed by another on representation, and so on. On the contrary, they are seen as interdependent: each concept is a possible point of entry to a given area of media education, which necessarily invokes all the others (Bazalgette, 1992). They therefore provide a way of organizing one's thinking about any activity or unit of work which might be undertaken – and it should be emphasized that they can be applied as much to *creative* activities (such as taking photographs) as they can to *analytical* ones (such as studying advertising or the news).

In order to illustrate how the key concepts work in practice, I now intend to consider three examples of curriculum planning in media education. These examples are all adapted from *The Media Book*, a textbook produced by the English and Media Centre in London (Grahame and Domaille, 2001). They are all aimed at students aged between eleven and fourteen. Each unit of work is designed to run across several lessons, and includes a range of classroom activities, which I have briefly summarized here. These activities include small-group and whole class discussion, direct instruction by the teacher, role-plays and simulations, close textual analysis, discursive writing and media production activities. There will be a more detailed discussion of these different teaching and learning strategies in the following chapter.

Example 1: teaching *The Simpsons*

This unit provides a good example of how one text (in this case, a television programme) can be used as a *case study*, addressing all the four key concepts identified above. The unit includes the following activities:

The title sequence   Students are asked to watch the title sequence closely several times, noting key elements. Group discussion then focuses on issues such as the visual style, the use of sound, the image of the Simpsons' home town, and the elements of the sequence that change in each programme. Students are then asked to write a summary of what we learn about *The Simpsons* from this sequence, and how it sets up expectations for the programme as a whole.

Background and context   Here students are given a brief introduction to the history of TV situation comedies featuring families, from *I Love Lucy* through to *Married with Children*. They are then asked to identify the differences and similarities, for example in terms of social class, in terms of the types of families, and in terms of the settings. They are then given an introduction to *The Simpsons*, and asked to consider how it differs from other programmes in this genre.

Character   Students are asked to produce a character study of one *Simpsons* character, and compare their own analysis with that contained in the programme's publicity materials.

Comedy   Following a screening of a single episode, students are asked to break down the plot and identify the nature of the humour in each incident. Students are encouraged to think about the different types of humour (satire, slapstick, absurdity, 'black' comedy and so on), and then carry out a further analysis of an episode of their choice.

Conventions   Building on their analysis of the two episodes, students are asked to consider how the programme uses – and also departs from – the conventions of its genre. For instance, they are asked about how it uses the conventions of situation comedy; how it uses animation to 'break the rules' of verisimilitude; and the extent to which it can be seen as 'realistic'. They are then asked to write a detailed critical analysis of one episode.

Industry   Here students are provided with some information about the production process (scripting, animation, overseas sales, scheduling, merchandising, and so on). They are then asked to study the cover of a *Simpsons* videotape, and find out the roles played by different companies in production and marketing. Finally, they are asked to carry out some research on *Simpsons* merchandise, considering how it is targeted at different audiences and how it is bound by the copyright requirements of the production company.

Debates   Students are presented with a range of statements about *The Simpsons*, ranging from positive newspaper reviews to the criticisms voiced by President Bush. They are then asked to evaluate and debate these statements in the light of their own responses, focusing particularly on the idea that the programme presents 'negative role models'.

Simulation   Finally, students are asked (in groups) to undertake a simulation, in which they produce an outline of an animated family show that is specific to their national context. They are asked to devise characters, settings and sample storylines, and think about ways of promoting their show through merchandising. In addition to reporting back to the whole class, they also have to produce a written rationale for their proposals.

This unit addresses all four key concepts through an integrated study of one text. The aspects covered would include the following:

* *Production*: production processes, merchandising, international distribution.
* *Language*: genre (the sitcom), form (animation), codes and conventions.
* *Representation*: realism, stereotyping, moral values, images of the family.
* *Audience*: targeting audiences, interpretations, influences, pleasures (comedy).

Example 2: selling youth

This unit is organized more thematically, in that it focuses on a genre (advertising) and a theme ('youth') that cut across several media. It focuses on advertising that specifically targets young people, and the broader issues to do with consumer culture that it raises. It includes the following activities:

Reading ads　The unit begins with a description produced by a drinks manufacturer of a particular drink, 'product X'. Students are asked to identify product X from the range of drinks produced by this company. In doing so, they are asked to think about how advertisements define the image and qualities of products, how particular audiences are targeted, and how these are reflected in the design of product logos.

Creating the image　The students go on to brainstorm ideas for selling product X (now identified as a drink called Juice Up), and then compare this with real ads for the product. They then undertake a detailed analysis of three ads from the Juice Up campaign, focusing on the visual techniques, editing and soundtrack. They are asked to think particularly about how the product is targeted at a youth audience, how this is reflected in its marketing and branding, and how young people are represented in the ads.

Marketing　The students are given an article from an advertising trade newspaper concerned with the Juice Up campaign, and asked to consider how the marketing campaign was conceived by the advertising agency and the company. Discussion here focuses on issues such as the scheduling and placement of the ads, and what the producers assume about their audience.

Scheduling　Students are asked to watch as many TV advertising breaks as possible at home. They are then asked to consider the range of ads that target their age group, and where these are most likely to be scheduled.

Catching the audience　On the basis of their viewing at home, students are asked to identify which ads are most effective at catching their attention, and how they achieve this. They identify the ads they personally liked the most, and what they liked about them; and then share the results with the whole class. In the process, they consider the assumptions that are made about themselves as a target audience, and the extent to which they are accurate.

The advertiser's perspective　Students read a series of statements made by an advertising agency executive about the youth audience. Students are asked to debate these statements, and then assess them against their viewing of a series of ads produced by the agency in question. Following group discussion, students are then asked to produce a written essay analysing a particular campaign of their choice, and discussing how it attempts to target the youth audience. They are asked to consider the kinds of images and identities such campaigns are selling to their own age group.

Making ads The final activity in this unit consists of a simulation, in which students are asked to assume the role of an advertising agency responsible for marketing a new breakfast cereal product aimed at their own age group. They are given a description of the product, and asked to identify its potential appeal, both to the target audience and to their parents, who will actually be buying it. Through 'brainstorming', they identify the image or 'personality' of the product, and consider likely marketing strategies. They then go on to devise a logo and packaging design, a script or storyboard for a television ad, and to suggest where and when it should be scheduled. In presenting their ideas, they are asked to explain how their campaign is targeted, and how their strategy is designed to appeal to the audience.

Like the previous unit, this unit addresses all four key concepts through an integrated study of one media theme. The aspects covered would include the following:

- *Production*: the work of advertising agencies, TV schedulers and commercial companies.
- *Language*: the codes and conventions of advertising, the creation of a 'product image'.
- *Representation*: images of young people and the values they are seen to represent.
- *Audience*: targeting audiences, influences, pleasures and preferences.

Example 3: photography and identity

This unit looks at photography and documentary film, and raises questions about how they are used to represent and construct identities. The focus here is therefore much less on popular 'mass' media than the two previous units. The unit includes the following activities:

Portraits Students are shown a series of pictures from the personal album of a fourteen-year-old girl. They are asked to discuss the differences between the images, for example in terms of where and why they were taken, the different poses and expressions, and the different types of image (for example, snapshots, formal portraits, family groups, etc.). They are also asked to match the girl's own captions to the photographs.

Making a photo-documentary   They are then asked to sequence the photographs to make a short 'photo-documentary' about the girl, and to debate the different ways this might be done. They are asked to create a script for a soundtrack, and to suggest music that might be used. They are then invited to compare their productions, debating how the girl herself might have wanted the images to be arranged for different audiences. This activity introduces the key question about how accurate or truthful photography can be.

Exploring a documentary   The students then watch a short BBC documentary called *Photo-You*, which is about photo-booths of the kind that are often found in railway stations or airports. Before viewing they are asked to consider the different functions of documentaries as a genre (such as teaching, offering a personal view, persuading, entertaining, etc.). They are then asked to identify examples of how *Photo-You* and other documentaries achieve these purposes.

Documentary conventions   Students are then introduced to a range of techniques used in documentaries (such as interviews, archive compilations, reconstructions, voice-over narration, etc.) and asked to identify which of them are used in *Photo-You*, and the effects they produce.

Editing   Students are asked to undertake a close analysis of *Photo-You*, one sequence at a time. Questions are asked at each stage about the choices made by the film-makers, the different techniques used, the placement of the camera, the selection of images and sounds, and so on. They are then asked to 're-edit' the film using a series of still images provided on a CD-ROM. In groups, they are asked to produce a version of the film that will instruct people on how to get good pictures in a photo-booth, persuade people of the benefits of installing photo-booths, or train people to look after and clean photo-booths. Having considered these alternatives, they are then asked to write to the film's director with a personal response to the film.

Commentaries   Here the students are asked to write a commentary for another short piece of film, about a graduation ceremony at Oxford University. Again, groups are asked to write commentaries reflecting different views, and then compare them, thinking about how the commentary can change the meaning of the images.

Writing a proposal Here the students work towards a proposal for a short documentary film, written for the commissioning editor of a TV station. They are invited to assess the director's proposal for *Photo-You*, and consider which aspects were omitted from the final film.

Simulating a documentary Finally, the students are asked to put together their proposal, which is for a five-minute film about 'a day in the life of our school'. They are given a mock memorandum from the commissioning editor, and asked to think through the criteria they will use in selecting which film will be made. Finally, they plan and make the film itself.

Here again, this unit addresses all four key concepts through an integrated study of one media issue. The aspects covered would include the following:

* *Production*: the work of documentary film-makers and com-missioning editors.
* *Language*: the codes and conventions of photography and documentary, the use of commentary, sound and images.
* *Representation*: images of individual identities and social institu-tions (the school).
* *Audience*: how documentaries attempt to teach, persuade, convince audiences of their truthfulness, and so on.

Conclusion: some general principles

This description indicates several general principles which char-acterize good practice in media education. These can be categor-ized under three headings: overall aims, curriculum planning and pedagogy.

Aims

In terms of the overall aims discussed in chapter 1, the approach adopted in these units is clearly oriented towards *preparation* rather than *protection*. The work does not begin from the assumption that students are passive victims of media manipulation, who are in need of inoculation against media influence. The second unit on advertising, for example, assumes that students are able to under-stand the ways in which they are targeted by advertisers, and to reflect on how their own choices and values as consumers may be informed by media images. The pleasures students experience from advertising are acknowledged and explored, but students are also assumed to be capable of making rational, informed decisions on their own behalf. None of the units really sets out to 'rescue' students from what are perceived as the negative effects of the media.

In general, therefore, much of the work is *deductive* rather than *inductive*: it is about students reaching their own conclusions from the evidence provided, rather than seeking to command their assent to a position that has been decided in advance. In the *Simpsons* unit, for example, students are presented with a range of arguments about the moral and political issues raised by the programme, and encouraged to reflect systematically upon them. Clearly, this ap-proach is not one that seeks to avoid or ignore complex issues; but its aim is not to provide a form of 'counter-propaganda'.

Curriculum planning

As I have noted, each of these units attempts to address all of the four key concepts in an integrated, holistic way. While different emphases emerge more strongly than others at different times, it is implicitly assumed that students need to understand how these different elements of the media are related. Thus, the first unit on *The Simpsons* addresses each of the key concepts, focusing in turn on representation, language, production and audience; and (as in the other units) the final activity effectively integrates these into a single, practical exploration of how they are related.

Differences of emphasis are of course inevitable: not all key aspects will be equally covered in each and every unit of work. The third unit on photography and documentary, for instance, is prob-ably stronger on aspects of media language than it is on produc-tion. However, it should be clear from these accounts that any one of the key aspects can (at least potentially) serve as a 'way in' to any of the others. Implicitly, therefore, meaning is seen to emerge from the *relationships* between the various aspects. Thus, the unit on advertising implicitly regards the production of 'youth culture' as something that emerges from a negotiation between the media industries and the needs and expectations of audiences. Likewise, the questions about realism raised in the unit on *The Simpsons* imply that viewers also make critical judgements about how the media represent the world: realism is not simply a property of texts, but also a perception on the part of viewers or readers.

Pedagogy

Within the three units described above, there is a diverse range of pedagogic strategies. These include: individual, small-group and whole-class work; provision of information by teachers and by students; critical analysis and practical media production; as well as strategies such as simulation, textual analysis and student research. In some respects, the approach could be described as 'student-centred', in that there is a strong emphasis on students sharing their own knowledge and opinions, and forming their own conclusions about the issues. All these units begin by assuming that students already know something about the topics to be addressed, and that their knowledge is both valid in itself and a useful resource for further reflection.

However, there is also a recognition that there are things that students do *not* know, and which they need to be taught. For example, the third unit on documentary explicitly sets out to teach about techniques of documentary film-making, and about the ways in which producers 'pitch' their ideas to television companies. In some instances (for example in relation to media language), this is a matter of making explicit what students already know implicitly – turning 'passive' knowledge into 'active' knowledge. This occurs through systematic analysis, and through sharing and comparison with peers. But in other instances (for example in relation to production), it involves directly teaching students information they do not already know. This occurs both through the direct provision of information by the teacher, and through research on the part of the students. These different teaching and learning strategies will be addressed in more detail in the following chapter.

5

Classroom Strategies

The course units outlined in the previous chapter use a range of teaching strategies. Few of these are specific to media education: some might just as easily be found in social education, or in history teaching, for example. However, media educators have steadily developed a repertoire of teaching techniques that are suited to particular aspects of the curriculum. In this chapter, we will look at six of these techniques: textual analysis, contextual analysis, case studies, translations, simulations and production. The first three of these are more analytical, while the last three are more practical. Here again, my account draws on published teaching materials, particularly those produced by the English and Media Centre (e.g. Grahame, 1991a; Grahame and Domaille, 2001) and the British Film Institute (e.g. Bazalgette, 1989; Bowker, 1991; British Film Institute, 2000). This is by no means an exhaustive selection of teaching techniques, but it gives a fair idea of the range of approaches that might be involved in any media education course. While many of these approaches might be tried with students of any age, my main emphasis is on those aged eleven to eighteen.

Implicit in these approaches are questions and assumptions about the nature of *learning*. As I have implied, students already have a great deal of knowledge about the media – almost certainly more than they have of other areas of the curriculum. There is some truth in the argument that, when it comes to media education, teachers are no longer the experts. Nevertheless, there is likely to be a great deal that students do not already know, and which it is important for teachers to teach. This relationship between existing knowledge and new knowledge, and its implications for learning, will be considered in detail in part III of this book.

Textual analysis

Textual analysis is probably the most familiar aspect of media education for teachers whose previous experience is in teaching literature or art. It is important to distinguish here between *textual* analysis and *content* analysis, although both are useful strategies for media teachers. Content analysis is well established as a method in the academic study of communication: it involves the quantitative analysis of a relatively large corpus of material using predetermined codes or categories. For example, students might count the proportions of image and text, or the amount of space devoted to advertising, in a range of newspapers; or they might conduct a 'head count' of the numbers of males and females in advertisements, or the kinds of role they occupy. This can prove time-consuming in the classroom, but it does offer a rigorous way of testing hypotheses and identifying overall patterns in a large sample.

By contrast, textual analysis offers depth rather than breadth. It tends to focus in great detail on single texts; and the texts selected are often quite short or limited in scope, such as single photographs, advertisements, opening sequences, trailers or music videos. Textual analysis involves close attention to detail, and rigorous questioning. Students need to be steered away from making instant judgements, and encouraged to provide evidence for their views. Analysis of this kind means 'making the familiar strange' – taking something that students may know very well and asking them to look very closely at how it has been put together, and to think about why it has been made in that way. In the process, students will come to understand that visual and audio-visual texts have to be 'read' like other texts.

Let us consider how students might undertake a textual analysis of a TV advertisement, for example. The approach that is often used in media education is mainly derived from semiotics, and consists of three stages (see Masterman, 1980). The analysis generally begins with *description*: students are asked to identify and list everything they can see and hear in the text. At this stage, the teacher may cover the video screen and ask students to listen carefully to the soundtrack: the students should then describe the type of music, the sound effects, the language, the speaker's tone of voice, the use of silence, and so on. The teacher may then turn off the sound and ask students to concentrate just on the images, for example by using 'freeze-frame' on the video. Here, the focus should be partly on identifying what is shown – the use of settings, 'body language', colour and so on – and partly on *how* it is shown – for instance, the use of camera angles, composition and lighting. Teachers may ask students to 'spot the shots', marking each change in shot and looking carefully at how shot transitions are created, and considering the pace and rhythm of the editing. Finally, students will be asked to consider how these various elements are combined in the text as a whole.

Only when this process of detailed description is complete should students move on to the second stage of textual analysis, where they are invited to consider the *meaning* of the text. Again, this should begin in a systematic way, looking at the connotations and associations invoked by the various elements of the text. For example, students might consider particular images or elements of the setting, or particular musical sequences, and identify what they remind them of. They might look at the way lighting or sound or colour is used to establish a particular mood or atmosphere, or how particular camera angles or movements place us as viewers in relation to the scene. One useful approach here is called the 'commutation test', where students are asked to imagine how the meaning would change if a particular element of the text were to change – for example, if the producers had used a different character or piece of music, or a different style of graphic design. 'Intertextuality' is also important here: students should be asked to think of other texts (or genres) to which this text seems to relate or refer.

Finally, students can move on to a third stage, where they are encouraged to make *judgements* about the text as a whole. These judgements may relate to the values or ideologies they identify in the text. In the case of our TV advertisement, for example, we are likely to discover that the product is associated with qualities that are seen as positive in some way: the ad may claim that a product is 'natural' or 'homely' or 'sexy' or 'scientific', or that it will make the user into a better person – more powerful or sophisticated or attractive, for example. The analysis should enable students to understand how this claim has been made, and to make an informed judgement about the values that it invokes. These judgements may also relate to the 'quality' of the text – in other words, how effective it has been in attempting to convince us of its claims, or to convey its meaning. 'Quality' in this sense is also about aesthetic pleasure; and one result of the analysis should be that students are able to understand *how* the text has managed (or indeed failed) to create feelings of excitement or glamour or energy, for example.

Of course, this is not to imply that textual analysis is always such a well-regulated process: as we shall see in more detail in chapter 7, there may be a great deal of negotiation and debate between students over the meaning of a particular text, and about their judgements of it. The aim is not for students to agree on their conclusions, but for them to be systematic and rigorous in their analysis.

Textual analysis obviously involves students acquiring a technical vocabulary (or 'metalanguage'), for example in order to describe different types of camera angles or shot transitions. However, it is very important that such analysis does not degenerate into a routine, mechanical activity: it should be used sparingly, and in relation to other activities. Textual analysis should also have a practical dimension. Students might be asked to 'deconstruct' an image into its component parts, labelling each part with an analytical commentary, or to construct storyboards from moving image texts. This can lead on to constructing montages of 'found' images, or storyboarding photo-strips or short video sequences. Taken in isolation, textual analysis can seem rather like the teaching of formal grammar: if it is to be meaningful for students, it needs to be applied to real texts in real contexts, and explored in practical ways.

Contextual analysis

Textual analysis works by removing texts from the contexts in which they are usually encountered. While this can be a powerful way of 'making the familiar strange', it also has its dangers. Close attention to *context* will enable us to understand the connections between particular forms of media language and two other key aspects of media education: production and audience.

One useful technique here is to encourage students to focus on the elements of a text that they might usually ignore. For example, the opening and closing sequences of movies or TV programmes can provide important information about how the text is targeted at a particular audience, and the different roles in the production process. Title sequences on television, for example, are used to identify and 'sell' the programme to its intended audience. They may offer a succinct summary of the programme's most significant 'appeals' to its audience – which may include characters, settings or typical storylines. Detailed textual analysis of the music or editing, for example, can reveal a great deal about the producers' assumptions about their audience. Title or closing credit sequences also contain information about who produced the text, the companies that own and distribute it, the various roles involved in making it, and so on. Identifying these can alert students to the financial (and perhaps ideological) interests it may represent. This technique is often most effective when there is a comparative dimension – for instance, when comparing the title sequences of two examples of a given TV genre that are aimed at different target audiences; or when looking at the companies that produce and distribute two contrasting representations of a particular social issue.

Another technique is to gather information about how a given text was marketed and distributed to audiences. This might include looking at TV listings magazines, video catalogues, shop displays, film posters and ads, promotional web sites, trailers and press releases. Media companies will often provide a 'press kit' that can be mined for such information. Students should evaluate this material, paying attention to the claims made about the text and the methods being used to promote it. In many instances, they will become aware of the extent of cross-media marketing, and the connections between the various companies involved – which may operate on a global scale. If possible, it is useful to compare such material from different cultures – for example, by considering how a given film was marketed in two different countries.

In addition, students should seek out information about how the text was received, using the trade press or the media pages in national newspapers, or the internet – for example, to find data on TV ratings, box office receipts and reviews. This will encourage students to consider the effectiveness of the text in reaching its target audience. However, students should also be encouraged to think about how this kind of information is gathered, and how reliable it is; and about the ways in which it is fed back into future planning. In some instances, students will be alerted to the ways in which media companies deliberately court controversy in order to sell their products. Taken together, these kinds of activities should help students develop an awareness of the economic motivations behind the media industries, and the often competitive, risky nature of the enterprise.

These activities are often easiest to undertake in relation to visual media, although contextual information of this kind is available for a range of other media. The popular music industry is particularly fruitful here: students can begin by studying CD covers, posters and advertising, and move on to look at the range of merchandising (both 'official' and 'unofficial') that surrounds successful acts. This material often provides a very clear indication of how particular audiences are targeted, and how products are differentiated from each other in the marketplace. The music industry trade press, record companies' press packs, fan web sites and fanzines can also be used to explore the connections between the various companies involved, and the struggles that sometimes occur between music fans and the industry. It may also be interesting for students to consider how particular acts may have attempted to change (or widen) their audience over time, and how this is reflected in the ways in which they are packaged and marketed.

This kind of contextual analysis draws students away from a narrow focus on textual explication. It encourages them to recognize that media texts do not simply appear from nowhere, but that promotion and marketing are crucially important aspects of the ways in which texts find audiences. At the same time, it is important that students do not fall into the view that such activities are merely a form of conspiracy to manipulate the public. In this respect, it is important to consider examples of media products that fail to reach audiences, or to generate profit (which constitute by far the majority); and to consider how audiences can appropriate and change meanings – sometimes in ways that the media industries might not favour.

Case studies

This broadly contextual approach features more strongly in the third technique, case study. Here, students are encouraged to conduct in-depth research into a media topic of their choice. Of course, it is important that media educators should respond to their students' enthusiasms, and to contemporary controversies; but this can be very demanding and time-consuming. In some instances, teachers may be able to gather the necessary information; but in many cases, students will need to do this themselves. Independent research and investigation of this kind should therefore play an important role in media education.

The simplest kind of case study focuses on the production, marketing and consumption of a particular text. To some extent, this is an extension of the kind of contextual analysis discussed above. The launch of new media products provides a particularly useful opportunity for this kind of case study: students might focus on the launch of a new TV show or youth magazine, the release of a new feature film, or a current advertising campaign, for example.

Students may gather information of the kind identified above and (if possible) arrange to speak to producers.

A second kind of case study involves a cross-media investigation of a particular issue. For example, students might choose to explore the use of animals in advertising, selecting particular examples for close study, using the trade press, looking at audience responses, and consulting with relevant pressure groups and regulatory bodies. Alternatively, students might choose to focus on the media coverage of a particular event, such as an election or a major sporting event, or a local news story. Here, they might study how stories are circulated, as each medium feeds off the others.

A third approach involves investigating media audiences. For example, students might develop and administer small-scale questionnaires or 'media diaries' looking at patterns of media use, or conduct observational studies or interviews with particular audience groups – possibly focused on a particular text or genre. Students could be encouraged to compare their findings with those of published audience research (for example, the TV ratings), and to present them in a range of visual as well as written formats. They might also make use of the range of fan web sites, discussion groups and forums on the internet.

Finally, students might choose to investigate the work of a single media company or organization. This need not be a major global company: it could equally well be a small organization run by a minority group, a local newspaper or a regulatory body, who might be more willing to provide information. If students are undertaking 'work experience', this study could be conducted via observation. Here again, students will need to use 'insider' sources, such as industry reference books, the trade press and company PR materials.

While these different types of case study have different emphases, they present important opportunities to address the *relationships between* several of the key concepts. A case study of *Big Brother*, for example, might usefully cover:

- *Production*: the production process, the broadcasters and sponsors, cross-media marketing, global sales
- *Language*: editing, visual style, the generic mix of documentary, soap opera and game show
- *Representation*: 'realism' and falsehood, performance, the construction of characters, moral values
- *Audiences*: ratings, newspaper reviews, 'interactive TV', audience response.

Work on a case study of this kind thus involves a range of sources of data. In addition to watching and analysing extracts from the show, students would be looking at other media coverage, reading publicity put out by the production company, visiting the web sites, reading the trade press and researching other people's responses to the programme.

The case study approach clearly requires students to develop skills as 'researchers' – skills that are not frequently taught on the school curriculum. These skills are partly a matter of gathering information – for example, by using libraries or the internet, or making enquiries with media companies, or by conducting surveys or observational studies. However, they are also to do with *evaluating* such information. Students may find it relatively easy to locate material on the internet, for example; but they need to make some careful and informed judgements about how far such material can be trusted. Here, as with any other media text, students need to be aware that the material they have gathered is a *representation* that has been produced by people who will obviously have particular interests; and they therefore need to assess this material critically. Likewise, when undertaking audience research, students need to reflect upon the inherent limitations and biases of their chosen methods, and the representativeness of their samples.

Finally, it is important that students recognize that a case study is an *example* – it is, precisely, a case study of broader issues or tendencies. Media education is not a licence for students simply to accumulate vast amounts of information about their media enthusiasms. They need to be encouraged to recognize the broader issues that are at stake in them. In this respect, it is important that students are encouraged to present their research to the teacher and to their peers at regular intervals, and to present a summary of their key findings. Debate and questioning should encourage a more distanced, reflective approach.

Translations

This approach focuses primarily on questions of media language and representation, but it can also involve the more contextual issues addressed above. 'Translation' is essentially concerned with the differences that arise when a given source text is employed in different media or in different genres. The approach can be both analytical and practical.

The more analytical approach involves students investigating the treatment of a given issue or the use of a given source text in two different media, or for two different audiences. This might mean examining how a key moment in a fictional print text has been dealt with in two different film adaptations; or comparing how a given theme has been dealt with in fictional and factual forms. Students can systematically examine which elements remain the same between the two versions, and which are changed – and, most importantly, why this might have occurred. In the process, students will be considering how ideas and issues are represented in different ways in different genres or media forms, or for different audiences; and how a given text can be presented in a variety of ways.

Thus, in the case of fiction, they should develop a clearer understanding of how different media deal with features such as character construction, setting, time and narration. They may come to recognize that what can be communicated in one medium may be impossible to show in another. In the case of factual material, they should consider how different treatments in different media inevitably lead to a partial or 'biased' view of the world. For example, students might choose a group of people who tend to be presented in the media in distinctive ways, such as refugees. They could gather and analyse a range of material in different media (such as news coverage, material from refugee charities and pressure groups, even fictional material), comparing the kinds of information that can be conveyed in each. This kind of activity also shows how the intended audience of a text can affect its ideological or moral message.

The more practical approach involves students themselves 'translating' a text from one medium to another – from a newspaper story to a TV news item, or a short story to a film sequence, or vice-versa. If production facilities are not available, students might translate a print text into a script or illustrated storyboard. This kind of work enables students to realize the possibilities and limitations of different media, and the ways in which meanings can change when they are presented in different forms or transposed from one medium to another. This provides a very practical way of addressing questions about the 'codes and conventions' of different forms of media language. In the case of translating fiction from print into film or video, for example, students may have to address the difficulties posed by first-person narration, or changes in the narrative point of view. Conversely, translating from film to print can pose challenges in finding verbal equivalents for the use of sound and visuals to create atmosphere and suspense.

In both cases, it is important to address the contextual issues identified above. The constraints and possibilities of different media are not solely determined by the characteristics of the media themselves: they also depend upon the production context, and on the intended audience. One of the problems with the use of 'the film of the book' in literature teaching is that these issues are frequently ignored. A 'classic' literary text is compared with a mass-market film adaptation; and the latter is, almost inevitably, found to be lacking. Yet millions more people have seen Baz Luhrmann's *Romeo and Juliet* than have ever seen Shakespeare's original text performed on stage; and the particular qualities and achievements of each of them need to be assessed in terms of the different audiences they are seeking to reach, and their overall aims. As this implies, media analysis should be both textual *and* contextual.

Simulations

Simulation is a very popular technique in media teaching. Several examples of this approach were briefly mentioned in the previous chapter. Simulation is a form of role-play: it involves putting students into the position of media producers, albeit in an essentially fictional way. Simulation is particularly useful for addressing questions about production – for example, about production roles and processes within the media industries, and about how media producers balance financial, technological and institutional constraints in their work. Students are generally presented with a series of choices to make or problems to solve, and then encouraged to reflect upon the consequences of their decisions, in comparison with those of other groups within the class. The teacher may also act 'in role' as a commissioning editor or executive producer.

Simulations do not necessarily need to proceed to the stage of production itself. Thus, students might be asked to act as TV programme makers tendering proposals to a broadcaster for a new series in a given genre – a children's series, for example. Here, they will be required to produce a description of the series, outlining its appeal for its target audience, as well as character sketches, plot summaries and costings. Alternatively, they might be asked to introduce a range of hypothetical new characters to an existing programme (such as a soap opera), or to develop a new location; or to take an existing text and 're-package' it for a different audience; or to create a 'spin-off', perhaps in a different medium. These approaches can obviously be applied to other media: students might become authors seeking to sell proposals for a new 'blockbuster' novel to a major publisher, or journalists seeking to launch a new magazine title.

In some cases, this approach can become quite elaborate. For instance, there are several published simulations about the popular music industry, in which students are asked to form an imaginary band, get them signed with a record company, seek relevant publicity and media exposure, and so on. In this kind of simulation, different groups in the class may take roles representing different groups of personnel: managers, agents, record companies, radio stations, and so on. The same approach has been used in relation to the film industry. Here, groups of students act as competing production companies: they have to develop script ideas, identify marketable stars and directors, and draw up budgets. These ideas must then be 'pitched' or 'sold' to another group of students acting as potential financial backers. Here, students will come to recognize that success depends not just on the originality or appeal of the idea itself, but also on the 'package' that is presented, and its potential for merchandising and global sales.

Students can also simulate the activities of other aspects of the media industries. For example, they might be given a TV scheduling exercise, in which they are asked to timetable a given selection of programmes into an evening's viewing, perhaps in competition with another channel whose schedule has already been fixed. This encourages students to think about the ways in which different audiences are targeted at different times of day, and about how channels establish a distinctive identity. Regulation is another aspect of the industry that can be explored in this way. For example, students might be presented with examples of films that have to be classified or certificated according to certain age bands, and asked to provide justifications for their decisions.

In some instances, simulations will be carried through to the production stage. For example, questions about the selection and construction of news can be addressed very effectively through a practical simulation. Here, students act as a production team (editors, producers, newsreaders) and are presented with a steady flood of incoming stories of various kinds over a period of several hours (or lessons). Production constraints – for instance, in the form of last-minute items and instructions from station executives

– are also thrown in. The students are required to select, edit and sequence the stories into a short news bulletin (for radio or TV) aimed at a particular target audience, which is then recorded 'live' at a pre-determined time.

Another approach that is frequently used is the 'photoplay'. Here, students are given a series of still images and invited to select and sequence them to form a storyboard for a moving image sequence. Such activities can be used to explore how editing is employed to construct mood and atmosphere; or to construct different types of narrative from the same material. Different groups of students in the class can also be briefed to create different end products, and the results compared. Such materials are now available using CD-ROM technology (rather than scissors and glue); and some of these materials also use moving images and sound, thus enabling students to explore the effects of different combinations or sequences.

The obvious advantage of simulations is that they offer a direct, 'hands-on' experience of aspects of media that are often difficult to teach about in other ways. For example, there is a risk that teaching about media production and the media industries can become heavily information-laden; and in this area, simulation provides a much more active, accessible approach. Simulating media production for different target audiences, and thinking how to attract and reach them, can also provide an engaging way of approaching this area, which can sometimes appear rather 'abstract'.

However, as with case studies, one of the key issues for teachers here is to enable students to realize the broader issues at stake. The personal immediacy of a simulation can make it hard for students to distance themselves from what is happening, and to reflect upon the consequences of the choices they have made. 'Debriefing' is particularly important in this respect: students need to be encouraged to evaluate their own and each other's work, and to consider the similarities and differences between the 'unreal' world of the simulation and the real world of the media industries.

The value of a simulation also depends very much on the nature and quality of the 'input' – that is, the ways in which students are informed about the area of media they are working on, and the constraints that are built in to the process. Students need to be effectively briefed about the nature of their particular role and the institutional circumstances they are operating within; they need to be presented with problems that are sufficiently challenging; and their choices should genuinely make a difference. A simulation should not be regarded as just a form of play acting.

Production

To a greater or lesser extent, most of the approaches discussed so far involve some form of media production. Practical, hands-on use of media technology frequently offers the most direct, engaging and effective way of exploring a given topic. It is also the aspect of media education that is most likely to generate enthusiasm from students. Practical work offers a comparatively 'safe' space, in which students can explore their emotional investments in the media, and represent their own enthusiasms and concerns. As I have argued, the notion of 'media literacy' necessarily implies that 'reading' the media and 'writing' the media should be inextricably connected. For all these reasons, media production is a central and indispensable aspect of media education – although it is often the most challenging one for teachers.

As we shall see in more detail in chapter 8, some media educators are rather sceptical about the educational value of production work. They argue that students' productions are often little more than a mindless imitation of mainstream media. However, recent research has questioned this view. Researchers have shown that students' uses of popular media forms and genres frequently display a clear understanding of 'media language', and a form of ironic distance which is at least potentially 'critical'. By making these dimensions of their work explicit, and through subsequently reflecting upon them, students can be encouraged to develop a more thoughtful approach to concepts such as representation, which are sometimes dealt with in rather mechanistic terms.

The advent of digital technology has created significant new opportunities here. In many cases, this technology is both less expensive and easier to use than the technology it is replacing. For instance, editing video on a computer is much more straightforward than using older analogue equipment, while digital still cameras offer instant images much more cheaply than traditional cameras. In many instances, it is also possible for students to produce extremely 'professional' results; and the internet now makes it possible for them to distribute their productions to wider audiences. As I shall indicate in more detail in chapter 11, these developments have several important implications in terms of learning. At least in principle, they can offer a much more intuitive and 'playful' way of developing key areas of understanding, and encourage a more reflective approach.

However, media production need not involve access to 'high-tech' equipment. A great deal can be achieved using cheap disposable cameras, or even pens, scissors and glue. Furthermore, it is important to keep production activities small-scale and manageable, particularly in the early stages. Students will avoid disappointment if they understand the limitations of the available technology and adjust their ambitions accordingly. As with any other form of 'writing', production skills need to be acquired in a structured, gradual way: students who launch enthusiastically into making their own feature films will learn little apart from failure. In the early stages, activities should build a step at a time, from textual analysis towards exploratory hands-on experience with technology, and then on to small-scale, modest productions, such as trailers or opening sequences, rather than 'complete' texts.

Yet, particularly as media technology is changing so rapidly, it is becoming harder for teachers to specify what and how students should be learning in this field. Production is an area where teachers have to cede some of their authority and control to students, and allow them a space for exploration – and for many teachers, this is difficult to achieve. However, there are certain general caveats that should be raised here.

Firstly, it is important to acknowledge that – even in the most well-resourced schools – media production work can present significant problems in terms of classroom management. Teachers will have to develop ways of rationing students' access to equipment, and ensuring that the inevitable technological obstacles can be adequately dealt with. Production work generally involves students working in groups over a relatively long time; and this often requires high-level skills in communication and in time-management. Students need to learn to set their own targets, to work to deadlines, to resolve disputes, to allocate responsibilities among the group, and so on. Furthermore, students may already have different levels of expertise in production, gained from their experiences outside school. If certain groups of students are not to dominate, these differences need to be explicitly addressed rather than left to chance.

Secondly, media production work needs to be effectively integrated with the kinds of critical analysis students are undertaking elsewhere in their courses. The aims and parameters of production work should be defined from the outset, and clearly agreed with students. Teachers need to be aware of the conceptual issues that the project is intending to address, and ensure that these issues are constantly brought to students' attention. This is partly a matter of well-timed and effective intervention by the teacher. Students need to be regularly encouraged to distance themselves from what they are doing, and to reflect upon the consequences of the choices they are making. This can be a formal requirement, which is built in to the process: students can be required to have regular 'production meetings' with the teacher, and even to draw up a form of 'contract' which will promote ongoing self-evaluation and review of the project as it proceeds.

Self-evaluation is particularly crucial here. In evaluating their own and each other's practical production work, and audience responses to it, students are encouraged to consider the relationship between intentions and results, and hence to recognize some of the complexity of meaning making. Far from reducing production to a mere illustration of theory, this can enable students to generate new theoretical insights. Thus, as with simulations, it is vital that students should 'debrief' at the end of the process, and formally evaluate their work. This can be difficult to achieve immediately, so it is often wise to leave time for students' emotional involvement in the work to cool. Undertaking this kind of evaluation in the context of a whole-class discussion, and taking account of the responses of other audiences (if these can be found), is also a very valuable way of helping students to achieve this.

Perhaps the key point here is that – in the context of *media education* – production is not an end in itself. Of course, media education should enable young people to 'express themselves' creatively or artistically, and to use media to communicate; but it is not primarily a matter of training them in technical skills. In the context of media education, production must be accompanied by systematic reflection and self-evaluation; and students must be encouraged to make informed decisions and choices about what they are doing. Media education aims to produce *critical* participation in media, not participation for its own sake.

Conclusion

The accounts of classroom strategies in this chapter have implicitly reflected a certain set of assumptions about the nature of teaching and learning in media education. Broadly speaking, they all begin by recognizing the validity of what students *already* know about the media; and they all involve 'active learning' on the part of students. Nevertheless, they also implicitly assume that there are things students do *not* know, and that they need to learn. They all entail the acquisition of new skills and knowledge, either through direct instruction from the teacher or through investigation and research by students themselves. Media education is not therefore simply a matter of 'celebrating' students' knowledge; nor indeed is it a matter of replacing that knowledge with the 'objective' analysis of the teacher. On the contrary, it must necessarily involve an ongoing dialogue between them.

Of course, the reality of classroom practice is bound to be more complex than the simplified prescriptions I have outlined here. Good teaching is not ultimately reducible to a set of 'techniques'. As we shall see in part III of this book, looking at how such methods are actually used in practice raises some very awkward questions about the fundamental aims of media education. What *counts* as a truly 'critical' perspective is not something that can simply be imposed through the exercise of teacherly authority. On the contrary, it is very much up for negotiation, both between teachers and students and among students themselves.

6

Locating Media Education

As I suggested in chapter 1, the aims and methods of media education are likely to depend not only on broad philosophical or political motivations, but also on pragmatic considerations of educational policy. Although it has a long history, media education is still generally perceived as a 'new' curriculum area; and as such, it has had to struggle for a place alongside more established subjects or areas of work. In the process, different 'versions' of media education have emerged, which reflect the characteristics and constraints of the contexts in which they are formed.

In this chapter, I outline a range of curriculum locations in which media education has developed, and the advantages and limitations of each. My primary focus is on the situation in schools in the UK, although it should be possible to draw parallels and connections with the situation in other countries as well. As I shall indicate, the prospects for media education are largely determined by the overall structure of the education system: factors such as the degree of teacher autonomy, the control of assessment and curriculum and the distribution of funding exercise a significant influence on the potential for innovation. In the current context, this is leading some to look outside the formal education system; and so this chapter will conclude with a brief discussion of the alternative possibilities for 'informal' media education beyond the classroom.

A separate academic subject: Media Studies

The emergence of specialized media courses in UK schools dates back to the late 1960s, with the growth of what were once called 'cafeteria curricula' in the upper years of secondary schooling. At the start of Year 10 (age fourteen), students are required to opt from a range of specialist subjects which they will follow for two years until public examinations at age sixteen. Since the advent of a common system in the mid-1980s, these examinations have been called GCSE (General Certificate in Secondary Education). In making their option choices, students will typically 'drop' some subjects they have studied previously, but they will also have the chance to take up new specialist courses. They may then choose to continue with these in school years 12 and 13, to Advanced level (so-called AS and A2) examinations.

The first examined Film Studies courses were introduced in secondary schools in the UK in the late 1960s. Communications Studies and Television Studies followed in the early 1970s, with specialist Media Studies courses beginning in the mid-1970s. Over the intervening period, Media Studies has gradually overtaken these other options, although specialized Film and Communications Studies courses continue to be offered at A-level. Communications Studies has a somewhat wider brief, incorporating areas such as the psychology of communication which are rarely found on Media Studies syllabuses (for a review, see Burton and Dimbleby, 1993).

Over the past twenty years, and particularly in the last ten, specialist Media Studies courses have experienced a steady growth in student numbers. Nevertheless, the future prospects here are somewhat uneven. At the time of writing (2002), for example, the introduction of new AS-level examinations has led to a significant increase in student numbers; and it is likely that the number of examination entries at A2-level will continue to grow at the current rate of around 50 per cent each year. This development has also, of course, been supported by the phenomenal expansion of media courses in higher education. On the other hand, however, expansion at GCSE shows signs of levelling off, not so much because of a lack of student interest as because of a decline in the number of schools offering courses in the area. The reasons for this uneven development are worth explaining a little more fully, since they indicate the rather uneasy – and sometimes contradictory – conditions of educational innovation.

The argument that 'the curriculum is already overcrowded' has always been a very familiar one for media educators. Even in the more hospitable environment of the 1970s, it was often difficult for teachers to establish new optional courses against the competing demands of other curriculum subjects. New courses inevitably required investment in new equipment and resources, as well as a longer-term commitment to staffing. Despite their popularity with students, Media Studies courses have always remained vulnerable to cuts; and there has never been anything resembling a 'career structure' for specialist media teachers. All too often, Media Studies courses would be introduced by young and determined enthusiasts, only to fall by the wayside when such people moved on to other jobs.

In the current context, such constraints have become much more acute. Specialist Media Studies courses were initially developed during a period (in the 1970s and 1980s) in which teachers enjoyed a considerable degree of control over curriculum content and assessment. The 1988 Education Act saw a dramatic increase in centralized control of the curriculum, most obviously in the form of the National Curriculum; and while this has presented some opportunities for the development of media education in other curriculum areas (to be discussed below), it has led to a reduction in the time available for optional subjects. This, together with a decline in funding for training, advisory and support services, has begun to act as a brake on expansion at GCSE level.

On the other hand, years 12 and 13 – and hence Advanced level courses – fall outside the National Curriculum; and schools have increasingly found themselves in competition for students with other providers at this level, such as tertiary and further education colleges. In this educational 'free market', there is clearly an incentive to provide popular courses such as Media Studies – an argument which also explains the rapid growth of vocational and degree-level courses in the area.

As these observations suggest, the fate of specialist media courses depends very much upon the wider context of educational policy, and particularly on the control of the curriculum and of funding. Yet ultimately it would be false to pretend that Media Studies at this level remains anything more than a minority subject: as an optional course, confined to the upper years of the secondary school, it will only ever occupy a marginal role. Despite continuing growth, the number of students following specialist Media Studies courses at this level is significantly lower than for traditional subjects such as History or Geography. Even today, Media Studies is still regarded by some schools as a 'soft option' which is best suited to the academic underachiever; and this definition is reinforced by the fact that it is sometimes offered as an alternative to more 'academic' subjects such as English Literature.

Media education across the curriculum

Advocates of media education have often argued that it should be seen as an element of *all* curriculum subjects. Perhaps the most influential statement of this argument in the UK can be found in a report entitled *Popular Television and Schoolchildren* produced in 1983 by the Department of Education and Science (the report and responses to it can be found in Lusted and Drummond, 1985). In the light of its review of the programmes children were watching, the report argued that teaching about television was too important to be left to specialists: 'all teachers', it argued, 'should be involved in examining and discussing television programmes with young people'.

This notion of media education as a fundamental entitlement for all students took on a particular significance with the advent of the National Curriculum in the UK in the early 1990s; and it has been echoed in a number of other countries whose education systems have begun to move in a similar direction, such as Australia. Perhaps unsurprisingly, given its fairly marginal status and its somewhat 'political' profile, Media Studies was not included as a compulsory element of the National Curriculum; and this led media educators to search for opportunities in other curriculum locations. Media education was therefore promoted as a potential 'cross-curricular theme' and as a dimension of a number of other established subjects, most notably English (discussed below). In the event, some limited headway has been made here: there are identifiable elements of media education within the curriculum documents for areas such as History and Modern Languages, and most prominently within English – although whether and how such proposals are carried out in practice remains an open question.

Particularly in the context of primary schools, where there is still greater potential for a more integrated approach to the curriculum, media education has increasingly been promoted as a possible means of 'delivering' a wide range of subject-specific objectives (Bazalgette, 1989; Craggs, 1993; Marsh and Millard, 2000). Thus, many media education activities involve competencies such as literacy and numeracy, as well as skills in areas such as technology, problem-solving and research.

It is important to emphasize here that this argument can be applied as much to practical media production by students themselves as to the forms of critical analysis that take place in media classrooms. Lorac and Weiss (1981), for example, provide an account of media production activities in a wide range of curriculum areas, including Art, History and Science: such work, they argue, can assist in subject-specific learning, as well as developing more general 'social and communications skills'. On this account, media production becomes a *method of learning* which can be applied in many situations – an approach which has analogies, for example, with the notion of 'drama as a learning medium', and with the 'language across the curriculum' movement.

Box 6.1 illustrates some of the possibilities for media education work in four contrasting curriculum areas: History, Science, Foreign Languages and Music. Here again, these ideas draw on materials published by the English and Media Centre and the British Film Institute.

Box 6.1 Media education across the curriculum

In History students should study:

- How historical events and periods can be represented in different genres of media texts, both factual and fictional.
- How media texts are used as evidence in historical study, and how their value and limitations are assessed.
- How different sources and types of evidence may be combined and manipulated in media representations of the past.
- How historical figures have used media in order to exert influence or win power.
- The historical impact of changes and developments in communications media.

In Science students should study:

- The techniques used by media producers in order to represent scientific processes and the natural world.
- How scientists and scientific 'progress' are represented in popular culture.
- How scientific knowledge is conveyed in media debates about controversial issues, and how different interpretations are presented.
- How appeals to scientific credibility are used in advertising sales pitches.
- The scientific processes involved in specific forms of media technology, such as video or film projection.

In Foreign Languages students should study:

- How media in the country studied play with verbal language, for example in advertising.
- How media styles and institutions in other countries compare with those in the home country.
- How media convey current events in the country being studied, for example international stories in newspapers or sport programmes.
- The representation of national identity in media, including postcards and tourist brochures.
- The different ways in which the same media texts are marketed in different countries.

In Music students should study:

- How editing is co-ordinated with incidental music and non-musical sound in film and television.
- How generic forms of music are used to create atmosphere and 'cue' emotional responses among audiences.
- How different types of music are packaged and marketed to different audiences via radio and other media.
- How the music industry is related to other areas of the media industries.
- The use of visual images in publicity materials and record covers to create a 'brand image' for performers.

Aside from the general arguments identified in box 6.1, there are some more specific reasons for adopting this kind of cross-curricular approach. Thus, it can be pointed out that all teachers use media of different kinds – not only audio-visual media, but also textbooks and other print materials. For example, History teachers will routinely use films or photographs as sources of evidence alongside printed documents; Geography teachers will rely on anthropological accounts of life in other cultures, whether on video or in print; while Science teachers will use television as a way of demonstrating complex processes, or illustrating their effects, in ways that cannot be attempted in the classroom. Hence, it could be argued, if we are concerned to encourage students to be 'critical' of the media, or to use them in more informed ways, then surely this should be extended to the media they encounter inside the classroom. Again, this applies as much to media *production* as it does to the use of media as 'teaching aids'.

Furthermore, it could be argued that many students' existing knowledge of school subjects – their 'commonsense ideas' about science and technology, about other countries or about the past – are at least partly derived from the media in the first place. These media accounts may not, of course, necessarily claim to be factual. Students' perceptions of life in the nineteenth century may derive primarily from costume dramas, and their attitudes towards science and technology may owe most to science fiction. Yet, however invalid or irrelevant this knowledge may be seen to be, it is clearly something which teachers neglect at their peril.

Finally, it is possible to develop a more radical variant of this argument, in which media education comes to be seen as a challenge to dominant definitions of knowledge *per se*. Of course, it is possible to argue that the curriculum itself is a mediation: it is a constructed representation of the world, not a neutral reflection of it. By questioning the ways in which the world is represented, and hence the processes whereby knowledge is constructed, media education can be seen to challenge the dominant epistemology of the curriculum as a whole (Alvarado and Ferguson, 1983).

In practice, however, the notion of 'media education across the curriculum' does not necessarily imply such a radical stance. Indeed, some have argued that the term 'media education' implies a dilution of the radical political aims of Media Studies teaching in favour of a bland, inoffensive approach (Hart, 1992; Masterman, 1989) – or at least a view that 'anyone' can teach about television. There certainly remains a danger here that media education will be reduced to an instrumental role, and that teaching *about* the media will become confused with teaching *through* the media – a danger which may be increasing as media educators begin to respond to the challenges of new digital technologies (for further discussion, see chapter 11). As I have argued, it is important not to confuse media education with the use of media as 'teaching aids' – that is, as alternative means of conveying subject content. Likewise, using media production as a means of developing subject learning – for example, encouraging students to produce videos or CD-ROMs *about* aspects of Geography or Science – runs the risk of reducing media to a mere instrumental technique (Buckingham, 1992a).

A second criticism here is one which returns to the logistical considerations raised above. Particularly in secondary schools, where subject specialisms are much more institutionalized, the fate of cross-curricular movements has not generally been a positive one. The 'language across the curriculum' movement, which enjoyed widespread support in the 1970s in Britain, is now largely perceived to have faded away, even though it was often firmly based in departments of English. It is difficult to see how 'media education across the curriculum' is likely to succeed from a much weaker institutional base. It is for this reason that media educators have been inclined to regard the existence of a specialist Media Studies department as a prerequisite for the formulation – and particularly the *implementation* – of cross-curricular policies (see Robson, Simmons and Sohn-Rethel, 1990).

Media education in language and literature teaching

In the UK, as we have seen, media education has been a particular concern for teachers of English; and the same is true of teachers of language and literature in many other countries. In pragmatic terms, the subject of English would appear to be a safe place for teaching about the media and popular culture. English is an important part of the compulsory curriculum; and while it may be redefined in all sorts of ways, it is unlikely to be simply squeezed out. At least in principle, gaining a place for media education within English means that it will be a compulsory entitlement for all students, rather than merely an obscure specialism lingering on the margins. It is partly for this reason that much of the energy of media educators (particularly over the past decade) has focused on the attempt to integrate media teaching within the curriculum for English (see Bazalgette, 1991; Goodwyn, 1992; Hart and Hicks, 2001).

However, the argument is more far-reaching than this. Calling for greater attention to the media and popular culture within English is not merely a pragmatic concern. On the contrary, it implies a far-reaching philosophical and political challenge to English: it is an argument for fundamentally rethinking what the subject is about. In British schools and universities, the discipline of English was historically founded on assumptions about the social and psychological value of 'literature'. For the pioneers of English teaching, it was taken for granted that exposure to literature (of the right kind, and in the right kind of way) somehow refined one's sensibility, and thus made one individually a better person. It was clear that English was not just a matter of the mechanics of reading and writing. It was not primarily about 'skills', or about functional literacy. On the contrary, it was about creating a better society, a society which was enlightened rather than debased, and one in which civilized values would prevail (Doyle, 1986; Mulhern, 1979).

During the 1970s and 1980s, these founding assumptions came to be challenged by radical movements among English teachers concerned about the irrelevance of this conception of culture for their working-class, multicultural students. They were also challenged, somewhat more distantly, by the development of critical theory within higher education – a movement which attempted to broaden, if not wholly deconstruct, the notion of 'literature' itself (see e.g. Brooker and Humm, 1989). From both perspectives, the very notion of 'literature' – and hence a great deal of the 'civilizing mission' of English teaching – is inherently elitist; and by extension, the distinction between literary study and media education would have to be seen as spurious to begin with.

Yet in practice, while some media teachers in UK schools are trained in other disciplines (notably Art and Social Studies), most are initially qualified in English; and most specialist Media Studies teachers also remain teachers of English. Most English language and literature syllabuses in the UK include a requirement to address media such as advertising and newspapers; and a majority of English teachers are likely to cover aspects of popular television such as soap opera or situation comedy at some point (Dickson, 1994). Yet the term 'media' still often appears to be a synonym for anything that is *not* 'literature' – so that it is not uncommon to find popular fiction being studied in a Media Studies classroom, where it might be considered quite unacceptable within English. Furthermore, there remain significant differences in terms of how English teachers typically treat these different objects of study (see Buckingham, 1992b; Hart, 1998). Different kinds of questions tend to be asked, and different pedagogic approaches adopted, in the two fields, even where the same individual is responsible for both (Freedman, 1990).

Broadly speaking, English tends to be defined and organized in terms of activities or practices – in the case of the UK National Curriculum, for example, English means speaking, listening, reading and writing. By contrast, as we have seen, media education is defined in terms of concepts. Yet some of the 'key concepts' that English teachers will use when dealing with media texts are largely absent from their approach to 'literature'. The more 'sociological' emphases on media production and media audiences, for example, have no obvious equivalents in English teaching. However, there is no reason in principle why English teachers should not address, for example, the economic structure of the publishing industry, or the ways in which books are marketed and distributed to readers. Indeed, critics would argue that the neglect of these aspects in English teaching reflects an essentially individualistic approach to questions of cultural production and reception.

To a large extent, these continuing differences derive from the different estimations and motivations which attach to the categories of 'literature' and 'media' in the first place. Broadly speaking, 'literature' is seen to have humanizing effects on the reader: it encourages the development of sensitivity to language, culture and human relationships. By contrast, the media are often seen to have fundamentally negative effects: they manipulate and deceive readers into accepting false values, in ways which readers may be unable to resist. Thus, if literature teaching is primarily about developing students' responsiveness to something which is seen as fundamentally good for them, media teaching has tended to be defined as a matter of enabling them to resist or 'see through' something which is seen as fundamentally bad. For many English teachers, these underlying assumptions have proven quite resistant to change (Morgan, 1998a). At best, media education is often seen as a motivational tool – as a means to lead students on to conventional print literacy, or as a covert means of introducing them to the literary canon (Marsh and Millard, 2000).

Extending questions and approaches from media education to traditional aspects of literature teaching would result in a radically different approach, as box 6.2 implies (albeit in a somewhat provocative way!). Ultimately, however, there is a more fundamental need to rethink the aims and methods of language and literature teaching in the light of the challenges that media education represents. Indeed, it may be that, over the longer term, both English and media education in schools will become part of a more inclusive subject field (Buckingham and Sefton-Green, 1994).

Media education and ICTs

The advent of digital information and communication technologies (ICTs) poses significant new challenges for media educators. One cannot teach about the contemporary media without taking account of the role of the internet, computer games and the convergence between 'old' and 'new' media. These new media need to be integrated as *objects of study* alongside established media such

Box 6.2   Media education within English

In English, students should study:

- The economic operations of the publishing industry, and its integration with other media industries.
- The role of book reviewing, advertising, literary competitions, bookshops and book clubs as means of circulating and distributing books to potential readers.
- How the reputations (or 'brand identities') of particular writers – both living and dead – are created and sustained by the media.
- How print texts are adapted into a range of media in different historical periods and circumstances, and for different audiences.
- The comparative possibilities and limitations of different media, for example in terms of constructing character, authorial point of view, atmosphere, etc.
- Representation, fact and opinion in non-fictional print and other media texts.
- How different social groups are represented (or not represented) in print texts, and how this relates to the social position of their authors.
- How different audiences are targeted by the design and language used on book jackets, and in shop displays.
- The reading habits of different audience groups, and audience responses to print and other media texts.

as film, television and the press. However, these new technologies also have a significant potential in terms of media production. The increasing accessibility of digital image manipulation and digital editing, for example, allows students much more creative control than was available with 'old' technology; and they also make it possible to explore some of the more conceptual aspects of the production process (such as the selection and construction of images) in a much more direct and concrete way. As these technologies increasingly come to be used for creative purposes in other areas of the curriculum – such as Music and Art – the potential for collaboration between these different subject areas is bound to grow.

On the other hand, these technologies do seem to be regarded by some as an educational panacea; and like television in an earlier era, there is a risk that they will be seen as merely neutral and instrumental – as simply 'teaching aids'. In this context, it would seem to be vital to insist that 'digital literacy' should address the more 'critical' questions – for example, about production and representation – with which media educators have traditionally been concerned. Thus, rather than seeing the Web as a neutral source of 'information', students need to be asking questions about the sources of that information, the interests of its producers, and the ways in which it represents the world.

However, these new technologies will inevitably call into question the boundaries of 'media' as a discrete curriculum area – boundaries which are problematic in any case. As the media converge, the logic for separating verbal and visual media, or electronic technologies and non-electronic technologies, will come under increasing pressure. In the process, the boundaries between previously discrete areas of the curriculum – and particularly those which are broadly concerned with culture and communication – may come to seem quite obsolete.

At the same time, these technologies may also call into question the boundaries between the institution of the school and the many other contexts in which learning can occur. Digital cultures are significant sites of learning in their own right. Children's everyday uses of computer games or the internet involve a whole range of informal learning processes, in which there is often a highly democratic relationship between 'teachers' and 'learners'. Children learn to use these media largely through trial and error – through exploration, experimentation and play; and collaboration with others – both in face-to-face and virtual forms – is an essential element of the process. Traditional forms of teaching, which involve the transmission of a fixed body of information, are largely irrelevant here. At least for some of their advocates, ICTs offer a fundamental challenge to outdated notions of teaching and learning.

On one level, media educators are bound to respond pragmatically to these developments. In many countries, there is now a massive investment in providing ICTs in schools; and this can present significant opportunities that it would be wrong to ignore. Yet media educators also need to participate in the broader debate that surrounds these developments; and – as in the case of language and literature teaching – they may find themselves adopting a stance towards official educational ideologies that is necessarily critical. All these issues will be taken up in more detail in chapter 11.

Vocational media education

At least in the UK, training for employment in the media industries has historically been the responsibility of the industries themselves. In areas such as broadcasting and journalism, for example,
much of this work has been undertaken within 'on-the-job' training schemes. In this respect, the situation is very different from
that in other European countries (French and Richards, 1994) and
in North America (Scholle and Denski, 1994), where universities
have been major providers of vocational training, for example
in the form of 'journalism schools'. Yet even in those countries,
vocational training has largely been confined to further and higher
education – that is, to the post-sixteen age group: it has not yet
been widely seen as a responsibility of schools.

Nevertheless, the last decade has seen a major expansion in
so-called vocational media education in the UK. This move dates
back to government attempts, beginning in the early 1980s, to bring
the curriculum more into line with the requirements of employers
– a move which was justified through arguments about 'relevance'.
A bewildering and ever-changing array of new qualifications was
introduced over the following decade, although in recent years
there has been an attempt to rationalize provision (see Alvarado
and Bradshaw, 1992; Buckingham, 1995). While the main impact
of these developments has been in further and higher education,
schools have also become increasingly involved in providing
so-called vocational courses.

The response of media educators to these developments was
initially extremely hostile. Vocationalism was seen as a recipe for
reducing media education to a form of technical training, in which
the 'critical' dimension of media theory would be lost: Len
Masterman (1985), for example, described such courses as 'a desert
of know-thy-place technicism'. In the intervening years, however,
there has been a process of accommodation and compromise. Again,
this has partly been led by an economic logic: the intense competition for student numbers which characterizes the educational
'free market' has led to a significant increase in the provision of
media courses, which (at least for the moment) are proving extremely popular. Yet there is also a sense in which – despite earlier
fears – some of the new vocational courses have been seen to offer
the potential for *integrating* theory and practical production. Indeed, for some of their advocates, such courses have been regarded
as preferable to the political purism of an exclusive emphasis on

academic media theory (Hurd and Connell, 1989; Stafford, 1990, 1994). Either way, this more practical, production-based approach has undoubtedly come to influence the more strictly 'academic' courses available in schools.

Perhaps the most significant issue here, however, is whether such courses actually live up to their claims of providing access to employment in the media industries. On one level, the restructuring of the media industries in the wake of deregulation and of new technologies would appear to offer many new opportunities – perhaps particularly for social groups who have historically been under-represented there. Yet in practice, it is doubtful whether many so-called 'vocational' courses actually do fulfil their promise to equip students with adequate skills for jobs, or whether they are recognized to do so by the industry. In this respect, they might more honestly be described as *pre*-vocational courses (Buckingham, 1995).

Media education beyond the classroom

This chapter, and indeed this book as a whole, focus primarily upon media education within the formal education system, and particularly within secondary schools. Yet it is important to note that there may be many opportunities for 'informal' media education beyond the confines of the school classroom. Internationally, there would appear to be at least four major possibilities here.

Community media workshops

The use of media such as portable video within community work has a long history in many countries. It is often linked to broader arguments for democratization, not only of the media but also of the political process in general (Willener, Milliard and Ganty, 1976). In the context of liberation struggles in countries such as South Africa, for example, video and other media were actively used as tools of political struggle, and as a means of generating alternatives to government-controlled media (see Dowmunt, 1993). In the USA, by contrast, the provision of community cable access channels was for some time required by law, although the actual provision across the country is extremely variable; and of course such resources must be made freely available to individuals and political groups with a whole range of motivations. Nevertheless, the provision of community media of this kind is often seen as an essentially *educational* process, even if the extent to which educational aims are made explicit varies greatly. There is a great potential for young media professionals to be involved in such work, particularly those from disadvantaged groups who might not otherwise gain access to the media. (This area of work will be considered more fully in chapter 12.)

Churches

In many countries, churches have played a major role in promoting media education outside the formal education system. Such work has diverse motivations. In some cases, media education has been seen as a means of opposing the 'consumerist' and 'anti-Christian' values which are seen to be promoted by the media; while in others, it has been motivated by an ideological opposition to what is seen as US cultural imperialism. Some of the most interesting work here has been based on the 'consciousness-raising' strategies of liberation theology, and is tied to wider struggles for social transformation (Fuenzalida, 1992). In Western countries, there has also been a growing interest in media education among churches and religious organizations of various kinds; and while some of this has been based on similar 'liberationist' principles, some of it derives from the very different concerns of the so-called 'moral majority', and its preoccupation with what is seen as immorality and violence.

Independent activist groups

The history of 'media activism' has been even less well documented than the other approaches I have identified here; but it is clear that in many countries the media have been a focus of concern for a whole range of independent citizens' groups, many of which have used educational strategies alongside more directly activist ones. For such organizations concerned with children, media education has often been seen as part of their wider strategy. In the USA, for example, the organization Action for Children's Television spent more than two decades bringing pressure to bear on the government and media regulators in order to ensure adequate provision of children's television; yet its activities also included research and the publication of educational materials (Hendershot, 1999). Similar organizations exist in several countries, such as the Forum for Children's and Citizen's Television in Japan and the Alliance for Children and Television in Canada.

Media education with parents

In many of the above instances, the major focus for media education initiatives has been on parents. Many churches and activist organizations have produced advice literature aimed at parents, and in some cases educational materials designed to be used in the home. Again, the motivations here have been somewhat diverse. Much of the popular literature aimed at parents adopts a highly protectionist approach: for example, parents are offered strategies for reducing their children's television viewing, or for teaching their children to resist commercial messages. As critics have argued, such approaches are explicitly normative, and often seem intended to induce feelings of guilt among 'inadequate' parents (see Seiter, 1993) – and so seem almost bound to be ineffective. If parents are to be involved, they need to be seen as active participants, rather than simply being told what they should or should not be doing; and any educational initiatives aimed at parents need to take account both of cultural differences and of the sometimes difficult realities of child-rearing.

The diversity of this work inevitably makes it difficult to categorize and summarize; but it is clear that it cannot necessarily be aligned with 'progressive' social goals. While such informal approaches to media education tend to employ a rhetoric of 'liberation' or 'empowerment', they are also frequently characterized by the kind of defensiveness identified in chapter 1. As with 'formal' media education, the different national and institutional contexts for such work clearly exercise a determining influence on its aims and methods.

Nevertheless, as I have indicated, advocates of media education in many countries have increasingly acknowledged the importance of these more 'informal' sites of education. To some extent, this could be seen to arise from a recognition of the limited possibilities currently available within the formal school system; yet it also reflects a more general recognition of the growing importance of 'learning beyond the classroom' (Bentley, 1998). These issues will be addressed in more detail in chapter 12.

Conclusion

Despite the growing significance of the media, and the urgency of the case for media education, progress in this field has generally been slow or uneven. In some countries, one can see bursts of innovative activity that have not ultimately been sustained; while in others, advances in national policy have been painfully slow. Where media education does exist in any substantial form, it tends to take the form of an elective or optional area of the secondary school curriculum, rather than a compulsory element. The development of media education still seems to depend largely on the dedication and commitment of individual teachers, often working in isolation. And yet far too few teachers are being given the specialist training they need.

There are many reasons for this lack of progress. We can point to the relative – and in some instances increasing – conservatism of education systems; the continuing resistance to regarding popular culture as worthy of serious study; and the potentially threatening nature of the kinds of 'critical thinking' that are inherent in media education. When compared to the commercial and political drive to disseminate information and communication technologies in education, media education is now in danger of being left behind. Nevertheless, educational innovation of any kind is a complex process, and requires a range of strategies and tactics. It cannot be mandated, and it will not be brought about simply through the force or logic of the argument.

Each of the different locations for media education described in this chapter presents different challenges and opportunities. Yet ultimately, the prospects for educational change will be determined by the broader political climate, and by the logistical and economic constraints in which schools operate. It is beyond the scope of this book to offer detailed suggestions for strategy – let alone to engage with the specifics of educational policy-making. Experience in several countries suggests that promoting and developing media education depends upon the presence of a series of interdependent elements, and on partnerships between a range of interested parties (see Buckingham and Domaille, 2001; Pungente, 1989). Yet the strategies media teachers will need to adopt in promoting their field must surely reflect the specific circumstances and opportunities that present themselves; and thus they are bound to be diverse.

In the medium term at least, media education is still in need of some strong and persuasive advocacy. We need to keep making the case, and trying to ensure that it is heard. Yet advocacy should not be incompatible with self-criticism. We need to ensure that media education remains responsive to contemporary social and cultural developments; that it keeps pace with young people's changing experiences as media users; that it builds on the positive potential of technological change; and that the courses which are provided in its name are both coherent and of high quality. None of these outcomes can be guaranteed simply on the basis of enthusiasm; and none of them will arise simply because we insist that they are already happening. We should be constantly re-evaluating our own practice, and developing new frameworks and areas of concern. It is to exploring these issues that the following two parts of this book are devoted.

Part III

Media Learning

How do young people learn about the media? Part III draws on classroom-based research conducted by the author and his colleagues over the past ten years. It looks beyond what *should* happen, and considers some of the realities of teaching and learning in media classrooms. Chapter 7 looks at critical analysis, while chapter 8 looks at creative media production. Chapter 9 brings these two aspects of media education together, in an attempt to outline and illustrate a coherent theoretical model of media pedagogy.

7

Becoming Critical

The aims of media education have often been defined as a matter of developing students' 'critical' abilities. Media education, it is argued, is fundamentally concerned with the development of 'critical consciousness'. Through the process of critical analysis, media education is claimed to empower students, and to liberate them from the values and ideologies the media are assumed to impose upon them. 'The acid test of any media education programme', according to Len Masterman (1985: 25), 'is the extent to which students are critical in their own use and understanding of the media when the teacher is not there. The primary objective is not simply critical awareness and understanding, it is critical autonomy.'

But what is meant by the term 'critical' here? What distinguishes a 'critical' approach from one that is merely 'uncritical'? And who defines what *counts* as 'critical consciousness'? As Lawrence Grossberg (1987) has suggested, this use of the term 'critical' can reflect a dangerous kind of arrogance. In demonstrating our ability to define the truly 'critical' approach, we are making a powerful claim for our own authority. And if *we* are 'critical', those who do not share our views are, by implication, either ignorant and misguided or actively engaged in an attempt to obscure the truth.

To be sure, this emphasis on 'critical' reading is not confined to the political left. There are many right-wing politicians, for example, who are extremely critical of what they regard as the rampant left-wing bias of the media. Leavisite approaches to English teaching – which are frequently condemned by media educators – are centrally concerned with developing 'critical awareness', not least in relation to popular media. Even the most virulent advocates of traditional teaching methods would be unlikely to claim that they were interested in making students *un*critical.

Nevertheless, the term 'critical' – as in 'critical research' and 'critical pedagogy' – is often used by those on the political left as a kind of code word, an outwardly neutral euphemism for the politically unspeakable. As Grossberg (1987) argues, 'critical' researchers have often distinguished themselves from 'managerial' or 'administrative' researchers, who are assumed to be merely complicit with existing forms of social power. By contrast, 'critical' researchers are seen to have the monopoly on 'critical consciousness', exposing forms of oppression and mystification of which ordinary people are assumed to be unaware. Likewise, advocates of 'critical pedagogy' have generated a self-sustaining grand narrative of education as a form of political liberation. While claiming to speak on behalf of the oppressed, such authors continue to reserve the right to define others' best interests in their own terms – although they have been remarkably reticent when it comes to describing how their proposals might actually be implemented in practice (see Buckingham, 1996b; Gore, 1993; Luke and Gore, 1992).

In the case of media education, this rather self-aggrandizing 'critical' stance was particularly prevalent in the 1970s and 1980s. It was especially apparent in the notion of 'demystification', briefly discussed in chapter 1. According to Masterman (1980), media education was a 'demythologizing' process, which was concerned to make ideology 'visible' and hence to reveal the 'suppressed ideological function' of media texts. The implication here was that students were 'mystified' by the pleasures and illusions of the media into accepting ideologies that ran directly counter to their 'real' interests. Through a process of objective analysis, it was argued, the 'truth' would be revealed; and, once revealed, it was assumed that it would be automatically accepted. Here again, students were implicitly identified as members of a mass audience, that was helplessly duped by powerful media messages; and teachers were defined as members of a 'critical' vanguard, which alone was capable of liberating them (see Buckingham, 1986). As Robert Morgan (1998a) suggests, this process comes to be seen as a form of 'conversion'. Through the powers of analysis, students are seen to move from an unconscious to a conscious state, from being enslaved by bodily pleasures and emotional responses to being 'rational' and 'sceptical' in their dealings with the media – in short, from being 'uncritical' to being genuinely 'critical'.

This version of critical media analysis continues to be influential in media education, although in many respects it now seems to belong to an earlier era. It offers a set of analytical tools that can genuinely enable students to feel 'empowered' in their dealings with the media. Yet in practice, it often results in a situation in which only *one* truly 'critical' reading is privileged in the classroom – and that reading tends to be that of the teacher. In this chapter, I want to identify some of the problems with this approach, and argue for a more comprehensive form of critical analysis in media education.

The social functions of 'criticism'

As I suggested in chapter 3, children inevitably become aware of critical perspectives on the media as part of their everyday experience. Judgements about whether television is or is not 'realistic', for example, are part of the stock in trade of most viewers' discussions of their favourite programmes. To some extent, this can be seen as a function of children's general cognitive development. For example, the ability to 'decentre' – that is, to view the world from the perspective of others – is clearly entailed in children's growing ability to recognize the persuasive intentions of advertising (Young, 1990). And yet, as I have shown, critical judgements of this kind also serve particular social purposes. They enable children to present themselves as sophisticated viewers, who are able to 'see through' the medium, and hence to differentiate themselves from those who (by implication) cannot. Critical discussions of the media therefore provide important opportunities for 'identity work' – for laying claim to more prestigious or powerful social identities.

In my research, this has been particularly manifested in terms of age and social class. Thus, children will readily claim that *they* can tell the difference between television and the real world; but that children younger than themselves cannot, and hence are much more vulnerable to influence. Likewise, in the critical judgements of some middle-class children, it is possible to detect a similar attempt to distance themselves from invisible 'others' who are implicitly seen to consume the medium in a naïve and innocent – and therefore potentially dangerous – way.

Thus, I have frequently interviewed groups of middle-class children (particularly boys) for whom sneering at the shortcomings of popular television appeared to confer considerable peer-group status (e.g. Buckingham, 1993a; 2000b). There is often a degree of competition here, as the children vie to deliver the wittiest put-down of the most awful game shows, or to perform the most damning imitation of bad acting in the soaps. In such a context, admitting to liking anything – with the possible exception of 'adult' films – is much more difficult. In many instances, these children will admit to watching programmes only in order 'to see how stupid they are' – even though their detailed knowledge of them is often equal to that of self-declared fans. In this context, pleasure comes to be seen as an indication of weakness or inadequacy: it is something we have to 'own up to', preferably with a heavy dose of irony.

While this critical discourse is rarely phrased in explicit class terms, there is clearly a thin line between contempt for popular culture and contempt for its audience. This use of 'critical discourse' represents a valuable form of 'cultural capital', and a tangible demonstration of one's social distinction (cf. Bourdieu, 1984). Becoming critical offers middle-class children a means of distinguishing themselves from the 'others', and thereby of socializing themselves into class membership.

These findings pose some awkward questions for media educators. Indeed, one could suggest that – far from 'validating' popular culture – media education is itself complicit in this process of reinforcing class distinctions. In the slogan of Britain's now-defunct *Modern Review*, it could be seen to represent a form of 'low culture for high-brows' – a way of learning to 'talk posh' about popular culture. There is a genuine risk that the erudite analysis of popular culture will become merely a new, more fashionable form of 'cultural capital' – a new way for the middle classes to display their cultural and intellectual distinction, and to do so in pretentious language that serves precisely to exclude the people who feel that this culture belongs to them. In this respect, simply changing the *object* of study – studying Madonna rather than Milton, or the Spice Girls rather than Shakespeare – is far from being inherently subversive. Indeed, it can end up simply reinforcing cultural hierarchies, rather than challenging or undermining them.

This argument is perhaps unduly cynical; but it does point to some of the limitations of a merely critical stance – at least if such a stance is conceived in purely *negative* terms. As I have suggested, media education should not be conceived as an exercise in drawing attention to the shortcomings of the media – whether these are defined as moral, ideological or aesthetic. On the contrary, it should encourage students to acknowledge the complexity and diversity of their pleasures in the media; and to recognize the social basis of *all* such judgements of taste and value, including their own.

Critical language games

These questions about the limitations of a critical perspective are even more apparent in the context of the classroom. As I have noted, the extent to which my research interviews were themselves perceived as an 'educational' activity was itself a significant influence on the kinds of talk the children produced: the more children perceived there to be an 'educational' agenda, the more 'critical' they became. Criticizing the limitations of the media – rather than simply talking about the good bits in the video you saw last night – was clearly perceived by many as the required response. In this context, media criticism becomes a form of 'language game', a ritualized encounter that largely confirms the established positions of the participants – in this instance, as 'good students'.

The favoured use of *advertising* as an object of study in media education clearly reflects this (Morgan, 1998a). Advertising provides valuable opportunities for the kind of 'unmasking' of ideology that is central to the demystification approach. Of course, many advertisements repay close textual analysis: they are carefully and deliberately constructed, and often use a complex combination of visual and verbal techniques. In classroom terms, their relative brevity or small scale makes them a very convenient resource for addressing questions about 'media language'. Yet the study of advertising is often driven by broader motivations. Exposing the 'rhetoric' of advertising – the subtle ways in which it associates particular qualities with products – is often implicitly seen as a means of disabusing students of the values or ideologies it is seen to promote.

One of the problems here, however, is that this view of advertising coincides with a form of popular cynicism, which is easily available to children. Critics of advertising have traditionally presented it as a 'hidden persuader', which stimulates 'false needs', both for products that are deemed to be unnecessary or harmful and for consumer goods in general. As with so many other areas of the media, it is children who are assumed to be particularly at risk in this respect: advertisers are seen to exploit their vulnerability through dishonest or deceptive appeals, and thereby to cultivate a more generalized form of 'consumerism' or 'materialism'. However, research suggests that such views are highly overstated (Young, 1990). Evidence of the 'effects' of advertising – whether in relation to the purchasing of specific products, or in more general terms – is actually quite equivocal. While younger children may be uncertain about the persuasive intentions of advertising, most children become aware of this by around the age of seven or eight; and they quickly develop a set of 'cognitive defences' which enable them to resist and challenge the claims of advertisers.

Like many other researchers, I have repeatedly encountered a high degree of cynicism about advertising among children at around this age. While they undoubtedly gain considerable pleasure from repeating catch phrases, mimicking funny accents or singing advertising jingles, they will frequently mock and dismiss advertisements on the grounds of their implausibility or apparent dishonesty (Buckingham, 1993a). Far from exercising a hypnotic power over their innocent minds, advertising seems to be perceived by most children as a passing pleasure that they can take or leave. Of course, this should not be taken as evidence that advertising has *no* 'effects' on children (or indeed on adults). Their cynicism may be superficial, and their ability to resist advertising in the context of a research interview may well fail to translate into real life.

Nevertheless, this gives rise to some awkward contradictions when it comes to education. For critics of advertising, the teacher's job is quite simple – and indeed, extremely familiar: it is to *warn* children, and hence to enable them to defend themselves. Several children have described to me how this kind of message is reinforced at regular intervals throughout their school careers, for example through classroom projects that involve writing letters of complaint to the regulatory authorities about misleading claims in advertising. Even if this is not the teacher's intention, it is therefore very likely that students will perceive that it is. On the other hand, for the reasons I have indicated, students will probably have a good deal at stake in being seen to reject or 'see through' the appeals of advertising. Adopting the stance of the rational, 'wise consumer' offers a considerable degree of status, both in the eyes of the teacher and among the peer group; and this is a stance which the majority of students will adopt with little difficulty. This can easily result in a situation which is all too familiar in media education: where the teacher appears to be trying to teach students things which they believe they already know.

These contradictions were apparent in an early research study on teaching about advertising, conducted with eleven- to twelve-year-old students (Buckingham, Fraser and Mayman, 1990). Here, we devised a series of lessons in which the critical analysis of advertisements led into a practical simulation, in which students would produce their own. While our main focus here was on *media language*, we were also concerned to raise issues to do with *representation* – particularly gender representation – in advertising.

The analytical activities were largely based on the kinds of procedure described in chapter 5. We gave the students a small selection of magazine advertisements, together with a set of analytical questions to discuss in small groups; and subsequently undertook a whole-class analysis of a single TV advertisement, broken down frame by frame. In both cases, we attempted to begin with close description ('denotation'), followed by discussing the associations the images and words evoked ('connotation') and only finally moving on to judgements about ideological meaning (cf. Masterman, 1980).

The reality, however, was rather more messy. Both in small-group discussions and in teacher-led activities, there was a considerable amount of jockeying for position. Comprehensively dismissing particular advertisements (or aspects of them), or alternatively 'putting down' their imagined target audience, was the most effective form of power-play, particularly if it could be accomplished with a degree of cynical humour. As is often the case, analysis appeared to degenerate into an exercise in 'guessing what's in teacher's mind', particularly in the whole-class discussion. Even despite themselves, the teachers would repeat and reinforce 'correct' responses – or those which led in the preferred direction – and ignore or challenge those which did not. Despite our repeated insistence that there were 'no right answers', there clearly *were*; and it was these answers (or at least issues that we deemed legitimate topics for discussion) that had largely informed our selection of advertisements for analysis in the first place. For the students, obediently 'playing the game' was one option; although subverting it through flippant remarks or unduly literal observations was certainly another, which proved particularly attractive for some of the boys.

Here again, the middle-class students appeared to be more cynical about advertising than their working-class counterparts – although this was much more apparent in the whole-class discussions (with teacher to please) than in the small-group work with peers. Yet in some respects, all the students appeared to find the analytical activities much too *easy* – as though they were simply an exercise in stating the obvious. Meanwhile, the 'representation' agenda, which we had imagined would subtly emerge from the analysis, was readily apparent to many of the students, to the point where it was seen as something that could be satirized and subverted.

In some respects, the most interesting aspect of this project was the students' practical productions. Most of the advertisements they produced – which were for boys' hair care products – appeared to parody dominant conventions, suggesting that they already had a fairly sophisticated understanding of the 'language' of advertising. At the same time, the simulation appeared to allow a relatively safe space, in which potentially difficult issues such as sexuality could be dealt with in a fairly distanced and harmless way. However, what was most significant for the students themselves was not the conceptual issues we had intended to raise (for example, to do with gender representation), but the social and interpersonal aspects of the work, and the enjoyment it involved. Even in terms of what they learned about the media, it was clear that the practical work provided an opportunity for *play* with media forms and conventions which effectively exceeded our more rationalistic aims. (These issues will be discussed in more detail in chapters 8 and 10.)

While the students were well aware of the persuasive intentions of advertisers, some of them appeared to know rather less about the economic functions of advertising for the media industries – an area that was neglected in our teaching. Yet ultimately, it is hard to avoid the conclusion that – at least in the critical analysis – we were largely teaching students what they already knew. This is not to say that nothing was learned: the discipline of having to pay close attention to specific aspects of texts that might usually be ignored was clearly unfamiliar, and is something that should be developed incrementally over the longer term. Nevertheless, this study clearly shows that critical analysis cannot be regarded as a neutral or objective procedure. On the contrary, it can become a site of struggle, in which the debate about textual meaning reflects broader relationships of power between the participants.

Approaching 'ideology'

Several of these difficulties come to the fore when issues of 'representation' (or, in terms of the British Film Institute's model, 'messages and values') are more central to the analysis. Judith Williamson's article 'How does Girl Number Twenty understand ideology?' (1981/2) raises a series of questions here that are still very relevant for media educators (see Turnbull, 1998). 'Girl Number Twenty' is Sissy Jupe, from Dickens's novel *Hard Times*; and Williamson's specific reference is to the scene where the authoritarian rationalist Mr Gradgrind challenges Sissy to define a horse. Sissy, whose experience of horses has been gained from the circus in which she lives, is unable to satisfy him – in contrast to Billy Bitzer, 'the colourless boy', whose dictionary definition of the 'gramnivorous quadruped' does the trick. For Williamson, the central question here is that of the relationship between analytical knowledge and personal experience; and her implication is that, like Gradgrind's obsession with 'facts', media teachers' preoccupation with ideological analysis largely fails to connect with students' lived experience – and hence also fails to make much difference to them.

Williamson's concerns arise from her experience of teaching undergraduates, although they raise issues that also apply to much younger students. She describes how studying soap operas and the popular press in her first-year Media and Communications class seemed merely to reinforce students' beliefs about the 'ignorance of the masses'; and how one of the male students on her course 'Representation of women in the media' engaged in a sustained and effective critique of the ideology of women's magazines, which seemed merely to confirm the view that women must be stupid to enjoy such things in the first place. Here again, critical discourse appears to serve as a marker of distinction, a means of distancing oneself from the delusions of the mass audience – a process which is defined, at least partly, in terms of gender and social class. Meanwhile, students who might have had more invested in these representations were effectively silenced.

As Williamson argues, analysis alone will not necessarily change students' attitudes. Unless the discussion of ideology in the media is related to students' own experiences and identities, it will remain a purely academic exercise: media students will 'do' images of women in the media in the same way as English students are required to do medieval poetry, or History students the age of the Tudors. In the process, there is a danger that ideology will be seen as 'what *other* people think, and the only explanation for why they believe such "lies" or "propaganda" is because they are stupid'.

Williamson's article raises several troubling questions, not all of which she resolves (for further discussion, see Buckingham, 1986; Lusted, 1986; Richards, 1990; Turnbull, 1998). Certainly, my own attempts to work through some of these difficulties in the classroom were far from unproblematic. Changing the focus from 'images of women' to 'images of men', for example, might have undermined some of the complacent positions Williamson's male students were able to adopt; but in practice, it seemed far easier for boys – and for myself as a male teacher – to adopt a safe, ironic stance. And while attempting to broach the question of homoerotic desire in the display of the male body might be a challenging seminar topic for postgraduates, it is (to say the least) a rather more intimidating prospect for most adolescent boys. As I shall argue in more detail in the following chapter, creative production work may provide a more constructive way forward in tackling such issues.

In some respects, the processes Williamson describes might now be seen as a manifestation of 'political correctness' – or perhaps as 'the curse of the lefty teacher'. Once students have recognized what such teachers want (and it is generally not too difficult), they have two basic options. Either they can choose to play the game, in which case the lesson becomes merely a rehearsal of 'politically correct' positions; or alternatively, they may refuse to do so – not necessarily because they reject the teacher's views, but merely because they wish to challenge their authority, and thereby amuse themselves. In my experience, both strategies may also be informed by the dimension of social class. A middle-class teacher who attempts to impose 'politically correct' beliefs on working-class students is likely to encounter resistance, not necessarily because the students have consciously articulated beliefs that are under attack, but merely because they perceive it as yet another instance of 'trendy' middle-class people telling them what to think (Buckingham, 1986).

Sue Turnbull (1998) traces similar contradictions in her analysis of teaching about the media with ethnic minority students in an Australian high school. She found that the teachers were generally disapproving of the young women's enthusiasm for romance, male pop stars, soap operas and so on. The teachers' views reflected both a feminist critique of the 'objectification of women' in popular culture and an argument that the girls should set their sights on academic success and professional careers, rather than romance and early marriage. Yet far from simply swallowing the anti-feminist ideology of the media (as the teachers supposed), the students adopted a much more complex attitude. While occasionally ridiculing romance, they also valued it because it addressed them as sexualized adults rather than (like school) as children; and because it represented a gesture of independence in relation to their parents' aspirations for arranged marriages. Rather than constructing these students as deluded and in need of teacherly liberation, therefore, Turnbull suggests that their uses of media provided one way of 'living the contradictions' of their current social experiences.

Of course, 'playing the game' has limitations of its own. In my experience of teaching media in higher education, I have found that – despite my intentions – ideological analysis all too frequently degenerates into a kind of political competition. Here, the strength of one's condemnation of the racist or sexist values one claims to have identified in the text is taken as evidence of the unassailable authority of one's own political position. In this language game, dissenters are simply defined as hopeless liberals. The tendency to 'up the ante' in this way precisely precludes the possibility that students might genuinely examine or explore their own positions, or the complexity of their own readings.

Julian Sefton-Green's account of teaching about *The Cosby Show* in an ethnically mixed London school in the late 1980s provides some indication of how this process might be manifested among younger students – again, despite the intentions of the teacher (Sefton-Green, 1990). One lesson he describes, with a group of fourteen- to fifteen-year-olds, was effectively hijacked by two black girls, who proceeded to outline what Sefton-Green calls 'a mono-lithic theory of media racism'. The students mounted an extended critique of the absence of 'realistic' black characters on television; and they argued that this operated to reinforce the racist attitudes of white audiences. As Sefton-Green suggests, their argument was consistent and articulate, and it clearly connected with a wider political perspective; yet it was also a drastic oversimplification of the much more nuanced and complex analysis the class had been engaging in over the course of the preceding lessons. The 'con-spiracy theory' the students felt required to produce had no place for 'liberal' representations like *The Cosby Show* (which the class had been analysing in some detail) or for their more subtle dis-cussions of the 'realism' and 'unrealism' of such programmes. The critical discourse enabled the students to assume power in the class-room, in a way that effectively silenced the other students – and indeed their teacher; but it also failed to do justice to the com-plexity of their own understandings of the media.

Similar issues are raised by Hyeon-Seon Jeong (2001) in her ana-lysis of a series of lessons about 'images of women' conducted with a group of A-level students (aged sixteen to seventeen) in one London school. Jeong shows that, despite the appearance of rigorous 'linguistic' analysis, the discussions tended to arrive at a single, pre-determined ideological judgement, derived from exist-ing (and indeed somewhat outdated) academic arguments. This was achieved only through some close policing of the discussion by the teacher, particularly in relation to the boys. Although the material that was being studied was fairly complex, the argument was constantly reduced to simplistic conclusions about the negat-ive influence of the media: women's magazines, which were the primary focus of study, were implicitly accused of a straightforward form of *victimization* of women readers. This pre-defined critical position effectively prevented the students from arriving at a more nuanced account which did justice to their everyday readings and uses of these texts.

The most revealing moments here were those in which the 'official' critical discourse of the classroom was disrupted by the intrusion of a more 'personal' approach. Here, the students and the teacher appeared to abandon their prescribed positions, and to speak as 'audiences' rather than as 'media critics'. For example, one discussion was diverted into a debate about the TV series *Ally McBeal*, in which both teacher and students engaged in much more emotional and informal evaluations of the central character. Unlike the analysis in the more formal part of the lesson, the debate here centred precisely on the *ambivalence* of Ally – her combination of professional competence and personal need. In some ways, a great deal more was raised here than in the critical analysis of the magazines; but ultimately it appeared that both teachers and students were expected to set these more personal investments aside as they took up the critical roles that were marked out for them. As a result, Jeong suggests, both appeared to be expected to subscribe to a rather simplistic account of how the media operated in their own lives.

The studies I have summarized here provide some challenging criticisms of the ritualized 'language games' that often seem to constitute ideological analysis in media education. In particular, they draw attention to what such analysis frequently tends to exclude. The adoption of a critical position frequently appears to imply automatic *condemnation* of the media and all their works. From this position, the media can only be seen as uniformly negative, both in the 'messages' they contain and in their effects on audiences. This is a position which seems to have significant problems in accounting for the existence – and, I would assert, the growth and contemporary dominance – of media that are more 'liberal' or even simply contradictory in their ideological stance (such as *The Cosby Show* or *Ally McBeal*). From this position, the fact that the media are not feminist and revolutionary necessarily means that they are agents of patriarchy and reaction (Lovell, 1983). 'Liberalism' can only be seen as a token gesture or a cunning trick on the part of the media conspiracy.

Furthermore, this position is one in which media audiences are implicitly seen as victims of media manipulation. Of course, adopting the official critical position serves as a means of exempting oneself from such charges, and hence of claiming a political 'high ground'. In the process, however, students' (and teachers') own experiences as audiences – and in particular, their pleasurable investments in the media – frequently have to be marginalized or disavowed. As in several of the studies quoted here, this can result simply in silence; but it can also result in 'unacceptable' forms of resistance – sexist jokes or inappropriate laughter, for example – that teachers may interpret precisely as evidence of the enormity of the struggle that they are attempting to engage in. In these respects, the critical position can easily become self-confirming – and, indeed, self-righteous.

Learning critical discourse

So what is happening when students *acquire* these critical discourses? On one level, they are gaining access to socially approved, 'legit-imate' ways of talking about the media. As I have suggested, employing critical discourse represents a powerful claim to social status: to be critical is to be powerful – or at least to *feel* powerful. Media students will quite frequently attest to the 'life-changing' effects of such teaching: 'I'll never look at an advert in the same way again', they will tell you. Of course, this kind of statement might be seen as another form of teacher-pleasing, but it does reflect a quite genuine sense of 'empowerment' that cannot be denied. Talking about 'representation', 'genre' and 'ideology' – let alone 'intertextuality' and 'hegemony' – is therefore not just a matter of 'talking posh' (as I suggested earlier). Acquiring a metalanguage of this kind – that is, a language that enables us to describe how (media) language works – could be seen to have *cognitive* as well as *social* benefits. It doesn't just give us access to social status; it also enables us to think in more systematic and rigorous ways.

Our study of the development of one student's critical writing in English and in Media Studies (Buckingham and Sefton-Green, 1994: ch. 9) provides some support for this. Here we traced how the student, Stephen, gradually developed the ability to generalize about the texts he was discussing, to support his assertions with evid-ence, and to develop more abstract arguments. In the case of his Media Studies writing, he was able not merely to apply or illus-trate theories or concepts, but also to make reflexive judgements about them (for example, by questioning the notion of 'stereotyp-ing'). As might be expected, being 'critical' in the two subjects appeared to mean quite different things: while English empha-sized 'personal appreciation' and discrimination on the grounds of cultural value, Media Studies valued distanced analysis and explicit theoretical argument. Towards the end of his school career, Stephen was able to formulate the 'system' for critical writing in the two subjects in almost cynical terms; yet it was clear that he had also gained a kind of *authority* over his material that was both socially and intellectually empowering.

There are several broader issues here, to which I will be returning in chapter 9. In some respects, the crucial question is whether 'being critical' should be seen as a *state of mind* or as a *social practice*. On the one hand, it is possible to see Stephen's gradual mastery of the 'correct' terminology and linguistic structures of critical writing as a form of socialization: he is acquiring a form of 'cultural capital' that gives him access to the subject discipline, and hence to a form of social power. On the other hand, we can also see it in cognitive terms, as a matter of his developing control over his own thought processes, and of his growing conceptual sophistication. Yet, as I shall argue, it may be that we do not need to see this as an either/or choice – that is, in terms of a *dichotomy* between the subjective and the social.

Beyond criticism?

It has not been my intention in this chapter to suggest that 'criticism' *per se* should be merely abandoned. I have sought merely to demonstrate some of the limitations of established forms of critical analysis in media education. In a sense, my argument is that a good deal of what passes for criticism is actually not critical enough.

In conclusion, then, what are the implications of these arguments for how we might rethink and extend the practice of critical analysis in media education? There are several points to make here, which will be developed in more detail over the subsequent chapters. Most obviously, we need to devise forms of analysis that do not depend upon the production of singular, 'correct' readings, or on the imposition of teacherly authority. As I have implied, far too much of what passes for textual analysis in media classrooms is mechanistic and drily grammatical; and far too often, the results of the analysis are pre-ordained. We need to recognize that texts are read in a variety of different ways, and that these differences should form the starting point for classroom discussion, rather than being silenced or suppressed. This means allowing space for the 'personal' – for students (and teachers) to share their subjective interpretations, feelings and responses, and to describe and reflect upon their everyday experiences of the media outside the classroom.

As Turnbull (1998) suggests, this is particularly important when it comes to dealing with questions of representation and ideology. In our diverse, rapidly changing, multicultural societies, we need to be sensitive to the ways in which social differences (of class, ethnicity, gender and age) shape our experiences of the media; and we should beware of assuming that we know what the emotional and ideological significance of any media text might be for anyone else. In this context, and for the reasons I have outlined, using media education as a means of commanding assent to a given political or moral position is doomed to failure.

This is not to imply, however, that the classroom should become a kind of 'confessional', in which students are compelled to 'speak the truth' about their subjective relationships with the media (cf. Orner, 1992). Nor is it to suggest that we should simply celebrate the apparent authenticity of 'personal response', as is the case in some approaches to English teaching. As I have implied, 'personal' responses are inextricably embedded within the social, cultural and institutional contexts in which they occur. Adopting a social theory of literacy means enabling students to understand those contexts, and to recognize how their own responses are formed and produced. It means recognizing that meanings are not simply located in texts, waiting to be deciphered with the 'correct' tools of analysis; but that they are inevitably constructed within the social relations of everyday life.

To some degree, therefore, this perspective implies a more *comprehensively* critical or analytical approach, which integrates the various elements identified in chapter 4. Rather than requiring students to leave aside their subjective responses and experiences, as Masterman (1980) prescribes, it means positively *using* those responses as a resource for further analysis and debate. In chapter 9, I will describe some practical means of achieving this, through students' own audience research projects. In addition to enabling students to recognize the social basis of people's tastes and media practices (including their own), such projects can also help to dispel some of the crude assumptions about the 'mass audience' which frequently characterize critical debates about the media.

In addition to developing a more analytical and reflective consideration of *audiences*, this approach will also mean a closer attention to the area of *production*. As I have suggested, the critical stance often appears to require an essentially conspiratorial theory of media production, in which media producers are permanently engaged in a conscious attempt to mislead or manipulate their audiences. Here again, a thorough study of the economic and institutional contexts of media production, and of the nature of the production process, is bound to lead to a more sophisticated approach. Yet this kind of awareness can also be developed through enabling students to produce their own media texts. In creating their own representations, students are able to investigate media issues more directly and in a more open and playful manner, and hence to move beyond the security of ritualized condemnation.

To some degree, therefore, I am suggesting that we need to displace the text as the privileged focus of classroom study – an emphasis media education has clearly inherited from literature teaching (Morgan, 1996). This is not, of course, to suggest that we abandon the activity of textual explication; merely that we should situate it within a more comprehensive understanding of how the media operate. However, it is also to imply that critical analysis needs to be accompanied by creative production; and indeed, that creative production can be a means of generating new and more profound critical insights. The following chapter therefore moves on to look at media production in more detail, and to address some of the problems and challenges that it raises.

8

Getting Creative

My most lasting memories of my own early experiences of media teaching all relate to student production. As the person responsible for administering the media facilities in a large secondary school, my room became the focus for a strange mixture of groups and individuals who were driven by an enthusiasm for making their own media (nearly all of them boys, it must be said). There was fifteen-year-old Costas, who was producing his own Super-8mm. variants of Hammer Horror movies; hyperactive eleven-year-old Ben, who laboured for ages on plasticine animations; Chris and his friends, who worked for several years on their own magazines, and eventually moved on to crude computer animation; and sixteen-year-old Sam, who later turned his obsession with writing sci-fi scripts into a full-time job. When I subsequently introduced formal Media Studies courses, I found it hard to engage students in the mechanical forms of semiotic analysis that were then seen as compulsory; but what always managed to motivate them was the opportunity to take their own photographs and – eventually, struggling against the limitations of the equipment – to shoot and edit their own videos. I can still recall some of the elaborate semi-parodies of teenage magazines, 'youth programmes' and investigative documentaries that they produced.

Yet when I turned to the publications on media education that were then beginning to appear, I found a different story. The leading authors of that time largely seemed to condemn practical production as politically suspect and educationally worthless. In Len Masterman's highly influential *Teaching about Television* (1980), the chapter on production was the shortest in the book, and much of it was extraordinarily negative. What happens, Masterman asked, when you give students video cameras?

> In my experience an endless wilderness of dreary third-rate imitative 'pop'-shows, embarrassing video dramas, and derivative documentaries courageously condemning war or poverty, much of it condoned by teachers to whom technique is all and the medium the only message. (Masterman, 1980: 140)

What is quite striking about this quotation now, more than twenty years later, is its contempt for students' work, and its reliance on precisely the kind of Leavisite literary-critical criteria that the rest of Masterman's book sought to challenge. Yet this tone can also be found in other writings of the period. Bob Ferguson, writing in 1981, condemned students' video productions in similar terms:

> Many groups ended up just clowning around with the equipment ... the camera was often 'squirted' at its subject and the dizzy, boring and incoherent results thus obtained could be justified as experimentation. When plots were attempted they were puerile and ... often incorporated obligatory punch-ups in pubs and discotheques. (Ferguson, 1981: 44–5)

Significantly, Ferguson's main criticism was directed against the notion of 'creativity', an idea imported from Art and English teaching, which he condemned as mystical and individualistic. The emphasis on creative self-expression through media was seen to reflect a dangerous 'romanticisation of the working class': it led to work that was 'intellectually undemanding' and that merely institutionalized low expectations of students.

These kinds of criticism were echoed in many of the texts about media education published in the 1980s (e.g. Alvarado, Gutch and Wollen, 1987; Masterman, 1985); and they were later compounded by the rejection of what appeared to be a narrowly 'technicist' emphasis on production skills that was apparent in some of the new vocationally oriented media courses that began to emerge at this time. According to Masterman (1985), this kind of technical training represented 'a form of cultural reproduction in which dominant practices become naturalised'; it was a kind of ideological 'enslavement' which would produce 'deference and conformity'.

As my quotations suggest, these concerns were partly motivated by a fear of *imitation*, which in turn derived from a wider suspicion of the deceptive pleasures of popular culture. Imitation was seen to be an inherently *unthinking* process, through which the

'dominant ideologies' of media products would be simply intern-
alized and reproduced. An emphasis on student production was
therefore seen to be at odds with the radical political mission of
media education.

The only alternative, it would appear, was to encourage students
to produce 'oppositional' texts, which would directly challenge and
subvert these ideologies through the use of 'avant-garde' forms; or
alternatively to use production exercises in order to systematically 'deconstruct' the conventional norms of mainstream media
(Masterman, 1980). Thus, students might undertake exercises on
the conventions of TV interviews or news presentation, systematically isolating and experimenting with framing or camera positioning; or they might be required to produce 'exercises in style',
designed to demonstrate their understanding of the 'codes' of a
particular genre such as *film noir* or horror. This approach explicitly sought to oppose and subvert dominant forms of professional
practice; and in the process, the 'expressive' or 'creative' potential
of production was rigorously subordinated to the demonstration
of critical understanding.

Changing practices

Along with many other aspects of media education, this perspective on student production has been substantially challenged and
revised over the past two decades. There are several reasons for
this. Debates about the place of student production in media education have been bound up with wider claims about its status, and
about the status of those who study it. The emphasis on critical
analysis that emerged so strongly in the 1970s and early 1980s can
partly be explained as a claim for academic legitimacy – albeit one
made in highly traditional terms. Yet in some respects, these concerns were superseded by the advent of a common examination
system in the mid-1980s, in which subjects such as Media Studies
were no longer differentiated as being suitable only for 'lower-
ability' students. The new specialist syllabuses that began to emerge
at this time – like those that have succeeded them – all contain a
significant component of production work.

At the same time, of course, there have been significant developments in technology. When I started teaching, in the age of super-
8 cameras and reel-to-reel videotape, production was significantly
more difficult to organize in the classroom. Formidable obstacles
were posed by video that was never really portable, by projectors

that unfailingly chewed up your film, and by enlargers that were as easy to manipulate as dinosaurs. Editing meant 'crashing' from one machine to another, and the few editing suites that were rumoured to exist were jealously guarded by fearsome technicians with brown coats and extensive collections of soldering irons. In the era of palmcorders, photo-CDs and inexpensive computer graphics, it is hard to imagine how we ever managed to get anything finished. Of course, student production does not need to rely upon 'high-tech' media. A great deal of interesting and valuable work in schools continues to be achieved with pens, scissors and glue, with simple cassette recorders and point-and-shoot cameras. Nevertheless, technological developments have made more complex forms of practical production much more accessible and easy to manage (see Stafford, 1994); and, as we shall see in more detail in chapter 11, the use of digital technology – for example, for video editing – has potentially very significant consequences in terms of students' learning.

Broader changes in the media environment, of the kind described in chapter 2, have also had implications in terms of how we might define the *purpose* of production work, and hence evaluate its outcomes. For example, the distinction between 'dominant' and 'oppositional' practice that characterized rationales for student production in the 1970s and 1980s has become increasingly redundant. The aesthetic strategies of the avant-garde have steadily been incorporated into the mainstream, most obviously in advertising and music videos; and many of the institutional and economic distinctions between 'independent' and 'dominant' production have all but disappeared. The notion that there are fixed professional 'norms' that should be contested and deconstructed has become highly questionable; and the requirement that student productions should represent 'oppositional' practice seems increasingly meaningless.

As I have noted, media education has itself moved beyond the political protectionism of this kind of approach. The notion that the media simply transmit and impose monolithic 'dominant ideologies', and that media education should seek to 'liberate' students from mystification, has increasingly been questioned. Meanwhile, the practical emphasis of vocational and pre-vocational courses has increasingly influenced more 'academic' approaches to media teaching (see chapter 6); and in recent years, the growth of opportunities for 'informal' media production – for example in the context of youth and community-based projects – has also begun to feed into practice in schools (see chapter 12).

Thus, while some courses continue to be informed by the narrowly 'deconstructionist' stance of the early 1980s, production has now been largely accepted as a central element of media education, both in the context of specialist Media Studies courses and in other curriculum areas. Students following Media Studies courses in UK secondary schools are generally required to undertake at least two major production projects as part of their examination. They might produce a magazine or a newspaper, make a video or a web site, produce a photographic exhibition or an advertising campaign, or make a radio show; and they also have to produce a piece of writing to accompany this, which will explain their objectives, evaluate what they have achieved, and reflect on the process of production, in the light of the broader theories and critical approaches they will have encountered on the course. Such activities are often simulated: students are typically set tasks or assignments in which they are invited to 'become' fictional media producers within defined circumstances, which themselves raise broader theoretical issues or problems (for examples, see Grahame, 1994).

The limits of 'creativity'

Yet while some of the suspicions of earlier generations of media educators now appear misplaced, the concerns they raised about its aims and outcomes have not gone away. In particular, questions remain about the nature of *creativity*, and how it might best be developed. Ferguson's early criticisms of this idea, mentioned above, have been challenged by subsequent authors seeking to make the case for student production work (e.g. Stafford, 1990). Indeed, at the time of writing, 'creativity' is the current flavour of the month in British educational and cultural policy; and it is increasingly being used in rationales for media education (British Film Institute, 2000; Buckingham and Jones, 2001). Yet, as I have suggested (Buckingham, 2000c), 'creativity' is often very loosely defined here: the term seems to serve very different purposes for different users, while acting as a kind of 'magic ingredient' that is assumed to produce all sorts of transformative effects.

This usage of the term often seems to imply a *Romantic* conception of creativity. Here, creativity is seen in individualistic terms, as the emanation of some kind of 'personal vision' – a matter of an authentic 'self' finding its 'expression'. From this perspective, creativity is an essentially unmediated process, a spontaneous outpouring of feeling which is not subject to established conventions and structures. And creative products are seen as somehow self-sufficient: they 'speak for themselves', and hence any kind of analysis will only reduce or destroy them. In all these respects, true creativity is seen to involve a rejection or overcoming of constraints, whether social, formal or 'academic'.

This is an influential notion of creativity, although it is one that raises self-evident problems for education. As Julian Sefton-Green (2000a) points out, such a view seems to imply that creative individuals are born rather than made, and hence allows little place for teaching. From this perspective, creativity and education would have to be seen as inherently incompatible. In practice, therefore, 'creative' work in a range of subject areas (such as Art, Music and English) has been bound to adopt a rather different approach (Sefton-Green and Sinker, 2000). There has been a growing recognition of the social, collaborative dimensions of creative production; of the complex relationships between 'creative expression' and 'technical skills'; and of the importance of reflection and self-evaluation. The first two of these issues will be considered in the following sections of this chapter; the third will be addressed in detail in chapter 9.

The social worlds of production

In broad terms, it could be argued that all creative production is inevitably social. Even artists in their proverbial garrets cannot wholly isolate themselves from the world; and the distribution and reception of art are unavoidably governed by social and economic processes of various kinds (Becker, 1982; Bourdieu, 1984). Post-structuralist theory suggests that art inevitably emerges from a dialogue with others, even where they may not be physically present at the moment of production (Bakhtin, 1981).

This is bound to be the case in classrooms. Studies of children's creative writing in schools suggest that it often arises from a negotiation between the interests of the peer group (which are frequently drawn from popular culture) and the criteria of what counts as legitimate 'school writing' (Moss, 1989; Willett, 2001). Children will often include themselves and their peers in their stories as a way of defining identities and negotiating friendships – as they also do in media production projects (e.g. Buckingham and Sefton-Green, 1994: ch. 5). Anne Haas Dyson's research amply illustrates the social negotiations that occur when story-writing is linked to classroom drama and playground games (Dyson, 1997; and see chapter 10 below).

Thus, it would be false to imply that students necessarily present or express their 'true selves' in such activities. As some critics have argued, the common practice of autobiographical writing in English teaching seems to rest on a rather naïve view of writing as a means of access to some pristine, authentic self (Moss, 1989). Likewise, other authors have challenged the emphasis on 'student voice' in so-called critical pedagogy: the notion that students can be 'given' a voice by the teacher and that they will then use this to speak some kind of subjective truth is, they argue, an illusion (Orner, 1992).

By contrast, media educators have often sought to use production – particularly in the form of photography – as a means of exploring how the 'self' is constructed and represented (e.g. Dewdney and Lister, 1988; Spence, 1986). In our study of one such project (Buckingham and Sefton-Green, 1994: ch. 5), we traced how students consciously manipulated and played with various 'identities' through self-portraits and photo-stories using a range of familiar media genres. Perhaps the most interesting work here, however, was that which permitted a degree of play and fantasy – and indeed, of wish-fulfilment. In this case, several groups of students chose to create stories about 'taboo' issues such as gang violence – and even, in one memorable instance, male strippers – which implicitly allowed them to explore issues to do with the *social* dimensions of their identities, for example in relation to ethnicity and gender.

These issues are inevitably dramatized as a result of the *collaborative* nature of most media production. Of course, there are many areas of media production where collaborative work is not necessary; but in media education, there has always been a central emphasis on *group* production. There are several reasons for this. In the 'real world', of course, production often requires a range of specialist personnel – albeit often organized in hierarchical ways; and in simulating professional practice, students are frequently required to adopt defined production roles. Furthermore, media production – like other areas such as Drama – has been seen to provide important opportunities for developing more general 'social and communication skills' (Lorac and Weiss, 1981; Buckingham, Grahame and Sefton-Green, 1995: ch. 4). And while collaboration may not always be strictly necessary for the small-scale productions typically undertaken in schools, shortages of equipment may make it unavoidable.

While collaborative production may thus prove desirable and necessary, it nevertheless raises significant difficulties. Students come to the classroom with different levels of expertise and knowledge about the media, and with different motivations towards production. Gender is frequently an issue here (Drotner, 1989), although its significance will vary according to the medium being used. Studies of classroom projects on popular music, for example, have found that some boys tend to mobilize their specialist expertise as a means of intimidating or excluding girls, who are likely to have a rather more 'emotional' or 'aesthetic' approach to music (Buckingham and Sefton-Green, 1994: ch. 4; Buckingham, Grahame and Sefton-Green, 1995: ch. 5). On the other hand, projects that involve a stronger element of performance – such as those relating to soap opera (Buckingham, Grahame and Sefton-Green, 1995: ch. 7) – may result in a gendered division of labour, in which boys who are reluctant to perform tend to opt for more 'technical' roles.

In Jeong's (2001) study of one such project, she illustrates how students balanced the need for harmony within the group against the need to complete the work and gain good marks. Here, the male students' greater expertise in aspects of production resulted in a clear division of labour: while the boys made the 'creative' decisions, the girls were mainly responsible for the organizational 'housework'. Likewise, my own study of the production of a rap music video – albeit in the context of a youth work project rather than a school – illustrates how the girls in the group were marginalized by the boys (Buckingham, Grahame and Sefton-Green, 1995: ch. 4). On one level, this might be seen as an inevitable consequence of the male dominance of rap music; but it was also sanctioned by the failure of the tutors to intervene – an approach which, I suggest, was partly justified through sentimental appeals to the 'street credibility' of the young people who worked on the project.

Clearly, there are steps that teachers might take to prevent such difficulties. Providing agreed grounds and procedures for negotiation should prevent differences of opinion in the group from becoming mere 'personality clashes'. Explicitly providing opportunities for all students to experience a range of production roles (for example, by using single-sex groups, or by circulating responsibilities), and requiring students to share their existing expertise, should result in a more inclusive way of working. More difficult perhaps is to find media topics – or approaches to topics – that do not appear to 'cue' stereotypical expectations quite so automatically.

Nevertheless, the inherently social character of media production is not something that can be wished away. Indeed, as I shall describe in more detail in chapter 10, it can create all sorts of problems for teachers. In providing opportunities for production, teachers have to let go of the reins; and in doing so, they can unleash all sorts of tensions and conflicts that cannot easily be resolved.

Writing media

As I have noted, the metaphor of 'media literacy' implies that media education should include both 'reading' and 'writing'. But, as with print literacy, there is an ongoing debate about the most effective ways of teaching these two areas, and about how they should inter- act. In particular, there is the question of how we balance what psychologists call 'bottom–up' and 'top–down' processes. In the case of reading, do we prioritize the correct decoding of elements (phonics), or do we encourage the reader's search for meaning (as in the 'whole language' approach)? Likewise, in the case of writing, do we prioritize skills of orthography and sentence construction, or do we allow the free flow of 'emergent writing'?

Similar debates have occurred in relation to media production work in education (Sefton-Green, 1995). On the one hand are ap- proaches that prioritize the mastery of technical skills and of the 'grammar' of dominant media forms. This approach is particularly apparent in vocational courses, where students are schooled in the rules and routines of professional practice. Media production is taught here using a step-by-step approach, resulting in the gradual accretion of a fixed repertoire of skills and techniques (e.g. Dimbleby, Dimbleby and Whittington, 1994). On the other hand are approaches that emphasize self-expression and open-ended exploration. Here, media are often seen as a means of conveying the 'authentic voice' of young people. This approach is particularly apparent in the context of youth work (e.g. Dowmunt, 1980). As I shall indicate in more detail in chapter 12, these two approaches often seem to coexist, with rather awkward consequences.

On the face of it, it is hard to deny that media production in- volves a set of 'skills' that students need to learn. Media products (like other artistic forms) are constructed according to generic and linguistic conventions; and while these conventions may be flexible, and may change over time, it is ultimately impossible to create meaningful statements without them. Our research shows that stud- ents' early attempts at media production are often characterized by fairly basic 'mistakes' – in the sense that what they produce does not correspond to what they intended, or indeed to what they thought they 'saw' (Buckingham, Grahame and Sefton-Green, 1995). For example, many students' early attempts at photography are often entirely in long shot: the subject they are intending to focus upon occupies only a small area of the frame. Likewise, in editing, beginners will only gradually discover the need for 'rules' such as the 180 degree rule or the eyeline match (Bordwell and Thompson, 1979), unless – and, in some cases, even if – these are explicitly pointed out to them.

Jenny Grahame's study of a group of eleven-year-olds creating photo-stories points to the tentative nature of these early steps in 'media writing' (Buckingham, Grahame and Sefton-Green, 1995: ch. 2). In traditional fashion, this project was introduced with some analytical work on still images drawn from a variety of sources, and then with an analysis of a comic strip. Before taking their photographs, the students were also required to plan out a script and a storyboard. However, as is frequently the case, the students found it very hard to stick to their plans; and yet they were reluctant to take the opportunity to re-shoot any of their pictures, even though this was offered. Ultimately, the fact that the sequences 'made sense' to *them* was enough: the puzzled responses of their teachers, or concerns about communicating with a potential audience, seemed not to matter.

The dilemma, however, is *when* and *how* such 'technical' or 'linguistic' skills are to be learned. Skills cannot be taught in any lasting way if they are not set in the context of the students' attempts to communicate *meaning*. Decontextualized exercises in camera angles – like exercises in using prepositions or intransitive verbs – will not necessarily make very much sense, or indeed make very much difference to what students eventually produce, if they are unrelated to their own intentions and purposes. Furthermore (as with the teaching of reading), the ways in which we might break down these skills does not necessarily correspond to the ways in which students build them up: what appears to us to be a logical structure may well not correspond to the 'logics' with which students themselves make meaning.

Here again, the parallel with verbal language is potentially useful. Students of course possess large repertoires of knowledge about 'media language'. They are already fluent 'readers', even if they have yet to become 'writers'. Nevertheless, their existing knowledge is passive: it has to be made active in order for it to be used. They may know intuitively what a particular convention 'means', but not how that meaning is achieved. In other words, there has to be a kind of *translation* from the 'passive' knowledge that is derived from viewing or reading – or indeed from analysis – to the 'active' knowledge that is required for production or writing.

Of course, it could be argued that there are certain kinds of understandings that can *only* be fully achieved through the experience of production. For example, it is possible to come to 'understand' continuity editing through detailed frame-by-frame analysis of films; but the understanding that can be achieved through actually doing editing oneself is qualitatively different. Nevertheless, this process is one that inevitably requires some formal instruction. Students may be able to learn by doing; but if they are not enabled to reflect upon what they have done, it will be impossible for them to generalize from their experience to future situations. In this respect, then, learning has to involve a dialectical relationship between doing and analysing – or, to put it in media education terminology, between 'practice' and 'theory'.

This approach suggests that some familiar procedures and practices may need to be reconsidered. For example, teachers often make use of *storyboards* when teaching video production. In principle, this practice should enable students to think through the overall shape of their production in a systematic way; and it should also help them to 'think visually' about particular shots or sequences. Yet although storyboards are an essential element of professional practice (at least in some areas of the media), there is reason to doubt their value for students, particularly in the early stages. Younger students, who are unfamiliar with the form, often confuse storyboards with comic strips; while others are inhibited by a lack of confidence in their ability to draw. Perhaps more significantly, there are aspects of the production process – the positioning of cameras or the rhythm of editing, for example – that can only really be grasped through practical experience. It is only *after* such experiences that students may begin to see the purpose of 'modelling' them using pencil and paper. (For further discussion, see Buckingham, Grahame and Sefton-Green, 1995: ch. 8.)

As I shall argue in more detail in chapter 11, digital technology would seem to render much of this redundant; and even in the case of Grahame's photo-story activity, the use of digital still cameras would have permitted a much more inductive, 'trial-and-error' approach. To use the parallel with language teaching once more, this technology facilitates a process of 'drafting and redrafting' which was much harder to achieve with analogue technology; and by reducing the need for detailed advance planning, it also obviates some of the need for more 'abstract' forms of direct instruction.

Using genres

My argument here has attempted to move beyond the dichotomy between 'skills' and 'creativity' that has tended to characterize debates about media production. Implicitly, I am rejecting a view of language (and hence of 'media language') as something objectively given – as an abstract set of rules and conventions that should be explicitly taught. However, I am also rejecting a view of language as simply a vehicle for personal creativity and self-expression. Communication is possible only because of the shared ground of language; it is based in social experience, in a social dialogue with others, and it uses socially structured resources for producing meaning. To paraphrase a well-known saying, we do indeed make meanings; but we do so under conditions that are not of our own choosing.

Similar arguments can be applied, not just to the 'micro' level of composing images or editing, but also to the 'macro' level of media genres. As we have seen, much of the suspicion of earlier generations of media educators was based on a fear that – if left unsupervised – students would simply imitate dominant media forms. Simply 'copying' *Top of the Pops* (Ferguson, 1981) or even documentaries on social issues (Masterman, 1980) was seen as tantamount to complicity with the 'dominant ideology'.

One of the most obvious objections to this view is that imitation is an indispensable aspect of learning. Most practitioners in other art forms would have no problem at all with the idea that students should learn – at least in the early stages – by imitating more skilled exponents. The view of imitation as an essentially *unthinking* process belies the fact that it can demand – and indeed develop – a high level of analytical *and* practical skills. In literacy teaching, advocates of 'genre theory' have argued that students need to be given access to – and explicit instruction in – dominant language genres; and that attempts to deny them this, on the grounds that such genres are ideologically 'tainted', would be selling them short (Cope and Kalantzis, 1993).

A further objection here is that, when given the chance, students do not in fact reproduce 'dominant' forms in quite such a direct manner. A brief glance at even the most outwardly 'imitative' student productions would suggest that there is nearly always an element of negotiation, parody or critique. Furthermore, in using existing media forms or genres, students do not automatically take on the values those genres are seen to contain. On the contrary, they are actively and self-consciously re-working their prior knowledge of the media, often by means of parody or pastiche – a process which might be better understood as a form of 'intertextuality' or dialogic communication, rather than mere slavish imitation (Bakhtin, 1981). As we shall see in more detail in chapter 10, these parodic productions are often highly double-edged: they allow potentially 'incorrect' statements to be made and yet disclaimed at the same time, in ways that often cause problems for teachers.

Jenny Grahame's case study of a simulation on the marketing of popular music (Buckingham, Grahame and Sefton-Green, 1995: ch. 5) shows the positive uses to which 'imitation' can be put. Here, the students were invited to re-package examples of previously popular musical genres for contemporary audiences, by creating CD covers, magazines, video promos and radio shows. Like many Media Studies simulations, the project explicitly invited a form of 'reproduction' of dominant genres, and hence some understanding of their conventions; yet, in repositioning those genres for a different period and a different market, it also required those conventions to be manipulated and changed. These students – in this case, aged sixteen to seventeen – were extremely fluent in mobilizing the 'marketing-speak' of the professionals, even to the point of cynicism. As Grahame shows, there was a range of different *kinds* of 'imitation' going on here. At certain points, the students were indeed seeking merely to recreate familiar musical genres; yet they also showed an acute awareness of institutional constraints, and particularly of the tension between creativity (or innovation) and the need to generate profit. The students were *using* dominant genres, but they were doing so in a very knowing and self-reflexive way.

Likewise, Julian Sefton-Green's study of a project on soap opera conducted with thirteen- to fourteen-year-olds (Buckingham, Grahame and Sefton-Green, 1995: ch. 7) shows the value of working within a given genre with which the students are already familiar. Here, the students created a cast of characters through dramatic improvisation, and proceeded to bring them together in a series of short scenes, which were gradually 'firmed up' for filming. These students were well aware of the conventions of the genre, and capable of using them in a self-conscious rather than an 'unthinking' manner. In the process, however, they effectively 'discovered' why certain kinds of character and situation (such as a doctor's surgery) were necessary in order to generate meaningful narratives. Through 'play acting', the students explored a series of issues to do with realism and the representation of social issues that could then become an explicit focus for reflection and debate. Indeed, it was precisely the *differences* between what students could do using their own resources and the 'models' available to them on broadcast television that provoked much of the thinking here.

This latter example also illustrates a more general form of *hybridity* that frequently characterizes student productions. At least some of this process of generic mutation can be traced to the social context of the classroom. In this instance, there was an interesting coincidence between the familiar 'social problems' agenda of the soap opera genre and the ways in which such issues are typically raised in school subjects such as Social Education and Drama. As in Rebekah Willett's (2001) study of younger children's use of media in their creative writing, students frequently walk a difficult line between 'following school rules' and 'playing to the gallery' – that is, to the peer audience (see chapter 10).

In actively using and re-working dominant forms and conventions, students are bound to borrow from a number of other sources and forms. This is perhaps most evident in instances where they do not appear to possess – or at least to use – a *single* generic 'model'. This can occur where students are less familiar with the form they are using. For example, in a project involving the production of hypertext narratives, we found that the students tended to use models deriving from multiple-choice quizzes in teenage magazines, combined with elements of the 'make-your-own-adventure' story. Likewise, in our project on creating photo-stories, described above, students constructed narratives that drew upon and combined elements of a whole range of media (film, television, comics, books) and genres (horror, soap opera, crime drama, etc.) (Buckingham, Grahame and Sefton-Green, 1995: chs. 2 and 3). These kinds of production certainly incorporated elements of 'imitation'; however, the notion of 'intertextuality' – that is, the idea that texts are inextricably bound up in their relationships with other texts – might be seen as a more appropriate description of what is taking place here.

In other instances, however, the apparent lack of a generic 'model' can prove problematic. Our occasional attempts to encourage students to use more avant-garde forms have also raised significant problems for this reason – although of course it could be argued that the avant-garde is just as 'generic' as more popular forms. For example, one project involving the production of self-consciously 'analytical' media texts on the theme of representation resulted in somewhat abstract and schematic work (Buckingham and Sefton-Green, 1994: ch. 10). However, others have shown that such work can be productive for older students, particularly via the medium of the Web (Jones, 1999). Yet, perhaps ironically, it would seem that students need a familiar genre, at least as a point of departure or reference, if they are to do more than simply reproduce the teacher's agenda.

Conclusion

In this chapter, I have argued that production should be a central component of media education. While I have argued against the Romantic notions of 'creativity' and 'self-expression' which have sometimes informed student production, I have also implied that production work should be much more than a mere illustration of pre-determined 'theoretical' insights. I have also argued that student production is inherently and necessarily *social*, both in the sense that it is generally collaborative and in the sense that it uses socially available resources ('languages' and genres) for making meaning.

Of course, we cannot avoid setting an agenda of theoretical issues, not least in terms of how we frame and structure classroom assignments; and it is vital that these issues should be made explicit to students, rather than left for them to 'discover', as if by osmosis. Yet if students are not enabled to investigate these issues on their own terms, and to draw on their existing knowledge of (and pleasures in) the media, then the outcomes of such work will be little more than superficial. Much of the value of practical work lies in the fact that it allows students to explore their affective and subjective investments in the media, in a way which is much more difficult to achieve through critical analysis. If it is to be effective in this respect, we have to allow – and consciously construct – a space for play and experimentation, in which there are genuinely no 'right answers'.

This implies that production should be both frequent and recursive – and with the growing accessibility of the technology, this is increasingly becoming a realistic possibility. Rather than leading up to the Big Production Number (as is the case in some Media Studies syllabuses), students should be engaging in practical work on a regular basis, both in the form of longer projects and in frequent, small-scale activities, not all of which should be assessed. While these activities might take the form of 'exercises', there is an important place for unstructured social uses of the technology – or what might well resemble aimless 'messing around': this kind of

play is a vital first step that should be built upon, rather than
avoided. Equally, it is important that students have the opportunity to work across a range of media forms and technologies –
photography, video, desk-top publishing and so on.

To argue that practical work should be recursive in this way is
also to imply a particular relationship between process and product. The product should not be seen as the end of the process, but
as a stage within it – a starting point for reflection or a basis for
redrafting, rather than a summation and a demonstration of what
has been learned. As I have implied, reflection is a central and
indispensable aspect of practical work; but it is vital that it should
be built into the process, rather than simply enforced at the end.
This has implications in terms of how we sequence classroom activities. Rather than simply 'doing the theory' first and then using the
production work to illustrate it – as is frequently the case – there is
a strong argument for using practical work deductively, as a means
of generating fresh theoretical ideas. In order to achieve this, students need to have some genuine motivation to step back from their
productions, and to reflect upon their theoretical implications.
Reflection or self-evaluation of this kind has to be driven by something more than the abstract requirements of examiners – and it
too should be recursive, part of an ongoing cycle of action and
reflection. These latter issues will be taken up in more detail in the
following chapter.

9

Defining Pedagogy

The two previous chapters set out to question dominant approaches to teaching and learning in media education. In this chapter, I want to build upon the more positive arguments made there in order to outline a more comprehensive theory of 'media pedagogy'. In addition to discussing a range of theoretical perspectives, I also intend to show how they have been applied in concrete examples of classroom practice.

What *kind* of theory of learning do we need in media education? There is a wide range of competing theories available; and in principle, many of them have insights to offer here. Behaviourist theories, for example, are obviously ill-suited to explaining conceptual learning, or dealing with issues of meaning and identity; but they may help us to understand how students acquire some of the technical and communicative skills that are required for media production. Developmental theories appear to rest on a rather rationalistic account of learning; but they do alert us to some of the ways in which children's understanding of the media develops with age (see chapter 3). Theories of 'multiple intelligences' may provide a somewhat arbitrary map of the human mind; but they move us beyond narrow conceptions of intelligence, and point to areas of experience that are often neglected in formal schooling. Of course, these different theories are mutually incompatible; yet if we are prepared to be opportunistic about using them, they may well help to explain some of the aspects of teaching and learning with which we are concerned.

However, there are other areas of learning theory that appear to have more to offer here, and it is these I will focus on in this chapter. These theories all have limitations. Nevertheless, they may offer at least an indication of a more comprehensive – and, above all, practically *useful* – account of teaching and learning in media education.

Understanding conceptual learning

The model of 'key concepts' outlined in chapter 4 inevitably begs some difficult questions about students' learning. In particular, there is the question of what we take as *evidence* of conceptual understanding. What is the relationship between understanding and the language in which that understanding is embodied? Is students' ability to mobilize a particular academic discourse – for example, to talk about 'representation' and 'ideology' – itself a sufficient indication of understanding? Or – to put the question the other way around – does conceptual understanding necessarily *require* a specialist discourse in the first place?

In previous attempts to address these questions, I have been drawn to the work of the Soviet psychologist Lev Vygotsky (1962; 1978). Vygotsky's work offers many suggestive insights, rather than a fully finished theory; and partly for this reason, there are several 'versions' of Vygotsky in circulation. In this context, the value of Vygotsky's work derives from the fact that it seems to offer a *social* theory of consciousness and of learning. The development of the 'higher mental functions', according to Vygotsky, depends upon the linguistic (or, more broadly, semiotic) tools and signs that mediate social and psychological processes. Learning is, in this sense, a matter of the acquisition of symbolic codes, which are socially and historically defined. This theory can thus be aligned with the social theory of literacy outlined in chapter 3.

In terms of teaching, Vygotsky also appears to offer a way of moving beyond the sterile dichotomy between 'progressive' and 'traditional' approaches. Learning, from this perspective, is not simply about discovery and spontaneous growth; nor, on the other hand, is it about the passive reception of ideas transmitted by the teacher. Vygotsky makes an important distinction here between what students can understand without assistance, and what they can understand only with the help of others. Rather than waiting until children are 'ready', or applying a fixed model of 'ages and stages' (see chapter 3), teachers should be working in these 'zones of proximal development', 'scaffolding' students until they can understand without having to be supported. *Dialogue* between teacher and student, and between students themselves, is central to this process – although, of course, this is not to suggest that dialogue in itself guarantees that learning will occur.

Vygotsky's distinction between 'spontaneous' and 'scientific' concepts offers a useful means of explaining the relationship between students' existing knowledge about the media and the new knowledge made available by teachers (Buckingham, 1990). Briefly, spontaneous concepts are those developed through the child's own mental efforts, while scientific concepts are decisively influenced by adults, and arise from the process of teaching. Scientific concepts – which include social scientific concepts – are distinct from spontaneous concepts in two major respects. Firstly, they are characterized by a degree of distance from immediate experience: they involve an ability to generalize in systematic ways. Secondly, they involve self-reflection, or what psychologists term 'metacognition' – that is, attention not merely to the object to which the concept refers, but also to the thought process itself.

Thus, we might consider children's existing understanding of the media as a body of spontaneous concepts. While these concepts will become more systematic and generalized as they mature, media education might be seen to provide a body of scientific concepts which will enable them to think, and to use language (including 'media language'), in a much more conscious and deliberate way. The aim of media education, then, is not merely to enable children to 'read' – or make sense of – media texts, or to enable them to 'write' their own. It must also enable them to reflect systematically on the processes of reading and writing, to understand and to analyse their own experience as readers and writers.

The issue of children's judgements about the reality of television, discussed in chapter 3, provides an illustration of this. Through their everyday encounters with television, children gradually build up a set of spontaneous concepts that enable them to distinguish between the medium and the real world – and hence to decide how far they should trust what they watch, or take it seriously. In discussing such issues with others, they will be required to justify these judgements in the light of the available evidence, and hence to arrive at a more systematic and consistent set of criteria. And in media education, they will also encounter a set of social scientific concepts, such as 'stereotyping' and 'representation', that will enable them to develop a more self-conscious understanding of the process of mediation, and to speculate about its consequences.

Vygotsky's theory therefore has several important implications for media education. It stresses the value of students acquiring a 'scientific' *metalanguage*, in which they can describe and analyse the functions of (media) language; yet it also emphasizes the importance of teachers engaging with students' existing 'spontaneous' understandings. Reflection and self-evaluation are crucial elements in this respect. It is through reflection that students will be able to make their implicit 'spontaneous' knowledge about the media explicit, and then – with the aid of the teacher and of peers – to reformulate it in terms of broader 'scientific' concepts. Vygotsky argues against the 'direct teaching' of concepts – which he suggests will result in 'nothing but empty verbalism, a parrotlike repetition of words by the child'. Nevertheless, he does assert that children need to be introduced to the terminology of scientific concepts – in effect, to the academic discourse of the subject – and that they will only gradually take this on and come to use it as their own.

However, Vygotsky's distinction between spontaneous and scientific concepts is more problematic than might at first appear. To what extent is it simply a difference in degree, rather than in kind? Is it necessarily true to say that spontaneous concepts are always less systematic than scientific concepts, or that they develop in different ways? More significantly, we might ask whether the difference is merely to do with the social *contexts* from which they derive, and the conventions of the language in which they are couched, rather than something inherent in the concepts themselves. Interestingly, the words 'spontaneous' and 'scientific' could equally well be translated as 'everyday' and 'academic' (or 'scholarly'), which may be a more accurate reflection of these different origins (Gallimore and Tharp, 1990). As this implies, the language of scientific concepts, and the processes by which they are validated as scientific in the first place, are subject to particular social conventions; and a familiarity with these conventions is not equally available to all.

In some respects, therefore, Vygotsky's analysis here is insufficiently social. It does not seem to take account of the social interests that are at stake in the production and circulation of knowledge; nor does it fully acknowledge the relationships between language and social power, or the social functions and uses of language in everyday situations – including classrooms. It is not clear, for example, how Vygotskyan theory might account for some of the ritualized 'language games' described in chapter 7 – or indeed some of the questions raised there about the limitations of 'critical', social scientific perspectives. As James Wertsch (1990) has argued, Vygotsky's theory can usefully be extended here by drawing on the notion of 'speech genres', developed by his contemporary

Mikhail Bakhtin (1986). This focus on different types of speech, and the ways in which they are legitimized and used in different social contexts, begins to move us beyond Vygotsky's apparent privileging of the academic, 'scientific' mode.

Yet this also leads on to broader problems with Vygotsky's theory, and in particular with his emphasis on the 'higher mental functions' – in effect, on logic and the intellect. For example, Vygotsky's attempt to develop a social theory of mind led him and his colleague Luria to undertake extensive cross-cultural research, comparing the language and mental functioning of people in different regions of the Soviet Union. Yet their conclusion that 'primitive' peoples were lacking in the 'higher mental functions' merely points to the cultural bias of their own research. Furthermore, Vygotsky's theory also perpetuates the separation between 'cognitive' and 'affective' processes, and the comparative neglect of the latter, which is characteristic of cognitive psychology. In the case of media education, it may lead to a limited, rationalistic account of the learning process, which neglects the fundamental significance of students' emotional investments in the media; and as I have noted, this has been particularly apparent in some of the forms of 'critical analysis' that have often dominated media classrooms.

Towards a dynamic model

Despite these limitations (to which we shall return), Vygotsky's theory clearly implies a dynamic (or 'dialogic') approach to teaching and learning, in which students move back and forth between action and reflection. From this perspective, 'media learning' could be regarded as a three-stage process: it involves students making their existing knowledge explicit; it enables them to render that knowledge systematic, and to generalize from it; and it also encourages them to question the basis of that knowledge, and thereby to extend and move beyond it. At each stage, this is seen as a collaborative process: through the encounter with their peers and with the academic knowledge of the teacher, students progressively move towards greater control over their own thought processes. The act of moving between one language mode and another – for example, 'translating' or restating the insights gained through practical media production in the form of talk or writing – would seem to be a particularly important stage in this process.

An illustration from my own teaching might help to explain this. This is an activity I have used both with school students and with trainee teachers, often at a fairly early stage in their course. Students are asked, in groups, to take a number of photographs from a list which includes a range of generic possibilities. Depending on the context and the group, this might include more specific requirements – for example, an illustration for 'The Young Designer of the Year', an article for the *Sunday Times*, or an advertisement for the housing charity Shelter – or broader generic possibilities – a frame from a photo-story, or a record cover for a techno band. With school students, I have used this approach to introduce a unit of work on film stills and trailers: here, the students are asked to produce stills and publicity shots for films in specific genres such as horror, documentary and the musical. Once the photographs have been processed, they are initially returned to a different group, in order that they can try to identify which image is which: readings are then compared among the groups. In the original groups, students then put captions to their photographs, and label the particular conventions in the image that indicate which genre it comes from. In some instances, I have developed this work further, asking students to write more extended pieces that relate to the images (such as sleeve notes from the record album, or copy for the advertisement).

This activity obviously assumes an existing knowledge of generic conventions on the part of students – and of course, it is important to devise the assignment with that knowledge in mind. Yet in taking and subsequently captioning the photographs, students have to manipulate those conventions, which they often do through parody. And in subsequently reflecting on their work, they are being required to make their knowledge explicit, and to question it. In a sense, the exercise requires students to acknowledge consciously what they already know 'unconsciously'; yet it also encourages them to question how they know what they know, and where that knowledge comes from. The fact that this is a collaborative activity – both in devising the images and in subsequently gauging others' readings of them – is of course crucial to its success, since the students are continually having to justify their interpretations and choices to each other. Finally, this is an activity that involves an interaction between a number of different 'language modes' – and here I would include the visual language of photography, as well as talk and writing.

This approach is therefore based on a dialectical relationship between language *study* and language *use* – between critical analysis and practical production. This may well involve students acquiring a specialist terminology or metalanguage, for example in sharing and 'systematizing' what they may already know about camera angles and positions, or about the semiotics of dress or posture – in other words, their 'spontaneous' concepts. And it is also likely to involve considered intervention by teachers – for example, in encouraging students to compare different instances of the same genre, or to ask why particular images are seen to 'fail', and thereby to move them on to broader insights about the social and historical diversity of media language. Unlike many media production activities, however, it does not start with critical analysis and then move on to apply it; on the contrary, it encourages students to build 'theory' deductively, through reflecting on their own experience.

The model I have briefly outlined here overlaps with that more recently developed by advocates of 'multiliteracies' (Cope and Kalantzis, 2000). These authors argue that teaching and learning involve an interaction of four factors. The first, 'Situated Practice', refers to students' immersion in a community of learners engaged in authentic versions of a particular practice (such as reading or media production). This implies that some kinds of knowledge are best developed, not in the abstract, but in the context of particular activities. However, we do not simply 'learn by doing'; and immersion in practice does not necessarily lead to a degree of conscious control and awareness of what one is doing. This, they argue, requires a second element, 'Overt Instruction'. While this may include direct transmission of information by the teacher, it also includes less direct forms of intervention and 'scaffolding' that allow students to gain new knowledge and to organize what they are doing. It will therefore include the acquisition of metalanguages that allow more reflective generalization, of the kind described above.

The dynamic relationship between Situated Practice and Overt Instruction should promote conscious mastery of a particular practice. However, it does not necessarily enable students to recognize the social, cultural and ideological dimensions of that practice. It is here that students need a third dimension, 'Critical Framing', which will enable them to take a theoretical distance from what they have learned; to account for its social and cultural location; and to critique and extend it. Critical Framing implies 'making the familiar strange', and setting it within a broader historical context. This leads on to a final aspect, 'Transformed Practice'. This involves the implementation of new forms of practice in new contexts and for new purposes, building on the insights of earlier stages.

The multiliteracies model is somewhat vague on specifics, particularly when it comes to 'Transformed Practice'; but there are nevertheless some obvious parallels with the arguments I have been developing here. For example, in the previous chapter, I pointed to the need for a dynamic interplay between experiential learning-by-doing (Situated Practice) and the teaching of particular 'linguistic' or technical skills (Overt Instruction) – and I argued that this was best achieved through a process of reflection and self-evaluation. Likewise, in chapter 7, I argued that textual analysis (Situated Practice) alone was not enough, and that it needed to be combined with broader forms of contextual analysis, both in relation to audiences and in relation to production (Critical Framing). Transformed Practice – or what we might term 'reflective' or 'critical' practice – could be seen as one potential outcome of media education, for example in the form of innovative media productions.

In order to make these somewhat abstract formulations rather more concrete, the remaining sections of this chapter will describe some aspects of media education that appear to permit this 'dialogic' combination of different forms of learning. As we shall see, none of them is unproblematic, but they do at least begin to indicate some of the possibilities here.

Researching audiences: the social self

As we have seen, some advocates of media education suggest that students should be encouraged to leave aside their subjective judgements about the media, as a prerequisite for assuming a more 'objective', analytical approach (e.g. Masterman, 1980). This has led others to argue that media education has neglected or marginalized questions of cultural value and aesthetic judgement (e.g. Bazalgette, 1998). Yet, as any media teacher knows, it is actually very hard to prevent students from making such judgements: indeed, they are constantly debating and proclaiming the relative merits of different pop groups or soap operas. The point, as Raney and Hollands (2000: 21) argue, is not to ban the idea of value judgement, but to deepen and complicate our discussions about it.

In chapter 7, I suggested that teachers might productively *use* students' subjective judgements about the media, and their accounts of their everyday media experiences, as a valuable resource for further discussion and analysis. In addition to sharing and comparing their own responses, students can also gather those of others, and reflect on the differences between them. In the process, they might come to understand the social basis of all such judgements, including their own; and to recognize the ways in which media use is inevitably embedded within everyday routines and practices. Such activities should foster what Chris Richards (1998b) has called students' 'social self-understanding' – that is, their ability to understand their own location in the context of broader social and cultural relationships; and they should also promote a more questioning approach towards popular arguments about media 'effects'.

There are several classroom strategies that might be employed here. 'Media autobiographies', which involve students gathering and compiling evidence of their developing media tastes and interests, are a frequent starting point for media courses (Buckingham and Sefton-Green, 1994: ch. 6). Audience research projects, of the kind described in chapter 5, are also frequently undertaken (for examples, see Branston, 1991; Branston and Stafford, 1999; Duncan et al., 1996). Richard Beach (2000) provides a useful synopsis of recent developments in audience research, as well as some practical suggestions for teaching and some examples of undergraduate students' work in this field.

There are various researched accounts of this kind of activity, in a variety of settings. In his book *Teen Spirits*, Chris Richards (1998b) describes a 'Desert Island Discs' activity, which involved a group of sixteen- to seventeen-year-old students in selecting eight records to take with them to a fictional desert island. In justifying and reflecting on their choices, the students' writing inevitably shaded towards autobiography. On one level, this activity offered an opportunity for students to 'give voice' to pleasures and emotional responses in a way that rarely happens in classrooms; but it could also provide the basis for a more sociological analysis of the relationships between individual taste, the presentation of identity and broader factors such as gender and social class.

Sara Bragg (2000: ch. 3) describes a project in which she encouraged students in a similar age group to share and reflect on their experiences of watching horror films. This represented a deliberate break from the class teacher's regular approach, which involved introducing students to the historical 'canon' of classic horror movies. As Bragg suggests, however, this move was far from unproblematic. The students used the discussion, not as an opportunity to 'give voice' to their personal responses and enthusiasms, but as a means of staking out particular social identities. A kind of cultural hierarchy emerged in the discussion, led by particular dominant individuals, that valued certain *types* of horror films (notably 'psychological' horror) above others that were condemned as merely bloody and visceral – and hence as only appropriate for 'immature' viewers. In this situation, as in my own research (reported in chapter 3), the students were keen to calibrate themselves in terms of age, and to disclaim a childish self they had 'left behind'; and they were also seeking to locate themselves in relation to the school, as 'serious' students. In this case, it was only in a later development of the work, which involved students devising their own scenarios for 'remakes' of old horror movies, that some of the more 'tasteless' pleasures (and un-pleasures) of horror could be articulated.

Our own research in this area (Buckingham and Sefton-Green, 1994: ch. 6) points to further difficulties. In one case, groups of Year 10 students (aged fourteen to fifteen) carried out a small-scale audience research study at an early stage in their GCSE Media Studies course. Many of the projects reflected students' existing specialist interests in the media, and included studies of television viewing habits, musical tastes and newspaper reading. Studies often began with explicit hypotheses, for example about ethnic differences, or about differences between staff and students. However, most students found it problematic to verbalize and define sociological categories such as 'race' and 'class' explicitly. While they were acutely aware of such issues, they found it hard to translate this awareness into the public language of academic research. Thus, for many students, the initial problem they faced in constructing surveys was of labelling their 'subjects'. In the case of age and gender, this appeared comparatively straightforward; yet particularly with regard to 'race', students found it very difficult to decide how to describe themselves and their peers. Despite (or perhaps because of) the high level of ethnic diversity in the school, it seemed almost impossible to find a vocabulary in which to define racial differences. As these students were forced to acknowledge, even quantitative research of this kind is much more than a process of neutral description.

By contrast, a more 'personal' – and more productive – approach emerged from some of the 'media autobiographies' we undertook with this group, and from some of the more extended research studies undertaken by older students. A sense of personal engagement was particularly apparent in the projects undertaken by two British/Turkish girls. The first, Zerrin, set out to examine the media tastes of what she termed 'educated and non-educated' women living in Turkey. The research was conducted in both English and Turkish and was a mixture of interview and survey work, partly conducted during her summer holiday in Turkey. As Zerrin recognized (and as I have argued), the attempt to separate media use from the broader context of social practices and relationships is likely to prove reductive. In this respect, the research represented an opportunity for her to reflect upon aspects of her life that might well have been much harder for her to address in the more intrusive form of autobiographical writing.

Aylin, another British/Turkish student, chose to examine video usage amongst different generations of Turkish families living in North London. In particular, she wanted to explore the viewing of Turkish and American films amongst first- and second-generation immigrant families, and the ways in which Turkish films were used as a form of cultural maintenance and home language education (cf. Gillespie, 1995). Here again, the project acted as a way of reflecting on the relationships between gender and taste from a strongly personal perspective. Aylin effectively used the research as a way of writing about gender and power in her community. Adopting the position of researcher thus gave both students a sense of power over their material and an authoritative position from which they could reflect upon the range of social roles available to them.

These studies point to some of the benefits – as well as the potential difficulties – of this kind of practice. In principle at least, this kind of work can 'give voice' to students' personal experiences and pleasures. However, it should also seek to problematize this process, by locating them in relation to broader social factors. In a very practical way, it inevitably raises some of the theoretical and methodological dilemmas that plague 'real' researchers; and in this respect it can help students to question what *counts* as knowledge about media audiences. In terms of the models of media learning identified above, this approach clearly seeks to move outwards from the sharing of personal tastes towards a broader form of 'Critical Framing'.

Self-evaluation: from practice to theory

Another, quite different area of practice that is relevant here is that of students' self-evaluation of their own production work. Here again, students are encouraged to engage in a process of reflection on their own practice – to move from 'Situated Practice' towards 'Critical Framing'. As I have noted, examinations in Media Studies typically require students to produce a written essay to accompany their productions. Here, students are encouraged to reflect back on the process in the light of their own and others' readings of what they have produced. Did they communicate what they set out to communicate? Why did they make particular choices, and what effects did they have? How might an audience interpret what they have produced, and what can they learn from this? At least in principle, it is through this systematic process of written reflection that connections between 'theory' and 'practice' will be developed and made explicit.

In this context, writing appears to have a particular value, which derives at least partly from the specific characteristics of written communication, as compared with talk or other methods. Elsewhere, we have argued that much of the value of writing in this context derives precisely from its individual, private nature (Buckingham and Sefton-Green, 1994: ch. 8). This is not, however, to suggest that it is somehow asocial: on the contrary, it functions as a form of dialogue with an imagined other – or what one of the students in our study, Michael, aptly called a 'conversation with yourself'. Michael argued that, while he found writing difficult, it did serve as a prompt for reflection – it helped him to discover things that he didn't know he thought.

A further argument for the value of writing in this context can be drawn from work on 'Knowledge about Language'. In his theoretical overview of the area, John Richmond (1990) argues that self-conscious reflection upon the characteristics of language can be developed through the 'translation' between language modes. Writing about talk, or talk about reading, for example, can make the specific qualities of these different modes much more explicit, and thus contribute to the development of a systematic under-standing of how languages work (cf. my discussion of 'translation' in chapter 5). A similar argument could be made about the rela-tionship between media production and writing, which effectively involves a similar form of translation between one language mode and another. In the process, it could be argued, students are able to make their implicit knowledge explicit, to systematize it and thence to question it.

While it may be valuable in principle, however, this insistence on written evaluation is often more problematic in practice. One of the difficulties here is that this kind of self-evaluative writing is generally undertaken only for the purpose of assessment. Indeed, it is the written account or commentary that, in practice, represents the major form of evidence for the examiner of the conceptual understandings that were entailed or developed in the production process – and hence exerts a crucial influence on the allocation of grades. Thus it tends to be seen more as an exercise in self-justification designed to maximize marks in the examination than an 'honest' reflection on what took place. It also marks the point at which – again, for the purposes of assessment – a collective process must be individualized, and distinctions made between individual students. Yet the most successful students may be simply those who are best at presenting themselves; and in the process, self-evaluation may become little more than a form of impression management (see Buckingham, Fraser and Sefton-Green, 2000).

In her study of one extended production simulation, Jenny Grahame (1990) argues that a great deal of what is most valuable about student production work may be lost in the transition to writing. In this case, the students were working on the production of a TV programme for much younger children; and the activity generated a wealth of lively and innovative ideas. Yet many of the students who contributed most to the practical production, for example in terms of their technical or 'artistic' skills, or their role in group work, tended to lose out when it came to writing. One could well argue that, like other forms of assessment, the primary aim of insisting on writing is to discriminate in favour of students who have skills in particular forms of communication, and against those who have other abilities; and that this serves merely to perpetuate existing inequalities.

Grahame argues that one of the problems with this project – like many student production activities – was that the element of self-evaluation was conducted some time after the event. Of course, there may be good reasons for this: it is hard to step back from one's intense involvement in a production to reflect upon what is happening; and students may well need time to 'cool down' before they can arrive at a balanced and fair assessment of what they have achieved. However, as Grahame suggests, it is also important to build in regular opportunities for systematic 'debriefing', in which the connections between theory and practice can be forged. Rather than being extraneous, or tacked on at the end, evaluation should be a much more integral part of the process.

At the same time, it is vital to recognize the *difficulty* of what students are being asked to do here. The practice of self-evaluation seems to imply that the only thinking that counts is the thinking that can be made self-conscious – whereas of course one would not assume that a visual artist or a musician was necessarily best placed to explain or evaluate their own work, particularly in written form. As Grahame suggests, the insistence on the academic essay may reflect a teacherly insecurity: however open-ended production projects may be, we seem to need strategies that bring academic knowledge back to us in a safe and acceptable form. In a later publication, Grahame (1991b) suggests some interesting alternatives, using oral and visual methods, role-playing, group presentations, and so on, which might promote different kinds of reflection. And of course, it is vital that students should have opportunities for self-evaluation that are *not* tied to the requirements of formal assessment.

Ultimately, the fundamental issue here is to do with the *motivation* for self-evaluation. In my experience, written self-evaluation is often seen by students as an artificial, abstract requirement on the part of teachers or examiners. One way of moving beyond this is to capitalize on the potential of media for communicating with *real* audiences. Both in formal education and in informal settings, the audience for young people's media productions has tended to be extremely limited. In schools, such work is primarily produced for the teacher-as-examiner, and (more indirectly) for one's classmates. Likewise, the lack of an audience for young people's domestic media productions places significant constraints on what they are motivated to do (Sefton-Green and Buckingham, 1996). In principle, the attempt to communicate with a real audience, and the requirement to take on board their responses to your work, should make it easier for students to 'decentre' – to see their productions through others' eyes, and hence to adopt a more distanced perspective on what they have achieved.

This issue is explored in my own study of a project which, like Jenny Grahame's, involved the production of TV programmes – or in this case, trailers – for younger children (Buckingham, Grahame and Sefton-Green, 1995: ch. 6). In this instance, the students (aged fourteen to fifteen) were required to test out various pilot ideas with groups of younger students drawn from their target age group (eleven to twelve); and subsequently to gauge their responses to the finished products. Of course, the project was still a simulation: the students knew that the audience was only partly 'real', and so they were able to dismiss some of the responses of their audience groups where they were not in line with their own views. Nevertheless, the encounter with these partly real audiences did encourage them to justify their work, and to reflect on the gaps between what they had intended to communicate and what they had actually achieved, in a much more spontaneous way. As with Grahame's project, however, much of the complexity of these negotiations was lost when it came to the final written essay: here, many of the students attempted to efface the tensions and contradictions from which much of the most significant learning could have arisen.

The potential of this kind of approach is further developed in a more recent study (Buckingham and Harvey, 2001). Here, the students were involved in a 'video exchange' project between several countries. Viewing the other young people's productions, and getting some feedback on their own work, seemed to promote a kind of 'decentring' – and in some respects, the fact that the audience was not physically present may have encouraged this. Thinking about their own interpretations of the other young people's productions seemed to encourage the students to consider how other people might think about theirs. It led them to recognize that some of their intentions were not clear, or had changed as the work had progressed; and that some of the outcomes did not correspond to their intentions, and may have led to them being misinterpreted. The mere fact that there was a real audience out there – and indeed that they themselves were a real audience for other people's productions – helped them to evaluate their own work in a more thoughtful and critical way.

Almost thirty years ago, Murdock and Phelps (1973) were suggesting that students' assignments 'should be produced with a real audience or public in mind . . . the school, or, even better, the local neighbourhood'. In this respect – as we shall see in more detail in chapter 12 – media education can potentially cross the boundaries between formal education, everyday life and public culture (Morgan, 1998b). As I have suggested here, finding an audience – and reflecting on how that audience responds – can also have important implications in terms of learning.

Beyond the model

The theoretical models outlined in the earlier part of this chapter are far from unproblematic. Teachers have a right to be profoundly suspicious of such theories, and of the 'regimes of truth' that are used to regulate their work. As I have suggested, the realities of classroom practice are inevitably much more 'messy' and contradictory than the well-ordered universe of educational theory.

Nevertheless, the approach I am proposing here is essentially *dialogic*. It involves an ongoing dialogue or negotiation between students' existing knowledge and experience of the media and the new knowledge that is made available by teachers. It does not seek merely to 'validate' – let alone to celebrate – students' experiences, but to provide them with the means to reflect upon them, to realize how they might be different, and to move beyond them. Nor does it simply vindicate the academic – or even 'scientific' – perspective of the teacher. On the contrary, it implies that the knowledge teachers bring into the classroom, and the analytical tools and procedures they introduce, should themselves be subject to critical scrutiny and interrogation.

The approach is also *dynamic*, in the sense that it entails a constant shifting back and forth between different forms of learning – between action and reflection, between practice and theory, and between passionate engagement and distanced analysis. As I have argued, media education involves participation *and* understanding: it must enable young people to become active users and producers of media, but it must also enable them to comprehend the broader contexts in which the media are situated. Privileging any one of these terms above the other will inevitably result in a reductive experience of learning. Indeed, it is precisely in the interaction between them that much of the value of media education is to be found.

Part IV

New Directions

Part IV looks forward to some of the challenges that lie ahead for media educators. Chapter 10 extends the discussion of teaching and learning, drawing attention to some troubling questions emerging from recent studies of classroom practice. Chapter 11 considers the opportunities presented by new digital technologies; while chapter 12 looks at the potential for media education beyond the formal education system.

10

Politics, Pleasure and Play

In some ways, the very act of bringing children's popular culture into the classroom could be seen to create a whole series of problems. As I have suggested, education and the media have frequently been defined in opposition to each other. There has been a 'history of suspicion' in teachers' dealings with popular culture (Lusted, 1985); and in recent years, children's media have increasingly sought to undermine 'educational' values of seriousness and authority. If we are not attempting merely to condemn popular culture, or somehow to use or colonize it for our own purposes, to teach about it is bound to be seen as a profoundly ambivalent act. It will almost inevitably generate tensions and contradictions that cannot easily be contained.

This ambivalence is apparent in many contemporary discussions of media education. For example, in their book *Literacy and Popular Culture*, Jackie Marsh and Elaine Millard (2000) make a series of useful proposals for classroom projects with younger children. They present work on media and popular culture as a valid extension of literacy teaching; and they also see it as an important way of recognizing the 'cultural capital' of children, particularly working-class children. Yet although they challenge simplistic 'moral panics' about media effects, Marsh and Millard are clearly troubled by the values that popular culture is seen to promote; and they are unsure of how far they should be exercising their responsibility as teachers to offer moral or political guidance. For example, they offer some constructive ways of dealing with popular music in the classroom; but they continue to worry about whether they should comment on the misogyny of rap music, or the commercial manipulation of children by the music industry. Likewise, they recognize the growing importance of computer games, and provide some interesting ways of using them to develop children's understanding of narrative; yet they are still troubled by what they see as the 'hegemonic masculinity' of games culture, and the 'oppressive' forms of gender stereotyping that it promotes. Marsh and Millard recognize that self-righteous condemnation is likely to prove counterproductive; but they are ultimately uncertain as to how they should strike the balance between validation and critique.

In my view, the kind of conceptual framework I have outlined in this book provides at least a partial answer to these dilemmas. It offers a clear and comprehensive rationale for classroom activities that takes us well beyond the 'stereotype spotting' that sometimes passes for media education; and it should provide the basis for a more constructive form of dialogue between teachers and students, in which moral or political condemnation is ultimately redundant. From this perspective, effective media teaching is rather more than a matter of 'striking the balance' between teacherly criticism and the pleasures of children's culture.

Nevertheless, the worries and concerns that continue to trouble teachers like Marsh and Millard cannot simply be wished away. They arise partly from the fact that we are dealing with areas of experience that cannot be easily rationalized. But they also reflect the fact that there are limitations on what, as teachers, we can ever completely know about our students – and indeed, on what we have the *right* to know. As I shall indicate, this can sometimes make it very hard to know when and how we should intervene.

Postmodern identities?

The theoretical model of media pedagogy proposed in the previous chapter represents a very *provisional* settlement with some ongoing debates and developments. In this chapter, I take the discussion of teaching and learning a step further. In some ways, this chapter takes us to the outer limits of current thinking in the field – and indeed to places where some (perhaps myself included) may be less than willing to go.

The issues raised in this chapter also connect with broader social and cultural developments of the kind briefly identified in the first two chapters of this book. Theorists and commentators of many kinds have drawn attention to the increasing mobility and diversity of modern societies; the displacement of traditional patterns of work and domestic life; the fragmentation of established social groups; and the growing loss of faith in institutionalized authority. The contemporary world is also increasingly saturated by media of various kinds; and the media themselves have become significantly more diverse, more complex and more 'interactive'. In this context, it has been argued, the ways in which people form and construct their identities have fundamentally changed. Rather than identity being a kind of 'birthright' – something determined by one's social position and conditions of life – identities have now become much more diverse and fluid. Contemporary consumer culture is seen to provide a very diverse range of 'symbolic resources' – images and signs – that individuals can use to construct their own identities and to define their own lifestyles. The formation of identities is therefore seen not as an inexorable process of socialization, but as a process in which individuals are active and self-aware.

Of course, these changes are often overstated. Yet it cannot be denied that the experience of young people growing up in the contemporary media environment is now vastly different from that of the majority of their teachers. This in turn inevitably complicates the task of media educators. It places significant limits on what we can possibly know, and on how relevant our teaching can be. In place of the accessible 'common culture' of broadcast television, young people are now faced with a vast proliferation of media options, many of which may be unavailable – or at least incomprehensible – to us. We can no longer assume that our students will be sharing similar experiences with each other, let alone that they might do so with us. And we can no longer trust in a simplistic account of 'identity politics', in which media images are seen to have singular and predictable consequences in terms of our students' perceptions of their place in the world.

While media teachers clearly do need to keep pace with the enthusiasms of their students, they cannot hope to know more than they do – nor should they. Indeed, in my experience, personal preferences and investments in aspects of media can easily be a liability in the classroom: students are very likely to reject what you enjoy, particularly if you make that clear to them. Yet the 'generation gap' between teachers and students is not simply a matter of taste. It may also have much more far-reaching implications in terms of the theoretical assumptions that inform our teaching.

A good example of this is in teaching about representation. In an interesting reflection on her own teaching, Elizabeth Funge (1998) draws attention to the gap between her students' perceptions of gender in the media and the feminist theories on which much media education is based. She argues that '1970s feminism', with its emphasis on ideological deconstruction, simply fails to connect with contemporary gender politics – as embodied, for example, in the notion of 'girl power'. Analysing 'stereotypes' and the 'oppressive' objectification of the female body does not help us to understand the appeal of the Spice Girls or Lara Croft; nor, Funge argues, does it connect with her female students' 'insistent and quite powerful expression of their own sexuality'. These arguments might be extended by considering more recent representations of female sexuality – *Buffy the Vampire Slayer*, *Xena, Warrior Princess* or *Sex in the City*, perhaps – that seem to combine a heightened form of 'objectification' of the body with a powerful celebration of agency.

The implication here is not just that media educators need to engage with their students' changing media experiences. It is also that they need to recognize how those experiences are fundamentally different from their own – and that those differences may well have broader theoretical implications. The argument is not just that the media themselves are different, but also that the ways in which young people engage with them – the modalities of interpretation and engagement and investment – are also fundamentally changed. Funge argues that we are now in 'a new phase of representation', in which multiple readings and ambivalent reactions to media may be the norm. In this 'postmodern' context, she suggests, we need to recognize that media representations are more complex, and audiences more sophisticated, than was the case in earlier times. Contemporary representations of gender cannot be encompassed by outdated notions of 'stereotyping', 'negative images' and the 'male gaze' – although it is precisely these kinds of idea which, she argues, continue to circulate in media education.

To some extent, the argument here takes us back to Judith Williamson's (1981/2) concern about the lack of connection between ideological analysis and lived experience; although Funge also raises the important issue – which Williamson fails to address – about where any of this leaves the boys in her class. The more challenging question, however, is whether the ways in which young people now define and construct their gendered identities – and how they use the media in doing so – are significantly different from those of earlier times. The evidence here is bound to be difficult to establish, although some commentators on contemporary youth culture certainly suggest as much (e.g. McRobbie, 1994). Indeed, some feminist theorists have challenged the very notion of a fixed or essential gender identity, arguing rather that gender is a kind of performance or 'masquerade' (Butler, 1990); and of course the figure of Madonna has become the best-known popular icon of this 'postmodern' version of femininity (Schwichtenberg, 1993).

Yet even if we accept these arguments, it is debatable whether we can extend them to other areas of identity formation. There have been very significant shifts in the social position and experience of women over the past few decades, and it would be surprising if these were not reflected in media representations. Yet whether similar arguments might apply to 'race' and ethnicity, for example, is more questionable. Some commentators have certainly been inclined to celebrate what they see as the emergence of 'powerful' non-white personalities and characters, and more hybrid 'new ethnicities', in the media; but the continuing presence of racist rhetoric and assumptions is hard to ignore. Yet here again, the implications of this in terms of 'identity politics' – and for education – are unlikely to be straightforward.

Phil Cohen (1998) offers some useful reflections on these issues in his account of teaching about 'race' in the context of arts education. Cohen firmly rejects simplistic notions of 'positive images', arguing that they are based on a rationalistic approach, which regards racism as merely a result of irrationality or misinformation. Like Funge, he argues that images can be read in diverse and sometimes contradictory ways; and that the meanings attached to a notion such as 'race' are inherently unstable. Cohen argues that a more constructive starting point would be to recognize the elements of 'masquerade' – parody, mimicry, playful juxtaposition – that characterize some contemporary youth cultures; and he suggests that these can be used by students to subvert essentialized ethnic identities, and to generate more complex narratives of the self. His example, an image of an 'Indian Cowgirl Warrior', created by an ethnically mixed group of seven- and eight-year-old girls, is a distinctly hybrid, 'multicultural' creation which also gives voice to their resistance to racial injustice.

Behind both the studies I have mentioned here lies a broader dissatisfaction with 'modernist' conceptions of meaning and identity. They explicitly contest 'politically correct' teaching, which seeks to provide a form of 'counter-propaganda' to what is seen as the ideological delusions promoted by the mainstream media. They also imply that identity itself cannot be seen in singular terms, as something fixed or essential. They therefore suggest that prescriptive teaching strategies that try to legislate fixed meanings and impose 'correct' thoughts may miss much of the positive political potential of students' media cultures.

Playful pedagogies

Ultimately, these questions of politics and identity cannot be divorced from the crucial dimension of *pleasure*. As Roger Silverstone (1999) suggests, pleasure and play are central aspects of our relationships with the media. The non-rational, the bodily and the erotic are fundamental dimensions of social experience, yet they are often disavowed. Silverstone argues that popular culture has always offered an arena for play, in which these things could be sanctioned, if only temporarily. In the electronic media, we can find the same marked spaces for play, although the boundaries between play and seriousness are becoming more permeable and less distinct. And play, as he suggests, is also an opportunity to claim our individuality, to construct our identities through the roles we take and the rules we follow.

This playful – or 'ludic' – dimension has been a key emphasis in postmodern theory. In place of realist notions of representation, some postmodernists favour an irreverent play with meaning, in which seriousness and rationality are replaced by irony and parody. According to Usher and Edwards (1994: 15): ' "serious" modern culture aims to give a "truthful" representation of reality and thus to educate people into viewing the world in particular ways conducive to "progress" '. It is premised on the notion of mastery through rationality, and on the denial or suppression of desire. By contrast, postmodern culture subverts these totalizing discourses (which seek to explain the ultimate 'truth') through a kind of eclecticism and a refusal of fixed meanings. For some, this 'ludic' dimension of postmodernism is fundamental to its resistance towards an oppressive modernist *status quo* – although others argue that it is here that postmodernism most clearly displays its complicity with contemporary consumer culture.

As I have indicated, media production provides a space in which students can explore their pleasures and emotional investments in the media, in a way that is much more subjective and 'playful' than is the case with critical analysis. And, of course, production is itself often pleasurable, not least because of its collaborative nature: being part of a team, sharing your work with peers, having a laugh, dressing up and enjoying in-jokes, are absolutely central to the activity. At the same time, there is a sense in which many production projects reflect a kind of subversion or transgression of the rules of 'serious' educational endeavour; and as we shall see, this can have difficult consequences.

Perhaps not surprisingly, these playful dimensions of media education have been more successfully realized with younger children. In the context of literacy teaching, the work of Anne Haas Dyson (1997) and Rebekah Willett (2001) provides interesting insights into the ways in which children use elements of media and popular culture in their creative writing. In the classroom Dyson describes, the children engaged in a practice called 'Author's Theatre', in which they narrated and enlisted their classmates to act out their stories. In this context, the written story became a 'ticket to play': the Author's Theatre brought some of the informal play of the schoolyard into the classroom – and with it, the complex negotiation of social relationships and identities that such play necessarily entails. The children's extensive use of media characters and narratives (particularly superhero cartoons) in their writing thus became a means of defining and enacting their social identities, as well as a focus of potential tension between the official culture of the school and the unofficial culture of the children's everyday lives.

Similarly, Willett's (2001) study focuses on children's use of media themes and characters in the context of a 'process writing' classroom. The children drew enthusiastically on elements of their peer culture, such as the Spice Girls, computer games, and the movie *Titanic*; but Willett shows that they were doing much more than simply imitating media-based narratives. Indeed, despite the apparently open invitation to write, the children engaged in some quite tortuous negotiations in their efforts to align their use of media material with the 'rules' of school writing. Like Dyson, Willett shows how the use of media provides the basis for a kind of 'identity work', in which particular friendships as well as broader aspects of social identity (most obviously gender) are being negotiated and defined. (Other studies in this vein may be found in Marsh (1999) and Dyson (1999).)

In different ways, both authors address some of the teacherly anxieties that often surround children's use of media. Willett shows that boys' media enthusiasms – for example, for computer games – are less easily adapted to the preferred conventions of school writing than girls', and are more likely to provoke moralistic concerns about 'violence'. Dyson attempts to 'recover' aspects of popular culture, for example by comparing superhero cartoons to ancient Greek myths. However, she also subjects the texts on which the children draw – *X-Men*, *The Three Ninjas*, *Power Rangers* and so on – to some rather summary ideological judgements of her own, both about 'violence' and about 'stereotyping'.

These issues are addressed in a more direct way in a study by Donna Grace and Joseph Tobin (1998) of the use of video production in an elementary school in Hawaii. Here, the open-ended invitation to produce videotapes resulted in the children frequently transgressing the norms and conventions of school life. While many of the productions were quite unproblematic, others showed actions and situations, or used language, that the adults in authority considered rude, inappropriate or unacceptable. Many of these productions were influenced by popular culture, not only by children's cartoons and family movies, but also in some cases by horror films and 'taboo' programmes like *Beavis and Butthead*. As in the Rabelaisian 'carnival', the emphasis on laughter and parody, bodily functions, horrific violence and bad taste represented a playful inversion of traditional forms of order and authority (Bakhtin, 1968).

Grace and Tobin argue that, while 'progressive' educators may outwardly appear to encourage 'self-expression', they frequently attempt to constrain it. By contrast, this project did allow 'a place for pleasure', in which the children's humour and everyday interests could be recognized in the classroom. At the same time, several of the videos clearly – and in some instances, apparently self-consciously – violated the norms of 'political correctness'. Parodic representations of disabled characters and of native Hawaiian culture, or the reproduction of stereotypical views of gender and physical attractiveness, clearly made the adults who saw them uncomfortable. While Grace and Tobin acknowledge the difficulties here, they argue that this 'carnivalesque' approach allows such differences to be represented and addressed, rather than attempting to ignore them or wish them away.

Taken together, these studies make a strong case for the value of a more open-ended, 'playful' approach to media production. However, they also draw attention to some of its potential problems. All these studies focus on the children, and none describes the actual teaching process in any detail. In the case of Willett and Dyson, the primary aim of the activity is to encourage creative writing, rather than to develop children's understanding of the media. For Grace and Tobin, the aims are rather less clear. While they claim not to be celebrating the children's transgressions of classroom norms, they do not explain how teachers might *intervene* in this kind of activity, beyond using their 'intuition and judgement' to block projects that might prove unduly offensive. Yet the basis for any such intervention – and what children might be expected to *learn* from such activities – needs to be more clearly identified.

The politics of parody

In practice, very few media production activities in schools are as apparently open-ended as those I have just described. In the context of media education, the aims of production work are nearly always defined in conceptual terms. As in the activities described in chapter 8, production is generally seen as a concrete way of exploring issues to do with representation, institution or audience; and such activities often take the form of quite tightly structured simulations or 'exercises'. Nevertheless, production is an arena in which teachers necessarily cede some control to students; and what they choose to do with that control is not always to our liking. Even simulation activities can allow a sanctioned space for play, in which it becomes possible to speak the unspeakable, to flirt with what may be clearly recognized as politically incorrect – and, as we shall see, the political *consequences* of this are often complex and problematic.

As I noted in chapter 8, media educators have frequently expressed concern about the dangers of students imitating mainstream media. It seems to be assumed that if students imitate dominant forms, they will somehow inevitably and invisibly imbibe the ideologies those forms are seen to contain. Such arguments are based on rather simplistic assumptions about the ways in which students read and use the media; and they also seem to ignore much of what actually goes on in students' productions.

Where it does occur, imitation frequently involves *parody* – that is, a self-conscious and exaggerated use of dominant conventions for the sake of comic effects or ridicule. There are several reasons for this. Parody can provide an escape from the potential embarrassment that production work frequently seems to cause. Students recognize that their own work is unlikely ever to be as polished or authentic as the 'real thing'; and rather than being seen to fail, it is much more comfortable to pass off what you are doing as parody. For many, 'play acting' in a group is also a potentially uncomfortable situation; and so, here again, it is often easier to exaggerate for comic effect. And, as I shall indicate, parody can also provide a useful way of dealing with the ideological imperatives of teachers, since it allows one to use dominant forms while simultaneously disavowing any commitment to them.

Parody might thus be seen as the postmodern phenomenon *par excellence*. It rests on a kind of rejection of the fixity of meaning, and of the seriousness of authorship. It seems to be a matter of the

author's intention, but it also depends to some extent on the judgement of the reader. And if the reader does not recognize the signals
of the parodic intention, or the difference between the original and
the parody, this may have problematic consequences. It is not clear
how far we can trust what the author says about the work – since
the claim to parody can obviously function as a *post hoc* rationalization or justification. Parody potentially offers a freedom in which
nobody can be held to account for what they say. These ambigui-
ties may be particularly problematic where the authors are students
and the readers are their teachers.

Two of my own research studies point to some of the difficulties
that can arise here. The first was part of the 'real audience' simulation described in chapter 9 (Buckingham, Grahame and Sefton-
Green, 1995: ch. 6). One of the productions here, created by a group
of six fourteen-year-old boys, was a trailer for a situation comedy
entitled *Flat Broke*, about a group of ill-matched characters sharing
a flat. The characters were all perceived by the students themselves
as crude stereotypes: a violent man-hating feminist, a gay child-
molester, a Greek macho-man and a freeloading 'slut'. While there
were some objections from other members of the class (and ourselves as teachers) about its appropriateness for the target audience (eleven-year-olds), these were quickly swept aside; and indeed
one of the leading students in the group dismissed them as merely
a form of 'censorship'.

The most significant problem the group had to negotiate here
was an ideological one. In presenting their ideas to the class, the
students were noticeably more 'politically correct' in their descrip-
tions of the characters than they were when talking with each other.
The students insisted that the humour was even-handed, and that
in any case, a cast of 'outrageous stereotypes' was exactly what one
would expect in a situation comedy. Of course, the people whom
the students were primarily seeking to 'outrage' were ourselves as
teachers, and the wider institution of the school; and it is notable
here that the feminist character was given the surname of the (male)
class teacher. In a sense, the students saw the project as an opportunity to speak the unspeakable – to unleash the 'unpopular' and
subversive things that are normally restrained by the institution of
the school (cf. Britzman, 1991).

However, it would be mistaken to attempt to justify this kind
of work through some simple-minded notion of 'resistance'. The
leaders of this group were unashamedly homophobic, and justified
the inclusion of the predatory gay character on the basis that they

all 'hated gays'. The situation with the Greek character was more complex, in that the boy who devised and played him was also Greek; and while he strongly resisted the accusation that this portrayal was racist, it could certainly be seen as a kind of disavowal of his own ethnicity. One of the most significant difficulties here, however, was that the students were able to co-opt the arguments that one might have used to challenge them. In their written accounts, they themselves described the show as 'stereotyped' and even 'politically incorrect', and ultimately doubted whether it would be shown by a 'liberal' TV station. The fact that the activity was a simulation, and that they were placed in the role of *fictional* producers, enabled the students to reject the suggestion that the programme represented their 'own' views. The ambiguous nature of the production – as simultaneously fictional and real – effectively enabled them to have their cake and eat it.

The second study here (Buckingham and Sefton-Green, 1994: ch. 10) raises similar contradictions and dilemmas. *Slutmopolitan* was a systematic parody of the woman's magazine *Cosmopolitan* produced by four seventeen-year-old girls in another London school, as part of their A-level Media Studies coursework. The magazine comprised sixteen pages in full colour. There was a front cover based around a photograph of a cleavage adorned with an anti-nuclear pendant; an advert for 'Tina's Tights' comprising a shot of legs clad in 'tarty' fishnets; and a back cover in the form of a full-page advert for the chocolate bar Flake, in traditional fellatio style. Inside, there were a number of problem pages, including 'Dear Doreen', who dealt with 'the dreaded broken nail'; 'Clare's Clever Cookery Page', which described how to cook frozen peas, illustrated by a model in 'suggestive' poses; and 'Deirdre's Do-it-Yourself', which explained the complexities of changing a light bulb.

On one level, *Slutmopolitan* could be seen as a parodic deconstruction of a dominant media form, in which 'theoretical' issues of gender representation are quite explicitly addressed. Yet the pleasures of this project derived their energy not so much from theoretical critique as from the display of the body, a rude and vigorous sense of humour, and from the shared sense of 'having a laugh'. Here again, production provided a kind of ambiguity, a space for play, in which meanings could not be fixed once and for all.

Yet this ambiguity posed some problems, particularly when it came to assessment. Reading the students' written accounts, it became clear that the authors themselves did not always agree on the *target* of the parody: in some instances, it was the magazines, but in others it was their readers; for some, it was the conventional media representation of the 'slut', while for others it was simply real 'sluts' themselves. As this implies, the project seemed to function on several levels at once, from the point of view both of its creators and of ourselves as teachers. Indeed, this ambiguity was partly the point. The parodic dimension of the project implicitly positioned its target as 'other people'; yet it simultaneously permitted the girls to *become* those other people, or at least to recognize (and indulge) the 'otherness' in themselves. By providing opportunities to enact 'sluttish' behaviour, the project enabled the girls to display their sexuality (or a construction of their sexuality) in a semi-public forum. The resulting material could be seen as hopelessly sexist; yet it could also be seen as subversive – at least in the context of the girls' positioning as 'children' within the power-relations of the school.

Like the work described by Grace and Tobin (1998), *Slutmopolitan* could be seen as an example of the carnivalesque, subverting the respectable through a form of bodily transgression. Indeed, from the postmodern feminist perspective identified above, it could be regarded as a kind of celebration and a deconstruction of the masquerade of femininity. From this position, gender is seen, not just as a form of behaviour or a personal attribute, but in itself as a form of parody (Butler, 1990) – although even the most explicitly 'feminist' of the authors – and this is a label they would probably all have refused – would not have conceptualized the politics of their project in this way.

While such work offers a valuable alternative to the drily rationalistic emphases of some aspects of media education, therefore, it also poses some difficulties. Simply celebrating the pleasure of such work as a form of 'subversion' or 'transgression' of dominant norms fails to recognize that it can also reinforce existing inequalities and forms of oppression. Ultimately, it would be too much to claim that such work 'empowers' students – whatever we might take that to mean (cf. Ellsworth, 1989). It is difficult to ascertain what kind of *learning* might be going on here, and the relation of that learning to any kind of political consciousness. At best, we might argue that such work offers students a comparatively 'safe' space in which they can play with the range of identities that are available to them, and reflect upon their contradictory possibilities and consequences. But if that reflection is not at some point made explicit, it is hard to see how, as teachers, we can promote it or engage in a dialogue with it.

Working through pleasure?

Sara Bragg (2000) takes on many of these arguments in her investigation of sixteen- to seventeen-year-old students' work on the theme of horror. In some respects, horror could be seen as a 'limit case' here, since its appeal so clearly bypasses attempts at intellectual rationalization. Indeed, as Bragg suggests, it is a 'degraded' genre that is often accused of leading its fans into moral chaos. Bragg firmly rejects the defensive view of media education as a form of 'moral technology', for example in addressing the 'problem' of media violence (see also Bragg, 2001). So what are then the positive grounds for teaching about horror?

Bragg's answer is given most effectively in her analyses of student productions. One such production, a trailer for a serial killer film called *White Gloves*, produced by sixteen-year-old Lauren, displays several 'politically incorrect' characteristics akin to those in the parodies described above. The killer is Spanish, and his ethnicity is effectively seen as the sole motivation for his actions (he has 'some sort of chip' against the English); and his victims are helpless elderly women, who are implicitly regarded as dispensable. Lauren's production could undoubtedly be read as merely a reproduction of the patriarchal values of the slasher movie, in which men victimize powerless women. Yet Bragg argues that the contemporary horror genre cannot be reduced to simplistic formulae such as 'violence' or 'misogyny'; and that Lauren's work displays a very self-conscious control of its conventions that is far from 'unthinking' imitation.

More significantly, however, Bragg suggests that the experience of production enabled Lauren to work through some complex and difficult emotions and dilemmas. She argues that the figure of the male killer serves as a valuable cipher that allows her to explore – and yet simultaneously to disavow – a desire for control that is socially denied to her as a young woman. Lauren's trailer shows the killer struggling against his own violent impulses: his male power is not secure, in that the murders can be committed only through the agency of the white gloves. Bragg argues that the production offered Lauren shifting forms of identification – both with the killer and with the victims, but also as a distanced viewer and as the 'director' of the piece. This allowed her to step outside the identities available to her – as a young woman and as a student – and to take up new relationships to those around her, even if only temporarily.

A second example, Richard's *18 With a Bullet*, features a group of teenagers in the middle of the woods being systematically killed off by a psychopathic killer, who in the closing sequence is himself killed by a large bear. Here again, the scenario shows a confident grasp of horror conventions, and particularly those of the 'splatter movie'. Yet again, however, Bragg argues that the scenario and the trailer should not be seen merely as 'exercises' in genre. They also enable Richard to explore some unacknowledged fantasies of male masochism, albeit (in this case) with the distancing mechanism of humour. Meanwhile, Richard's accompanying essay tells a further story: while it might be dismissed by examiners as merely 'descriptive', it displays verve and irony in describing the improvised and *ad hoc* ways in which much learning happens.

Neither of these productions is explicitly parodic, in the manner of *Slutmopolitan*, although they do display a similar degree of control of generic conventions. To this extent they offer much that could form the basis for more explicit reflection and analysis. However, Bragg's argument seeks to move beyond such ultimately rationalistic aspirations. Attempting to assess such work merely in terms of what it tells us about students' 'conceptual understanding' is inevitably reductive; and forcing students to reflect upon it in the narrow regime of the traditional academic essay is to miss much of the significance of what takes place. Yet at the same time, Bragg is not arguing for production simply as a form of 'self-expression', or as a therapeutic opportunity to explore one's deeper psychic tensions. She directly challenges the notion that students should be seen to speak with a singular, authentic 'voice', and that they should be held accountable for what they say with it.

In some ways, these arguments could be seen as an extension of the criticisms I have raised in earlier chapters. Yet Bragg's account takes us beyond the 'modernist' paradigm in which most accounts of media education are situated – including, ultimately, my own. It challenges media educators' obsession with 'critical distance' and 'reasoned discussion', their implicit distrust of the emotional and the irrational, and their drive for final, definitive meanings. It disputes the idea that there can ever be a conscious, controlling ego at the heart of our learning; and it rejects the idea that teachers should be perpetually monitoring their students' moral or ideological progress, forcing them into the mode of the dutiful student.

So where does this argument lead? Following John Shotter (1993) and Sue Turnbull (1998), Bragg calls for a greater emphasis on the 'practical-moral knowledge' that is embedded within everyday activities and social relationships. This 'knowing of the third kind' is distinct from knowing *that* (a knowledge of facts or principles) and knowing *how* (a knowledge of techniques): it is neither abstract nor technical, but depends upon the judgements of others, and is the kind of knowledge that one can have only from within a specific social situation. From this 'ethical' perspective, responsibility for making cultural, moral or ideological judgements cannot lie with teachers alone; and students must be able to work with what they have and who they are, rather than in terms of what teachers might like them to be.

Conclusion

In the instances I have discussed in this chapter, young people seem to be engaging in new forms of learning that implicitly call into question the theoretical or 'critical' knowledge that media educators have traditionally sought to promote. They seem to be developing more playful – and perhaps 'postmodern' – conceptions of knowledge and learning that move beyond the limitations of the traditional, rationalistic academic mode.

Nevertheless, these studies also raise important questions that need to be more fully addressed. In bringing popular culture into the classroom, we inevitably also bring with it a whole range of desires and experiences that are often left unspoken in schools – or, where they are spoken, are often policed out of existence. The fact that this is inevitable does not make it any less uncomfortable. Teachers obviously have a responsibility to make the classroom a functioning and mutually respectful community; and they have the right to prevent behaviour that they believe may disrupt this. But merely attempting to censor what we believe to be politically or morally unacceptable – or subjecting it to a form of 'critical analysis' which does little more than command obedience and assent – is bound to prove counter-productive.

Yet to assert the value of play, or to acknowledge the limitations of a purely rationalistic approach, is not to suggest that media education should simply abandon the 'modernist' project of cultural criticism. However, it does need to reformulate it in a way that builds upon the new potential of postmodern culture, and the new forms of engagement with media that it offers young people. Media production may have a particularly important role here, since it seems to provide a means for students to explore and reflect upon their changing positions in contemporary media culture. It allows a space in which 'unspeakable' desires can be spoken and totalizing discourses transgressed and undermined. Nevertheless, it is vital that students be encouraged to *reflect* upon those processes, and to understand the conditions under which their own meanings and pleasures are produced; and in order to do so, they will need to develop a metalanguage, a form of critical discourse, in which to describe and analyse what is taking place. Some would undoubtedly see this as a betrayal of the 'ludic' dimension of postmodernity, and an attempt to contain it within conventional forms of academic seriousness and rationality. Personally, I cannot imagine how education itself might be otherwise.

11

Digital Literacies

The advent of digital technologies has presented significant new opportunities and challenges for media educators. On the one hand, these technologies provide a new set of objects and processes for study; and they make several aspects of media production much more accessible for students. Yet on the other, they often appear to be accompanied by a form of educational instrumentalism that implicitly regards technology as merely a neutral benefit. As well as capitalizing on the potential of digital technology, therefore, media educators also need to be insisting on some fundamental questions and principles.

As I suggested in chapter 2, these technological developments need to be seen in the context of broader social and economic changes. What we are seeing here is not so much a matter of new technologies displacing older ones, as a convergence of previously distinct cultural forms and practices. The technical possibility of 'digitizing' a diverse range of different forms of communication (not just writing, but visual and moving images, music, sound and speech) is part of a broader convergence of media, in which the boundaries between print, television and computer-generated media are beginning to break down. Yet these developments are also driven by a much more general move towards a market-led media system, in which the maximizing of profit takes precedence over public service imperatives.

The cultural and political consequences of these developments are quite double-edged, however. On one level, they reflect a growing concentration of power in the hands of a small number of global multimedia corporations. They also have significant implications in terms of equality of access, since these new media are not equally available to all. Despite the falling cost of equipment, the 'digital divide' between rich and poor continues to widen (Selfe, 2000). Yet these developments are also seen to have significant democratic possibilities. The advent of digital media production and the internet has helped to break down the distinction between interpersonal communication and mass communication. At least potentially, these developments enable 'consumers' to become 'producers', who can reproduce and publish material using technologies that were formerly the preserve of small elites.

Some have argued that these new technologies are inherently empowering for children. They are seen to offer new opportunities for self-expression that will 'liberate' children from adult control, and enable them to create their own cultures and communities (Katz, 1997). Children are often seen here as 'cyber-kids' who somehow possess a natural affinity with technology, and are automatically confident and autonomous in their dealings with digital media. Yet others are becoming alarmed at the prospect of an 'electronic generation gap', in which children are losing contact with the values of their parents. Centralized control – and even parental control – is becoming significantly harder to exert, as growing numbers of children have unsupervised access to these technologies in their bedrooms. Parents are bound to find it hard to decide between the appeals of marketers who trumpet the benefits of new technology and those of campaigners who play on their genuine anxieties about their children's welfare.

In the context of education, there is still widespread hype about the benefits of digital technology. Computers are aggressively marketed to parents and teachers as an educational medium – indeed, as *the* indispensable educational tool for the modern world (Buckingham, Scanlon and Sefton-Green, 2001). According to the sales pitches, computers offer children access to untold worlds of discovery, and reawaken their spontaneous desire to learn. For those who can afford to invest in them, they enable children to 'get ahead' in the educational race. Yet computers are largely seen here as delivery mechanisms – as neutral means of accessing 'information' that will somehow automatically bring about learning. 'Wiring up' schools is often seen to produce immediate benefits, irrespective of how these technologies are actually used.

Yet however problematic such claims may be, for most children computers are no longer primarily an educational medium. On the contrary, they are now a significant part of children's popular culture. Uses of computers in the home are massively dominated by video games; and leisure uses of the internet (for example in the form of chat rooms and entertainment sites) are becoming increasingly significant (Buckingham, 2002b). Schools are no longer children's first point of access to computers. Children are already living in a digital world; and so, as with 'older' media, we need to find ways of enabling them to understand and to participate actively in it.

Towards digital literacies

Of course, these new media must to some extent teach the skills that are needed to use and interpret them – just as books teach readers about how to read (Meek, 1988). Children's everyday uses of computer games or the internet involve a whole range of informal learning processes, in which participants are simultaneously 'teachers' and 'learners'. Children learn to use these media largely through trial and error – through exploration, experimentation and play; and collaboration with others – both in face-to-face and virtual forms – is an essential element of the process.

Playing a computer game, for example, involves an extensive series of cognitive processes: remembering, hypothesis testing, predicting and strategic planning. Players generally agree that the best computer games are those which offer the greatest cognitive challenges, and which precisely refuse to position them as 'children'. While game players are often deeply immersed in the virtual world of the game, dialogue and exchange with others is crucial. And game playing is also a 'multiliterate' activity: it involves interpreting complex three-dimensional visual environments, reading both on-screen and off-screen texts (such as games magazines) and processing auditory information. In the world of computer games, success ultimately derives from the disciplined and committed acquisition of skills and knowledge.

Likewise, participation in chat rooms requires very specific skills in language and interpersonal communication. Young people have to learn to 'read' subtle nuances, often on the basis of minimal cues. They have to learn the rules and etiquette of online communication, and to shift quickly between genres or language registers. Provided they are sensible about divulging personal information, chat rooms provide young people with a safe arena for rehearsing and exploring aspects of identity and personal relationships that may not be available elsewhere. Here again, much of the learning is carried out without explicit teaching: it involves active exploration, 'learning by doing', apprenticeship rather than direct instruction. Above all, it is profoundly social: it arises through immersion in a 'community of practice' (Lave and Wenger, 1991).

Compared with the demanding multimedia experiences many children have outside school, much classroom work is bound to appear unexciting. Even where they do use computers and other media in schools, many children complain that this is far too limited and restrictive (see Facer et al., forthcoming). Children who use the internet at home are already becoming critical users of information: they have a strong sense of their own autonomy and authority as learners, and they want to contribute rather than simply consume. Yet this is precisely what is so often denied to them in school.

Here again, we may be seeing a widening gulf between the styles of learning that are cultivated by formal schooling and those that characterize children's out-of-school experiences. Children are now immersed in a consumer culture that frequently positions them as active and autonomous; yet in school, a great deal of their learning is passive and teacher-directed. If schools fail to engage with young people's changing orientations and motivations towards learning, there is a significant danger that they will simply become peripheral to their lives. Indeed, some have argued that this situation is potentially explosive – perhaps particularly for boys, who may be highly self-confident users of technology but who are increasingly perceived as failures in the context of school learning. If the provision of technology in schools remains as restricted as it currently is, disaffection may simply become more widespread.

Nevertheless, it would be quite false to pretend that young people are already competent users of these new media, or that they necessarily know all they need to know. As in other areas, young people may have the advantage of a kind of wild confidence in their dealings with technology: unlike many adults, they are not in fear of the machine (Williams, 1999). Yet the majority of young people are far from being autonomous 'cyber kids': they are uncertain, they lack information, and they are often frustrated by the failure of the technology to achieve what it promises. We need to begin by trying to discover what young people actually do know; and we need to recognize that there may be a great deal they still need to learn.

At present, there is a lack of easily available support and advice that might enable young people to use these media critically and creatively. For example, the anonymity and ease of access afforded by the Web permits the dissemination of a whole range of false or unreliable information. In the case of health information or political news, for instance, the Web offers unprecedented opportunities for disseminating rumours and lies – with potentially very far-reaching consequences. Yet there are few sites that offer assistance in evaluating such material – and here too it is not always easy to judge how far they should be trusted.

'Consumer advice' and public information resources of this kind should certainly be supported through public funding; but ultimately schools will have to play a central role in enabling young people to deal with the challenges of the new digital world. In this sense, 'digital literacy' could be seen as one of the multiple literacies that are required by the contemporary media. Yet rather than simply adding digital literacy to the curriculum menu, we need a broader reconceptualization of what we mean by literacy itself.

As I argued in relation to 'media literacy' (chapter 3), this new conception of literacy is not merely 'functional'. The skills that children need in relation to digital media are not confined to those of information retrieval. They need more than lessons in how to use word processors or search engines. As with print, children also need to be able to evaluate and use information critically if they are to transform it into knowledge. Furthermore, digital literacy is more than simply a matter of protecting children from the dangers of digital media. As with older media, children need to be empowered to make informed choices on their own behalf, and to protect and regulate themselves. And just as print literacy involves writing as well as reading, digital literacy must involve creative production in new media as well as critical consumption.

The conceptual framework outlined in chapter 4 raises some fundamental questions that can and should be applied to digital media. Box 11.1 provides an indication (which is by no means exhaustive) of some of the issues that might be addressed here, specifically in relation to the World Wide Web. These kinds of questions can obviously be extended to other aspects of the internet such as chat rooms and e-mail, and to other areas of digital media, such as computer games. These different media undoubtedly raise new questions, particularly in relation to 'interactivity'; and they require new methods of analysis that will address these. The key point here is that none of them can be seen merely as neutral vehicles for 'information'. The Web, for example, is no longer an open-access, decentralized medium – if indeed it ever was. Like other media and forms of communication, it is actively used for particular motivations and purposes, at least some of which are essentially commercial. Whether we use these new media for

Box 11.1   The World Wide Web: issues for study

Production

- The technologies that are used to generate and disseminate material on the Web.
- The importance of commercial influences, and the role of advertising, promotion and sponsorship.
- The use of the internet by individuals or interest groups as a means of persuasion and influence.
- The relationships between the Web and other media such as television and computer games.

Representation

- The ways in which web sites claim to 'tell the truth', and establish their authenticity and authority.
- The presence or absence of particular viewpoints or aspects of experience.
- How readers can make judgements about reliability, bias and accuracy, for example by comparing web sites with each other or with other sources.

Language

- The use of visual and verbal 'rhetorics' in the design of web sites.
- How web sites are structured in order to encourage users to navigate in particular ways.
- How users are addressed: for example, in terms of formality and 'user-friendliness'.
- The kinds of 'interactivity' that are on offer, and the degrees of control and feedback they afford to the user.

Audience

- The ways in which users can be targeted by commercial appeals, both visibly and invisibly.
- How the Web is used to gather information about consumers.
- How different groups of people use the internet in their daily lives, and for what purposes.
- How individuals or groups interpret particular sites, and the pleasures they gain from using them.

education or entertainment, it is surely vital that we do so in an informed and critical way. A comprehensive form of 'digital literacy' will therefore need to address each of the broad areas I have identified.

Models of digital production

Of course, these understandings are not gained simply through analysis: they are also developed – in some instances, more effectively and enjoyably – through the experience of creative production. The growing accessibility of digital technology means that quite young children can easily produce multimedia texts, and even interactive hypermedia. Some children at least are likely to have access to such technology in their homes; and some may be using it for creative purposes, for example in video editing, manipulating images or creating music (Sefton-Green and Buckingham, 1996). It is in this area that some of the more far-reaching educational possibilities of digital technology may be found.

As with older media (Lorac and Weiss, 1981), multimedia authoring packages are now increasingly being used as a means of assisting subject learning in a range of curriculum areas. Here, students produce their own multimedia texts in the form of web sites or CD-ROMs, often combining written text, visual images, simple animation, audio and video material (Ordidge, 1999). Vivi Lachs (2000), for example, describes a range of production activities undertaken with primary school students in learning about science, geography or history. These projects generally involve children 're-presenting' their learning for an audience of younger children in the form of multimedia teaching materials. One of the most challenging aspects of this work is precisely the interactivity: the students have to think hard about how different users might interpret and use what they produce, and how they will navigate their way around. Yet although the children's productions frequently draw on elements of popular culture (such as computer games), the content of the productions is primarily factual and informational – and in this sense, the preferred genre is that of 'edu-tainment'.

Here again, it is important to make some fundamental distinctions. We need to differentiate between education *through* media and education *about* media – or in other words, between the use of media as a teaching aid and the study of media in their own right. The primary aim of using media production here is to assist subject learning, or to develop more generalized qualities such as motivation and collaboration, rather than to promote a more conceptual awareness of the media themselves. This is perfectly valid, but it is not media education.

Other potential uses of digital media have emerged from art education. These projects often involve the participation of 'digital artists' external to the school, and their primary emphasis is on the use of the media for self-expression and creative exploration. Thus, students will experiment with the possibilities of different art forms, and the ways in which they can be combined and manipulated using the computer, in exploring themes such as 'identity' and 'memory'. The implicit model here is that of the avant-garde multimedia art work, although (here again) students tend to 'import' elements of popular culture. This work can also involve an element of critical reflection, particularly where it entails communication with a wider audience.

Rebecca Sinker (1999), for example, describes an online multi-media project which set out to develop links between an infants' school and its community. The project was intended to mark the school's centenary, and to offer the children opportunities 'to investigate their own families, community, histories and experiences, exploring changes and celebrating diversity'. Using multimedia authoring software, the project brought together photography, video, drawing, story-telling, digital imaging, sound and text. Although outside experts were involved, the style of learning here was quite collaborative; and the control afforded by the technology encouraged a degree of critical reflection that might have been harder to achieve in other art forms. Perhaps most significantly, the results of the project (in the form of a web site) were available to a much wider audience than would normally have been the case with children's work.

As Sinker argues elsewhere, this form of multimedia production represents a form of 'learning-through-making' that is necessarily cross-disciplinary, even though it may derive initially from visual arts practice (Sinker, 2000). There is certainly a good deal of common ground here with media education, not only because of the use of electronic technology, but also because such work often explicitly addresses conceptual themes and issues, and engages with perspectives from critical theory. (For examples of such work, see Booth (1999) and Jones (1999).)

Nevertheless, there are two factors that distinguish the use of digital production in the context of media education. The first is the explicit focus on popular culture – or at least on finding ways of engaging with students' everyday experiences of digital media, rather than attempting to impose an alien 'artistic' or 'educational' practice. The second is the element of theoretical reflection – the dynamic relationship between practice and critical understanding that I have argued is crucial to the development of 'critical literacy'. In the context of media education, the aim is not primarily to develop technical skills, or to promote 'self-expression', but to encourage a more systematic understanding of how the media operate, and hence to promote more reflective ways of using the media. In these latter respects, digital technology does make a significant difference when compared with the analogue technology that preceded it; however, as we shall see, it also raises some new questions.

The meanings of 'access'

As I have noted, researchers have increasingly drawn attention to the existence of a 'digital divide' between the 'technology rich' and the 'technology poor'. Research in the UK in the late 1990s, for example, found that middle-class children were roughly three times more likely than working-class children to use multimedia computers at home, and eight times more likely to use the internet (Livingstone and Bovill, 1999). Schools can – and obviously should – play a role in equalizing access in this respect. However, it should be recognized that access is not just to do with technology, but also to do with cultural capital – that is, with the cultural skills and competencies that are needed to use that technology creatively and productively. When it comes to media production, it would be quite romantic to assume that young people have some kind of automatic expertise with technology, or that they will necessarily be able to learn to use it easily and quickly. Indeed, the majority of software programs students might use are designed for professionals, and are very time-consuming to learn. Here again, research suggests that middle-class children have significant advantages, as a result of their parents' greater experience of computers at work and their involvement in other social networks (see Facer et al., forthcoming).

Julian Sefton-Green (1999) describes the consequences of this in developing courses on Web design and computer games production in the context of a youth arts project. Young people, mainly from impoverished backgrounds, were recruited onto courses in both these areas; but the differences between the students' prior experiences of the two forms had a significant effect on how both courses developed. In the case of the Web work, the primary problem was the fact that virtually none of the students who attended these courses (in 1998) had ever used the Web before. By contrast, all the students came to the computer games courses with extensive 'consumer' knowledge about games. The students also had a sense of how the games industry worked and how the course might relate to media production in the real world – although some rather romantically hoped that the course might further their career aspirations. Nevertheless, they generally had a clear understanding of why and how games *as products* were designed and manufactured. By contrast, in the case of the Web courses, the students had no clear idea of what professional (or indeed amateur) Web producers might do, and only a very general sense that being competent to work in an online medium might have vocational relevance.

This prior knowledge led to very clear differences when it came to encouraging critical discussion, but it also had an influence on what students were able to produce. Neither group of students possessed basic skills in working with production software; but in the case of the Web course, they needed to develop basic skills in using browsers before moving on to devising their own pages and sites. Students tend to imagine only what they know they can actually make; as they become more proficient in technical skills, this in turn changes their capacity to imagine new possibilities. This was certainly apparent in the Web courses. Given that most students began with limited ideas about the Web itself, it was not surprising that the work they produced was limited in many respects. A further issue here is that – despite claims about the democratic potential of the Web – in reality most of the sites online are to some extent forms of advertising. Non-commercial online culture – particularly that produced by young people themselves – is much harder to find. As a result, the expressive models available to students are few and far between. Unsurprisingly, this argument did not apply to the games courses. Because they knew more about computer games, the students were quick to come up with ideas, sketches and scenarios for their work. They brought in a great deal of material from home and were clearly very motivated. The work they produced here showed a far greater sense of ownership. Although their technical control over the interactive programs was limited, this did not seem to inhibit their imagination. The key question here – as in relation to work with 'older' media – was to do with how far the students were actively using and re-working established genres, or merely striving to imitate them.

Andrew Jones (1999) provides a more detailed case study of Web production, in this case in the much more academic context of

A-level Media Studies. Here, a small group of students worked with multimedia artists to develop 'experimental' web sites exploring issues of ethnicity and identity. The work was strongly informed by the students' reading of media and cultural theory, which is required at this level; and the products themselves come close to a form of 'conceptual art' practice. However, these students were also relatively unfamiliar with the conventions of Web design – if indeed such conventions can yet be said to exist. This left them free to experiment, although, as Jones points out, their work was nevertheless limited by the paradigms and structures of the authoring software they were using. Here again, there was a sense in which the students needed an existing cultural form as a model, if only as something they would then go on to adapt or reject.

These studies suggest that getting 'hands-on' experience with digital technology is only the beginning. *Access* needs to be seen not merely in terms of access to technology or to technical skills, but also to *cultural forms of expression and communication*; and it needs to be acknowledged that students' access to (and familiarity with) those cultural forms is itself likely to be quite variable. This in turn has challenging implications in terms of how we teach, particularly in settings that are culturally and socially diverse.

Processes and products

Digital image manipulation or video editing are not just more efficient ways of doing the things that used to be done with analogue technology. They are certainly simpler and more flexible to use; and they enable students to achieve a 'professional' result much more easily. Yet there are some significant differences in the *process* of production that have much broader implications for students' learning.

Digital technology can make overt and visible some key aspects of the production process that often remain 'locked away' when using analogue technologies. This happens, firstly, at the point of generating images. For example, being able to take a whole series of shots on a digital camera, view them in the monitor and choose the ones you need can make apparent a whole series of points about the selection and construction of images that might otherwise have been mere theoretical exhortations on the part of the teacher. It is possible to learn through trial and error, without worrying about the possibility of losing or erasing images; and this can allow you to look back at earlier versions of your work, and reflect upon how and why your ideas have changed. In effect, the technology allows students to engage in a process of drafting and redrafting – and, in the process, of critical self-evaluation – that is similar to contemporary approaches to the teaching of writing. In principle, of course, these processes were possible with analogue technology, although they were always significantly more expensive (for example in the case of Polaroid cameras) and more extended in time.

This argument also applies to 'post-production'. Here again, complex issues about the selection, manipulation and combination of images (and, in the case of video, of sounds) can be addressed in a much more accessible way than was possible using analogue technology. This is not simply a matter of the ease of operating the software, or of the range of choices available – for example, the number of effects or shot transitions. (Indeed, the proliferation of such choices can become a distraction, particularly for relative beginners.) Software packages for image manipulation such as *Photoshop* make the process of constructing imagery (for example for film posters or adverts) much quicker and simpler than with the montage tools of the past (glue and scissors); and in the process, they can also quickly demonstrate the problematic status of photographs as evidence. Likewise, the benefit of digital editing programs such as *Premiere* is that they make the process of constructing meaning – and the choices that it entails – clearly visible. As a result, they may enable students to *conceptualize* the process in much more powerful ways. In this respect, much of what used to be tackled in very abstract and laborious ways through analysis and storyboarding can now be approached in a much more direct and flexible (not to mention pleasurable) way through production. In the process, the boundaries between critical analysis and practical production – or between 'theory' and 'practice' – are likely to become increasingly blurred.

These issues have been addressed in a series of empirical studies in this field. Julian Sefton-Green's early case study of digital production in the context of English teaching (Buckingham, Grahame and Sefton-Green, 1995: ch. 3) suggests that the technology permits a more systematic experimentation with possibilities, and hence a more conscious selection and construction of a final version, when compared with earlier methods. In one project, students produced film posters and edited trailers as part of a unit of work on the book and film of *The Outsiders*. By offering the students a high degree of control over the composition and editing of the images, and enabling them to engage with the work in very close detail, it encouraged them to explore a number of themes at stake in the original text, and to consider how it might be marketed for different audiences. Nevertheless, as Sefton-Green indicates, it is important for this knowledge to be made explicit; and this is not something the technology itself will automatically bring about.

Andrew Burn has conducted a series of studies looking at the impact of digital technology on students' engagement with the moving image. For example, he shows how using a digital package to 'grab' and then manipulate frames from films enables students to achieve greater analytical understanding of elements that might otherwise be noticed only in a much more condensed or subliminal way (Burn, 1999). In another study, students' digital editing of a film trailer is seen to offer a degree of flexibility and control – through reordering the shots, experimenting with shot transitions, stretching and condensing sequences, speeding up and slowing down – which is comparable to that afforded by writing (Burn and Reed, 1999). Editing and manipulating media images in this way, Burn argues, somehow mimics the infinite flexibility of the process of mental image-making or 'visual thinking'; and as the software develops, this process is likely to become increasingly intuitive.

Burn's ultimate objective here is to develop a comprehensive analysis of the 'grammar' of moving images, building on the account of still images developed by Kress and van Leeuwen (1996). In this respect, it takes us back to the discussion of 'media literacies' in chapter 3, and to some of the problems that surround the analogy between print and other media. Importantly, Burn uses functional linguistics rather than a more traditional form of grammar, which means that he is seeking to identify functional equivalents between media rather than parallels in terms of form or structure – so, for example, he seeks to identify the specific ways in which images are transformed, combined or 'fixed', rather than looking for visual equivalents of sentences, tenses or negatives (Burn and Parker, 2001). Whether or not this might add up to a 'grammar' remains to be seen; and even if it does, there are bound to be further questions about how that grammar might be taught. The interesting question here is whether the level of control afforded by digital technology somehow automatically encourages a more systematic approach. Burn's research certainly suggests that students quickly perceive the need for a technical metalanguage, which in turn helps their collaborative decision-making (Burn et al., 2001); although whether this necessarily encourages them to reflect on the broader cultural and social investments that are at stake in their productions is a more open question.

Technology and pedagogy

Both Burn and Sefton-Green make a powerful case for digital production as part of a more general 'empowerment' of media consumers. By offering greater democratic access to complex forms of media production, digital technology truly does enable students to become writers as well as readers of visual and audio-visual media – and indeed, begins to blur these settled distinctions. And it may be that the ability to manipulate and edit moving images in digital format offers a degree of flexibility and control that particularly lends itself to the kind of self-conscious reflection that I have argued is essential to media education and to 'critical literacy' more broadly.

This, at least, is the potential. Whether or not it is realized is not simply a matter of the technology: it is primarily a question of pedagogy. For example, it remains to be seen whether the advent of digital still cameras in the home will in itself make a significant difference to the conventional practice of popular photography – a practice which is predominantly a matter of selectively recording certain types of atypical family events (weddings, birthdays, holidays) as a means of constructing evidence of 'happy' social relationships. Digital technology does not necessarily challenge or make apparent these choices and selections, or encourage a dialogue about them. Indeed, it may simply facilitate indiscriminate use.

Likewise, it could be argued that the new range of choices made available by digital technology does not *necessarily* make the act of constructing an image any more conscious or deliberate. In the case of digital still cameras, for example, the ease with which filters and manipulations can be applied encourages the production of stylized images; but these may well continue to be seen as distinct from pictures presented as 'evidence' of reality. Unless these basic questions about selection and manipulation are built into the process, and made the focus of conscious reflection, these new choices may well become merely an excuse for arbitrary experimentation. Likewise, the high quality of digital video can encourage pride and a sense of ownership in the product which is very motivating for students. Pop videos, for example, lend themselves to digital production because of the ease of editing. Yet the fact that it is fairly straightforward to produce something that 'looks good' does not necessarily make the work any more coherent or effective in terms of communication. Indeed, 'good effects' can mask a lack of content – and even of *thought* about what the product is intending to communicate – particularly if they are accompanied by a powerful music track.

The key point here is that the potential benefits of digital technology will not be realized without informed intervention on the part of teachers – and, in a different way, of peers. There remains a need for reflection, deliberation and dialogue; and opportunities and requirements for these things need to be systematically built in to the process, even if they seem like a distraction from it.

In this respect, it seems particularly important to insist on the need for collaboration in digital production. As I have indicated (chapter 8), group work has been an established part of media education practice, not just for pragmatic and vocational reasons, but also for educational ones. These arguments do not easily apply to production work with digital media. Indeed, the use of digital technology often tends to *individualize* the process of production. A computer room, even one set up for creative art work, tends to involve students working individually at screens; and the teacher often has a more one-to-one relationship with individuals – although students may also work together as peer-tutors, especially to solve software problems. Attempts to build in group work often appear somewhat artificial; and students will sometimes seek to avoid dialogue and debate by dividing their labour into specialized functions that can be taken on by individuals. Particularly where there is a high level of access to the technology, the benefits of working together need to be made explicit and actively promoted. Set against the tendency towards individualization, group work needs to be perceived as a matter of mutual self-interest: students need to recognize that only by pooling resources, expertise and ideas can they get the job done.

Finally, there is the question of audience. As I have noted, the existence of a real audience can qualitatively change how students conceptualize production work, and what they learn from it. Digital technology seems to offer some important possibilities here. The internet provides – or may in future provide – significant opportunities for young people's work to find a wider audience. There are now a growing number of sites that feature images, video and audio material produced by young people (see Abbott, 1998; Stern, 1999). At present, the technological potential here is still a long way from its full realization, particularly when it comes to media such as internet radio (see Buckingham, Harvey and Sefton-Green, 1999). In the future, however, the internet is likely to offer many new possibilities for interaction and dialogue with audiences.

Nevertheless, it would be wrong to overstate this. The task of bringing students' work to the point of 'publication' is often quite time-consuming, and the work often looks and feels very different from 'professional' products (Booth, 1999). In reality, few schools have published their students' multimedia work, or made it more generally available via the internet; but this may partly reflect schools' growing concerns about their 'public image'. As I have implied, finding an audience – even a relatively small and local one – is just a stage in the process, rather than an end point; but, if seen in this way, it can have significant benefits in terms of students' motivation and their willingness to reflect upon their work.

In all these respects, therefore, digital technology appears to have important implications in terms of students' learning. Yet these changes will not occur automatically. Whether or not they are realized will obviously depend to some degree on the technology itself – on the design of the hardware and the software, and on whether they can actually deliver what they promise. However, it will also depend upon the social contexts and relationships into which it enters. The value of digital technology in this situation depends to a large extent on the *pedagogic* relationships that are established around it – for example, on how students are given access to the skills and competencies they need, how far they can control the process, and how far they can enter into a dialogue with their peers and teachers. It also depends, more broadly, on the *social* contexts that surround it – on the motivations of the students, on the ways in which cultural production relates to other aspects of their lives, on the audience for their productions, and so on. It is to a discussion of these issues – rather than to further excited speculation about the wonders of technology – that future attention needs to be directed.

12

New Sites of Learning

Over the past decade, there has been a growing acknowledgement that the school is not the only preserve of education; and that learning can and does occur in the workplace, in the home and in the context of leisure activities. These different contexts also entail different social relationships, and thus different conceptions of what counts as legitimate knowledge. There is an increasing recognition here that learning is not simply the consequence or the result of teaching, at least if we conceive of teaching as a process of more or less explicit instruction. And so the *forms* of education are changing, as well as the *sites* on which they occur.

In some respects, these developments are a matter of recognizing or acknowledging things that have always been the case; although that recognition does in itself represent a significant change, not just in how we conceive of education but also in how it is practised and socially legitimated. Most obviously, this recognition takes the form of a *credentializing* of achievements or competencies that would not previously have been subject to public measurement or assessment. We can now be awarded certificates and qualifications for acquiring skills in the workplace or in leisure activities that might previously have been seen as mere everyday accomplishments (Edwards, 1997). This recognition may also involve a *curriculariz-ing* of certain areas of everyday life, a transformation of aspects of experience into a form of explicit pedagogy. Thus, government agencies and commercial companies have recently become very interested in the potential of learning in the home; and parents are increasingly being encouraged to take on the role of teachers in providing explicit tuition for their children (Buckingham and Scanlon, 2003).

These kinds of issue feature prominently in current debates about lifelong learning, parental involvement in education, home schooling, accreditation of prior learning, distance learning, and so on. They are also central to many contemporary discussions of the role of information and communication technologies, where the internet is frequently touted as 'the school of the future'. These new forms of 'learning beyond the classroom' are seen to offer significant new possibilities, particularly for motivating young people who are disaffected from mainstream schooling. Authors such as Tom Bentley (1998) argue that 'informal' educational settings – such as neighbourhood learning centres, online networks and community action projects – can provide more active, relevant and flexible forms of learning that will equip young people more effectively for the challenges of the modern 'information society'.

Why are the media important in this context? On one level, we could argue that the media are by definition 'educational'; and that we can and should be attempting to understand both their curriculum and their pedagogy – that is, not just *what* they teach but also *how* they teach, and the social consequences this may have. This obviously applies not just to the educational functions of the news or the Discovery Channel, but also to those of Jerry Springer or WWF or Pokémon. Furthermore, one could argue that media cultures – that is, the everyday cultures of media use, of meaning-making and dialogue that surround the media – can be seen as 'learning cultures'. Fan culture provides many examples of the forms of teaching and learning that are entailed in people's social uses of the media (Jenkins, 1992); and online fandom in particular has been seen to exemplify a highly flexible and democratic style of learning (Baym, 2000).

The media are, in these respects, a kind of informal schooling – and one which most young people perceive as much more pleasurable and engaging than the formal schooling to which they are compulsorily subjected. Both as consumers and as producers of media, young people are engaging in forms of learning that are very different from those that are promoted in traditional sites of education such as schools. And yet the status and value of these new forms of learning remain highly problematic. In this chapter, I want to explore some of the implications of these arguments for media education. In particular, I want to consider the possibilities for media education 'beyond the classroom', in 'informal' community-based settings, and the different kinds of learning that this might entail.

Media education beyond the classroom

Self-evidently, media education should not be exclusively confined to schools. As I noted in chapter 6, there have been many important initiatives in the field that have involved parents, community organizations, churches and activist groups of many kinds. In order to be effective at a wider level, media educators clearly need to form partnerships with a range of organizations outside formal education.

Advocates of media education have often seen it as a means of building connections between schools and the wider community. Murdock and Phelps (1973), for example, suggest that school students' work could usefully be directed towards audiences beyond the school; while Len Masterman (1985) describes potential partnerships between schools and community-based 'media centres'. More recently, Chris Richards (1998c) has pointed to the more flexible and democratic styles of teaching and learning that might apply in the context of production studios or workplaces; while Bob Morgan (1998b) has likewise argued for taking media education 'back to the streets', for example by encouraging forms of media production that might 'make a difference' to local communities. By enabling young people to be other than 'school students', such approaches may encourage them to assume a greater degree of autonomy and control over their own learning.

Media production has often been seen as a staple tool of youth and community work. The origins of this approach probably lie in the early use of film as a means of 'cultural animation', for example in some of the projects carried out in collaboration with rural communities by the National Film Board of Canada. In the wake of the student activism of the late 1960s, there was a surge of interest in community-based media, particularly through the new medium of video (Boyle, 1997). The vast majority of these projects placed a strong emphasis on documentary realism. The central preoccupation was with *content*, with 'giving a voice' to groups whose perspectives had hitherto been ignored or unrepresented. While there were some exceptions, there was often a distinct lack of the formal experimentation that could be found in the other main use of portable video at that time – namely, the fine art practice of video makers such as Nam June Paik.

Some very grand claims have been made for the power of community media as a means of democratization and social liberation (e.g. Willener, Milliard and Ganty, 1976). Much of this work is informed by a belief in the progressive political potential of media production, particularly with under-privileged groups. Thus, it is argued, enabling young people to take control of the 'means of production' can empower them in relation to the adult world, and in relation to the media themselves (Dowmunt, 1980). They become active producers rather than passive consumers, able to give voice to their own concerns, and to create positive alternatives to dominant media representations.

However, such claims have proven remarkably difficult to substantiate in practice. As Caroline Heller (1978) points out, the barriers to democratizing the media are political and economic, rather than simply to do with technology. The experience of amateur production may easily have the opposite effect – of developing a deeper respect for the achievements of the professionals. Indeed, the major beneficiaries of the expansion in community media may well have been the multinational corporations who produce the equipment: community activists, Heller suggests, might be better advised to look to less expensive and smaller-scale means of furthering their aims.

Nevertheless, there has been growing enthusiasm in recent years for 'informal' youth and community settings as potential locations for arts and media education. Paul Willis (1990), for example, argues that schools are largely irrelevant to young people's creative engagement with popular culture, and proposes the establishment of new cultural organizations independent of formal education. The work of McLaughlin and Heath (1993), among others, in the USA has drawn attention to the role of community-based organizations in building self-esteem among groups of young people who have effectively abandoned – or been abandoned by – the formal education system. While this latter research has tended to focus on more traditional art forms, there are several community-based organizations that have sought to give young people access to opportunities for media production. Children's Express, for example, is a children's news agency with local branches in the UK and the USA that enables young people to create news stories for publication in local and national newspapers, and on broadcast television. The Educational Video Center in New York is one of the longest-established community-based organizations working with young people using video, particularly in documentary formats. And there are very many examples of projects using 'low-tech' media such as radio, wall newspapers and animation, as well as child-produced web sites, in many countries around the world. (For accounts of such work, see Von Feilitzen and Carlsson, 1999; and Tyner, 1998.)

There is also some evidence that media education can provide a bridge between the school and the wider community. In the UK, there is a growing number of 'specialist schools' formally designated by the government in the field of 'media arts'. In addition to curriculum development, these schools have a remit to develop community access and involvement, for example through after-school and weekend activities, holiday schemes, drop-in facilities and involvement in community media activities. One such school in Cambridge, for example, works with a local cable TV station to provide video facilities for local voluntary groups, and offers a cable TV broadcast outlet for the end products. Of course, the nature of the 'community' in these different settings is quite diverse; and community involvement means something very different in an impoverished, culturally diverse, inner-city neighbourhood as compared with a leafy suburb or country town. Interestingly, several of these schools are also beginning to use the internet as a means of developing new 'communities', both locally and globally, for instance through online magazines and international partnerships with other schools.

Of course, all these initiatives are constrained by the wider policy context on which their funding is based. In the UK, recent initiatives in arts funding have created significant new opportunities in this respect, although they have also presented some problems. Giving 'disaffected' young people access to participation in the arts and media increasingly seems to be seen as a panacea for a whole range of social ills. The benefits of the arts are partly defined here in psychological, individual terms; but they are also seen to have social and economic dimensions. The so-called 'creative industries' are seen as an expanding area of the economy, which can provide meaningful employment, particularly for those from socially excluded groups. In this way, it is argued, participation in the arts will build 'self-esteem' and release 'hidden talents', and thereby bring about the social and economic regeneration of disadvantaged communities (Buckingham, 2000c; Buckingham and Jones, 2001).

However, it is important to recognize that access means very different things for different social groups, in terms of what they do with the opportunity, how they are able to capitalize and build upon it, and in terms of potential outcomes. In our case studies of individual young people's involvement in such projects (Buckingham and Harvey, 2001), there have been clear differences between those who already possess social and educational capital and those who do not. An inside knowledge of youth culture is clearly a valuable commodity in some market situations; yet it is much harder to trade in this form of cultural capital if you do not also have social capital (that is, contacts and particular kinds of 'social skills') and a certain degree of formal educational capital (such as a degree of literacy) as well. Access to media production may be perceived by working-class kids as a means of developing 'really useful knowledge' (Cohen, 1990), but how it translates into eventual employment is more problematic. Evidence from surveys suggests that the majority of young people who enter employment in the media industries do so by virtue of social contacts, and are effectively working for nothing or relying on a private income (British Film Institute, 1998). Again, this is clearly more of a possibility for some social groups than for others.

These kinds of initiative therefore raise a series of questions that need to be addressed. These are partly to do with whether this kind of 'informal' education in the arts and media is capable of delivering the broader social objectives it is charged with delivering. They are also to do with issues of access and equality – to do with who the imagined objects of these interventions might be, and who stands to gain from the benefits they make available. And finally, they are to do with the nature of the learning that is being called for or promoted, and how it might be enabled to happen.

Media and youth work

One influential version of this 'informal' approach can be found in the work of the Cockpit Cultural Studies Department, which is documented in some detail by Andrew Dewdney and Martin Lister (1988). During the late 1970s and 1980s, the Cockpit undertook a series of projects using practical photography, primarily with working-class young people in London schools and youth centres. Rather than emphasizing the aesthetic or technical aspects of the medium, this approach aimed to capitalize on the status of photography as a genuinely popular social practice. Building on everyday uses of photography (such as the snapshot and the family album), the Cockpit team sought to move beyond the limitations of traditional 'amateur photography', and to devise an approach which was based in the cultural forms which are most valued by young people themselves. The central focus of much of this work was the notion of youth culture as 'style'. Following the work of academic writers such as Dick Hebdige (1979), style was seen here as the terrain on which young people actively construct and explore their own cultural identities. Thus, many projects focused on aspects of fashion, self-image and subcultural identity. This approach aimed to enable young people to investigate the relationships between who they 'are' and how they are represented; and hence it clearly did attempt to move beyond documentary realism. It was not simply about young people 'expressing themselves' or communicating their perspectives and concerns. On the contrary, it involved a self-conscious and reflexive emphasis on the *process* of representation itself.

In many respects, the work of the Cockpit team offers not just a developed alternative to academic Media Studies in schools, but also a direct challenge to it. Dewdney and Lister argue that Media Studies' drive for academic legitimacy has effectively under-mined its 'best and most democratic elements': in the process, it has fallen prey to a didactic and schematic approach, and a form of 'theoreticism' – that is, a privileging of theory for its own sake. In their view, media education would be able to fulfil its radical potential much more easily in a less restricted institutional context, and using much more open-ended teaching methods. Ultimately, they appear to suggest that we should be abandoning the search for academic status, and seeking to define media education, not as 'work', but as an extension of leisure.

Thus, while some of the Cockpit work took place in schools, it was largely consigned to the margins of the formal curriculum, for example in the form of 'life skills' work with disaffected school leavers. Even this work tended to import the ethos of youth and community work into the school, while the institutional apparatus of the school was largely perceived as a constraint that had to be resisted or evaded. Thus, Dewdney and Lister note 'the remote-ness of the school as a social institution from the social worlds of young people' and argue for 'the need to look beyond the school to other institutions in the communities in which young people live as the next stage in building cultural practices with them'.

Nevertheless, the use of the word 'institutions' is significant here. In the UK, the youth service – in which this kind of work has mostly been located – is funded by local government to make insti-tutionalized provision for young people, both in the form of youth centres and clubs, and by supporting voluntary sector projects. It would be a mistake to assume that these are merely neutral spaces, in which radical interventions are somehow magically possible. On the contrary, the historical study of local authority youth provision would suggest that it functions primarily as a means of keeping troublesome youth off the streets – and in this context, the term 'youth' implicitly refers to young people who are working-class, often black and predominantly male (Nava, 1984). Of course, it would be simplistic to regard the youth service – or indeed schools – as merely a form of 'soft policing', but the arguments can clearly cut both ways.

In their retrospective account of the Cockpit work, Dewdney and Lister also identify a number of difficulties and unresolved issues in their approach. They acknowledge the dangers of focusing exclusively on 'spectacular' youth cultures, and the limitations of a simplistic validation of these young people's 'resistance' to middle-class authority. As they note, radical teachers cannot simply affirm young people's perspectives merely by announcing that they are 'on the same side'. Particularly within the context of school (although not *only* there), young people may often reject this kind of approach as merely patronizing.

Ultimately, however, Dewdney and Lister fail to resolve the crucial question of what students might actually be *learning* from this kind of work, beyond merely acquiring technical skills. The danger of their approach is one that has been identified in critiques of 'progressive' pedagogy much more broadly. In seeking to validate students' perspectives and concerns, does it not end up simply leaving them where they already are? While this process of validation might prove to be progressive (or perhaps therapeutic) for teachers, it is more important to investigate what it might be doing for the students themselves. Advocates of the Cockpit approach have produced some persuasive analyses of students' work, which make use of semiotic and post-structuralist theory (e.g. Chappell, 1984; Cohen, 1990). But the extent to which these insights were available to the students themselves, or in what form, remains highly debatable. Dewdney and Lister acknowledge the need to 'problematise', to 'make students think about what is being celebrated', and to enable them to be 'self-reflexive' about their own work – an emphasis that I would see as crucially important. Yet they provide few indications of how this might be achieved in practice, without merely recuperating it back into the academic (or, in their terms, 'magisterial') mode of conventional schooling. Indeed, the non-interventionist teaching style on which the approach is based would seem to preclude such 'teacherly' interference.

Media and 'informal' learning

The questions raised by Dewdney's and Lister's work are still highly relevant, particularly in the light of the growing interest in 'informal' arts and media education. Does working with 'students' cultures' necessarily have progressive political consequences? To what extent does the apparently non-interventionist style of teaching actually embody a 'hidden curriculum' – an unstated set of prescriptions and constraints? How far is it possible here to enable students to ask critical questions about their own work, or to reflect back on the production process itself? And what, ultimately, do young people *learn* from this kind of activity?

To date, there have been very few empirical research studies that have sought to address these questions. My own research (Buckingham, Grahame and Sefton-Green, 1995: ch. 4) points to the gap between rhetoric and reality in some of this work. This study was conducted in a local youth project, and focused on a mixed group of young people producing a rap music video. On one level, the project appeared very 'student-centred': the young people were asked to define the topics they would address, and to devise their own approach through working in small groups. The predominant ethos here was one of 'learning-by-doing'; and the tutors generally avoided anything resembling direct instruction, perhaps on the grounds that this would appear authoritarian – although ultimately it was the determined intervention of the staff, at a relatively late stage, that finally 'rescued' the production. This 'hands-off' approach implicitly sanctioned a certain division of labour, in which the young women were largely confined to decorative or supporting roles, and several felt distinctly marginalized. Furthermore, the staff did not appear to have any very effective ways of enabling the young people to develop the *content* of their video. The primary aim appeared to be to assemble a video that 'looked good'; and as the project progressed, more unconventional ideas were steadily abandoned, in favour of a much more obviously generic product.

Of course, several of these problems might be seen as simply a manifestation of the dominant ethos of youth work. Many young people who attend such projects define them precisely in terms of their *opposition* to school: they are primarily about 'hanging out' with friends rather than anything resembling 'work'. Likewise, the approach of most youth workers is defined in terms of their opposition to teachers: however much specialist expertise they may have, they are generally keen to avoid the implication that they are authority figures, or indeed anything other than older friends. The difficulty here is that this can result in a kind of abdication of teaching. In this instance, this was compounded by the tutors' choice of media genres. Choosing a music video meant that all sorts of 'mistakes' could be edited together and carried along by the rhythm of the song. Likewise, a reasonably acceptable-sounding rap could be generated fairly easily by the group. Yet producing a coherent music video or an effective rap track requires a high degree of artistry, discipline and technical skill; and there were few attempts to develop these things in this project. On the contrary, there appeared to be an implicit assumption that these genres belonged to young people, and emerged spontaneously without form or structure from their everyday experiences. This is a patronizing approach which, in my view, sells young people short.

Hyeon-Seon Jeong (2001) provides a case study of a similar youth project that develops some of these issues. She observed an introductory video production course, in which the students engaged in a brief interview exercise, followed by a more extended drama production. In this context, Jeong identifies a tension between two competing institutional aims. On the one hand, the tutors on the project saw themselves as youth workers; and as such, their aim was to provide the 'disadvantaged' young people with a 'creative refuge' from the pressures of inner city life, where they could build their self-esteem and 'find a voice' with which to represent themselves and their concerns. On the other hand, however, the project also claimed to provide young people with training for eventual employment in the media industries – an emphasis that is increasingly important in the funding of such initiatives, at least in the UK. Here, the aim was to provide the young people with instruction in handling equipment, in specialist terminology, and in the routines and procedures of professional practice. Video production was therefore intended to serve here both as a form of social education and as a form of vocational training.

As Jeong shows, the tension between these two rationales led to some rather contradictory and unsatisfactory teaching strategies. In practice, the *content* of these productions did not appear to matter very much: the tutors encouraged the young people to volunteer ideas and vote on them (hence 'proving' that they were definitely their own), but they made very few attempts to develop or question those ideas. The young people were told that they would have the opportunity to show 'what young people are really about', and in fact some fairly complex issues were raised by the work they produced; but these were not at any point made the focus of explicit reflection or debate. Here again, the students were pressured to produce 'politically correct' representations, and to 'subvert' stereotypical views; but the implications and consequences of this were not discussed. Ultimately, despite the tutors' occasional lip-service to media theory, the work was primarily intended to function as a set of technical 'exercises'.

Of course, this is not to say that these young people learned nothing at all from these projects – although in practice, much of their learning would have been confined to technical skills. As I suggested in chapter 8, there is undoubtedly a balance that needs to be found here between instruction and 'learning-by-doing' (Situated Practice); and given the contexts in which they occur, these kinds of project are bound to be relatively 'student-centred'. Yet to imply that this is somehow incompatible with direct instruction, or with providing a clear structure for group activities, is to take the lazy way out. Furthermore, despite an apparent commitment to 'political correctness' here, there was an almost total lack of 'Critical Framing' – that is, of any discussion of the social and political dimensions of the work the students produced.

In some respects, however, the most striking absence here was of any means of developing the *content* of students' productions. In my experience, few young people attend such courses because they are burning with something to say: they want to learn how to make a video, not a statement about the world. Yet if they are going to learn how to use the medium, it is vital that the content is important to them, and that they have an audience to whom they wish to convey it – even if this is something they discover during the production process itself. Learning to communicate in a given medium is more than just a technical process: it involves setting out to achieve particular purposes or effects. If the content does not matter – or is not *made* to matter – then the technical or communicative skills that are developed are likely to be fairly superficial.

Evaluation

The studies discussed above do puncture some of the optimism that tends to characterize discussions of this field, particularly among policy-makers (see Buckingham, 2000c). There is undoubtedly much better practice taking place. Yet much of this work remains to be documented and evaluated; and (perhaps understandably) most published accounts of it are characterized by self-justification rather than critical rigour. For policy-makers, such work often seems to be valued more for what *appears* to be happening than what is actually being achieved. As Sara Selwood (1997) has argued, such projects often seem to be regarded merely as 'a form of temporary social service for young people who are disadvantaged or "excluded" ': they may serve as a means of keeping young people out of trouble, but they may achieve little more. Yet, as I have implied, there are significant questions about the *educational* criteria that should be used to evaluate such work.

For example, it is often far from clear whether such projects are to be evaluated in terms of the process or the product. As I have implied, media educators in schools have tended to prioritize the process – and in particular, the conceptual learning that the process should bring about. In the more informal context of youth work, the criteria for evaluation are often somewhat vague. Media production activities are frequently described in terms of their ability to promote 'social and communication skills', or to develop 'self-esteem' and 'self-awareness'; but the criteria by which these things might be identified and measured are rarely well defined. Likewise, it is often far from clear how we might assess the value or quality of the work the young people produce. Comparison with the work of 'professionals', or the use of 'expert juries' in the manner of a film festival, may be inappropriate or positively misleading. Is 'quality' simply in the eye of the producer, or is it also determined by audiences – and if so, *which* audiences? To what extent do we take account here of the involvement of adults – for example, in editing or providing specialist expertise, or in the drive to create an acceptable finished product?

Some of these issues have been addressed by the most advanced work in this field in the United States. Steve Goodman (1998), for example, describes how the student video-makers in his project keep detailed journals and portfolios of their work in progress, and use structured protocols for evaluation. Students are also required to demonstrate what they have learned to a panel made up of parents, media producers, teachers and other students; and the criteria for evaluation are collectively agreed by several members of the wider community. In this context, the tutors have also devised effective means of enabling students to develop the *content* of their work, through collaborative research and debate; and many of the productions seek to make clear statements about social issues in the local neighbourhood.

By contrast, most practice in this field in the UK seems to adopt a much less rigorous approach. Much of the reason for this is because of the short-term nature of many of the projects and the lack of specialist training for staff. A recent report on the informal youth media production sector (Harvey, Skinner and Parker, 2002) draws attention to a number of such endemic problems. The projects surveyed have a wide variety of aims and modes of working, as well as very different levels of resourcing. Yet there is a lack of strategic, long-term funding, and of networks for sharing experience and good practice. Evaluation is often carried out on the basis of 'head counting', or in terms of narrowly measurable outcomes, rather than in any depth. In the UK at least, there is also very little infrastructure for the distribution or exhibition of young people's work, which means that much of it never reaches the wider audience it might deserve.

Despite their limitations, however, these kinds of 'informal' media education project undoubtedly can offer valuable opportunities for learning and creative work; and there is therefore a great deal that media teachers in schools can learn from them. There is a need to build closer connections between such projects and the work of teachers in schools, and to encourage a more general debate about the styles of learning that are most appropriate in the different contexts. Ultimately, however, such projects will only ever reach a small minority. As Hall and Newbury (1999) suggest, the school curriculum remains a much more significant force in shaping young people's cultural activities and perceptions; and it should therefore surely remain the key site for intervention.

Towards deschooling?

The 'informal' media education discussed in this chapter is one aspect of a much broader move to develop new forms of 'learning beyond the classroom'. While this appears to be a contemporary preoccupation, it actually has a long history. Indeed, it is now thirty years since Ivan Illich (1973) called for the 'deschooling' of society. Looking back to Illich's proposals, one can find a very similar argument for alternative forms of learning to those I have noted here. Illich claims that much of the most significant learning arises not as a result of teaching but in more informal settings; and he calls on all social institutions, including workplaces, to recognize their potential educational role. In terms that are very reminiscent of contemporary arguments about 'situated learning' (Lave and Wenger, 1991), Illich argues that most learning is not the result of instruction, but of 'unhindered participation in a meaningful setting'.

Illich's metaphors for replacements for the school seem equally contemporary. He talks about webs and networks, and even looks forward to the role of computer technology in creating them. He imagines a situation in which individual learners would be able to make contact with others with similar interests via computerized databases. In this situation, teachers would be freely chosen rather than imposed: they would serve as network administrators or facilitators, offering guidance when requested to do so. In many ways, Illich is imagining the internet – or at least some people's fantasy version of the internet.

Yet however attractive this vision may be, it raises the obvious question of how we get there from here. As an anarchist, Illich rejects all types of institutionalized provision as merely forms of state surveillance and control; but if they were to be implemented, his alternatives would clearly require quite extensive state regulation. In a capitalist society, access to educational resources is bound to involve the exchange of labour time for money, and hence the generation of profit. Indeed, in most countries, private companies are now increasingly taking over areas of leisure and cultural provision that were previously the responsibility of national or local government; and many public organizations have reorganized themselves according to commercial principles. In the field of education, these developments are most apparent in the gradual privatization of public schooling, and the increasing involvement of private corporations – not least media companies – in the 'education market' (Buckingham and Scanlon, 2003).

In most industrialized countries, education is now much more the consumer commodity Illich so powerfully condemns. In the UK, for example, educational policy continues to be driven by a reductive conception of 'standards'. National testing and the publication of league tables of schools' examination results has generated a new 'consumer culture' that is characterized by high levels of competition and anxiety, both among children and among parents. Leisure providers – sports centres, museums, youth clubs, community arts projects – are also increasingly required to justify themselves in narrowly educational terms. It might be more accurate to describe these developments as a form of *re*-schooling, rather than deschooling. They represent an extension of the competitive ethos of formal education into areas of everyday life, rather than a broader view of what counts as learning.

Illich's view of computers as a means of networking and sharing skills and resources has to some extent been borne out by recent developments. Enthusiasts rightly point to the development of informal, democratic 'learning communities' on the internet, and to the potential for communication across boundaries of age and culture. But the increasing penetration of information and communication technologies into all areas of social life – not least education – is primarily being driven by capitalism's relentless search for new markets. In some respects, the internet is the ultimate fulfilment of individualized, niche marketing; and there is a growing polarization between those who have access to technology and those who do not. Far from leading to the deschooled utopia of the network society, these developments may result in a privatized educational dystopia – a form of educational consumerism that is governed by market forces, and characterized by increasing levels of competitiveness and inequality. And we may see the emergence of an educational 'underclass' that is effectively excluded from access, not merely to economic capital but to social and cultural capital as well.

It would be too much to claim that media education alone can reverse or counteract these tendencies, as previous generations of media educators may have hoped. Contemporary media teachers have a much more realistic estimation of its potential, and are inclined to adopt a rather less missionary approach. Yet wherever we may be heading, the media will undoubtedly be playing a central role in social, economic and political life. Now more than ever, young people need to be equipped with the ability to understand and to participate actively in the media culture that surrounds them. The case for media education has never been more urgent than it is today.

References

Abbott, C. (1998) 'Making connections: young people and the internet', in Sefton-Green, J. (ed.) *Digital Diversions: Youth Culture in the Age of Multimedia* London: UCL Press.

Abrams, M. (1956) 'Child audiences for television in Great Britain', *Journalism Quarterly* 33: 35–41.

Alexander, A., Ryan, M. and Munoz, P. (1984) 'Creating a learning context: investigations on the interactions of siblings during television viewing', *Critical Studies in Mass Communication* 194: 345–64.

Alvarado, M. and Boyd-Barrett, O. (eds) (1992) *Media Education: An Introduction* London: British Film Institute/Open University Press.

Alvarado, M. and Bradshaw, W. (1992) 'The creative tradition: teaching film and TV production', in Alvarado, M. and Boyd-Barrett, O. (eds) (1992) *Media Education: An Introduction* London: British Film Institute/ Open University Press.

Alvarado, M. and Ferguson, B. (1983) 'Media Studies, the curriculum and discursivity' *Screen* 24(3): 20–34.

Alvarado, M., Collins, R. and Donald, J. (1993) *The Screen Education Reader* London: Routledge.

Alvarado, M., Gutch, R. and Wollen, T. (1987) *Learning the Media* London: Macmillan.

Anderson, J. (1980) 'The theoretical lineage of critical viewing curricula', *Journal of Communication* 30(3): 64–70.

Bakhtin, M. (1968) *Rabelais and his World* Cambridge, MA: MIT Press.

Bakhtin, M. (1981) *The Dialogic Imagination* Austin, TX: University of Texas Press.

Bakhtin, M. (1986) *Speech Genres and Other Late Essays* Austin, TX: University of Texas Press.

Barton, D. (1994) *Literacy: An Introduction to the Ecology of Written Language* Oxford: Blackwell Publishers.

Baym, N. (2000) *Tune In, Log Out: Soaps, Fandom and Online Community* London: Sage.

Bazalgette, C. (1988) ' "They changed the picture in the middle of the fight": new kinds of literacy', in Meek, M. and Mills, C. (eds) *Language and Literacy in the Primary School* London: Falmer.

Bazalgette, C. (ed.) (1989) *Primary Media Education: A Curriculum Statement* London: British Film Institute.

Bazalgette, C. (1991) *Media Education* London: Hodder and Stoughton.

Bazalgette, C. (1992) 'Key aspects of media education', in Alvarado, M. and Boyd-Barrett, O. (eds) (1992) *Media Education: An Introduction* London: British Film Institute/Open University Press.

Bazalgette, C. (1998) 'Still only 1898', *Media Education Journal* 24: 2–9.

Bazalgette, C. and Buckingham, D. (eds) (1995) *In Front of the Children: Screen Entertainment and Young Audiences* London: British Film Institute.

Bazalgette, C., Bévort, E. and Saviano, J. (eds) (1992) *New Directions: Media Education Worldwide* London: British Film Institute.

Beach, R. (2000) 'Using media ethnographies to study response to media as activity', in Watts Pailliotet, A. and Mosenthal, P. (eds) *Reconceptualizing Literacy in the Media Age* Stamford, CT: JAI Press.

Becker, H. (1982) *Art Worlds* Berkeley: University of California Press.

Bentley, T. (1998) *Learning beyond the Classroom* London: Routledge.

Booth, J. (1999) '*PhotoWork*: a case study in educational publishing for and by young people', in Sefton-Green, J. (ed.) *Young People, Creativity and New Technologies* London: Routledge.

Bordwell, D. and Thompson, K. (1979) *Film Art* New York: McGraw-Hill.

Bourdieu, P. (1984) *Distinction: A Social Critique of the Judgement of Taste* London: Routledge and Kegan Paul.

Bowker, J. (ed.) (1991) *Secondary Media Education: A Curriculum Statement* London: British Film Institute.

Boyle, D. (1997) *Subject to Change: Guerrilla Television Revisited* New York: Oxford University Press.

Bragg, S. (2000) 'Media Violence and Education: A Study of Youth Audiences and the Horror Genre', PhD thesis, Institute of Education, University of London.

Bragg, S. (2001) 'Just what the doctors ordered? Media regulation, education and the "problem" of media violence', in Barker, M. and Petley, J. (eds) *Ill Effects: The Media/Violence Debate*, (2nd edn) London: Routledge.

Branston, G. (1991) 'Audience', in Lusted, D. (ed.) *The Media Studies Book: A Guide for Teachers* London: Routledge.

Branston, G. and Stafford, R. (1999) *The Media Student's Book*, 2nd edn London: Routledge.

British Film Institute (1998) *Media Industries Tracking Study Report* London: British Film Institute.

British Film Institute (2000) *Moving Images in the Classroom: A Secondary Teacher's Guide to Using Film and Television* London: British Film Institute.

Britzman, D. (1991) 'Decentering discourses in teacher education: or, the unleashing of unpopular things', *Journal of Education* 173(3): 60–80.

Brooker, P. and Humm, P. (1989) *Dialogue and Difference: English into the Nineties* London: Routledge.

Brown, J. (1991) *Television 'Critical Viewing Skills' Education: Major Media Literacy Projects in the United States and Selected Countries* Hillsdale, NJ: Erlbaum.

Buckingham, D. (1986) 'Against demystification', *Screen* 27(5): 80–95.

Buckingham, D. (1990) 'Making it explicit; towards a theory of media learning', in Buckingham, D. (ed.) *Watching Media Learning: Making Sense of Media Education* London: Falmer.

Buckingham, D. (1992a) 'Practical work', in Alvarado, M. and Boyd-Barrett, O. (eds) (1992) *Media Education: An Introduction* London: British Film Institute/Open University Press.

Buckingham, D. (1992b) 'English and Media Studies: making the difference', in Alvarado, M. and Boyd-Barrett, O. (eds) (1992) *Media Education: An Introduction* London: British Film Institute/Open University Press.

Buckingham, D. (1993a) *Children Talking Television: The Making of Television Literacy* London: Falmer.

Buckingham, D. (1993b) *Changing Literacies: Media Education and Modern Culture* London: Tufnell Press.

Buckingham, D. (1995) 'Media education and the media industries: bridging the gaps?' *Journal of Educational Television* 21(1): 7–22.

Buckingham, D. (1996a) *Moving Images: Understanding Children's Emotional Responses to Television* Manchester: Manchester University Press.

Buckingham, D. (1996b) 'Critical pedagogy and media education: a theory in search of a practice', *Journal of Curriculum Studies* 28(6): 627–50.

Buckingham, D. (ed.) (1998) *Teaching Popular Culture: Beyond Radical Pedagogy* London: UCL Press.

Buckingham, D. (2000a) *After the Death of Childhood: Growing Up in the Age of Electronic Media* Cambridge: Polity.

Buckingham, D. (2000b) *The Making of Citizens: Young People, News and Politics* London: Routledge.

Buckingham, D. (2000c) 'Creative futures? Youth, the arts and social inclusion', *Education and Social Justice* 2(3): 6–11.

Buckingham, D. (ed.) (2002a) *Small Screens: Television for Children* Leicester: Leicester University Press.

Buckingham, D. (2002b) 'The electronic generation: children and new media', in Lievrouw, L. and Livingstone, S. (eds) *Handbook of New Media* London: Sage.

Buckingham, D. and Domaille, K. (2001) *Report on the Global Media Education Survey* Paris: UNESCO.

Buckingham, D. and Harvey, I. (2001) 'Imagining the audience: language, creativity and communication in youth media production', *Journal of Educational Media* 26(3): 173–84.

Buckingham, D. and Jones, K. (2001) 'New Labour's cultural turn: some tensions in contemporary educational and cultural policy', *Journal of Education Policy* 16(1): 1–14.

Buckingham, D. and Scanlon, M. (2003) *Education, Entertainment and Learning in the Home* Buckingham: Open University Press.

Buckingham, D. and Sefton-Green, J. (1994) *Cultural Studies Goes to School: Reading and Teaching Popular Media* London: Taylor and Francis.

Buckingham, D. and Sefton-Green, J. (1997) 'From regulation to education', *English and Media Magazine* 36: 28–32.

Buckingham, D. and Sefton-Green, J. (2003) 'Gotta catch 'em all: structure, agency and pedagogy in children's media culture', *Media, Culture and Society* 25(3).

Buckingham, D., Fraser, P. and Mayman, N. (1990) 'Stepping into the void: beginning classroom research in media education', in Buckingham, D. (ed.) *Watching Media Learning: Making Sense of Media Education* London: Falmer.

Buckingham, D., Fraser, P. and Sefton-Green, J. (2000) 'Making the grade: evaluating student production in Media Studies', in Sefton-Green, J. and Sinker, R. (eds) *Evaluating Creativity: Making and Learning by Young People* London: Routledge.

Buckingham, D., Grahame, J. and Sefton-Green, J. (1995) *Making Media: Practical Production in Media Education* London: English and Media Centre.

Buckingham, D., Harvey, I. and Sefton-Green, J. (1999) 'The difference is digital? Digital technology and student media production', *Convergence* 5(4): 10–20.

Buckingham, D., Scanlon, M. and Sefton-Green, J. (2001) 'Selling the Digital Dream: Marketing Educational Technologies to Teachers and Parents', in Loveless, A. and Ellis, V. (eds) *ICT, Pedagogy and the Curriculum: Subject to Change* London: Routledge.

Buckingham, D., Davies, H., Jones, K. and Kelley, P. (1999) *Children's Television in Britain: History, Discourse and Policy* London: British Film Institute.

Burn, A. (1999) 'Grabbing the werewolf: digital freezeframes, the cinematic still and technologies of the social', *Convergence* 5(4): 80–101.

Burn, A. and Parker, D. (2001) 'Making your mark: digital inscription, animation, and a new visual semiotic', *Education, Communication and Information* 1(2): 155–79.

Burn, A. and Reed, K. (1999) 'Digiteens: media literacies and digital technologies in the secondary classroom', *English in Education* 33(2): 5–20.

Burn, A., Brindley, S., Durran, J., Kelsall, C., Sweetlove, J. and Tuohey, C. (2001) ' "The rush of images": a research report into digital editing and the moving image', *English in Education* 35(2): 34–48.

Burton, R. and Dimbleby, R. (1993) *Teaching Communications* London: Macmillan.

Butler, J. (1990) *Gender Trouble: Feminism and the Subversion of Identity* London: Routledge.

Center for Media Education (1997) *Web of Deception: Threats to Children from Online Marketing* Washington, DC: Center for Media Education.

Chandler, D. (1997) 'Children's understanding of what is "real" on television: a review of the literature', *Journal of Educational Media* 23(1): 65–80.

Chappell, A. (1984) 'Family fortunes', in McRobbie, A. and Nava, M. (eds) *Gender and Generation* London: Macmillan.

Cohen, P. (1990) *Really Useful Knowledge* Stoke-on-Trent: Trentham.

Cohen, P. (1998) 'Tricks of the trade: on teaching arts and "race" in the classroom', in Buckingham, D. (ed.) *Teaching Popular Culture: Beyond Radical Pedagogy* London: UCL Press.

Cope, B. and Kalantzis, M. (eds) (1993) *The Powers of Literacy: A Genre Approach to Teaching Writing* London: Taylor and Francis.

Cope, B. and Kalantzis, M. (eds) (2000) *Multiliteracies: Literacy Learning and the Design of Social Futures* London: Routledge.

Craggs, C. (1993) *Media Education in the Primary School* London: Routledge.

Davies, H., Buckingham, D. and Kelley, P. (2000) 'In the worst possible taste: children, television and cultural value', *European Journal of Cultural Studies* 3(1): 5–25.

Davies, M. M. (1997) *Fact, Fake and Fantasy* Mahwah, NJ: Erlbaum.

Del Vecchio, G. (1997) *Creating Ever-Cool: A Marketer's Guide to a Kid's Heart* Gretna, LA: Pelican.

Department of Education and Science (1963) *Half our Future* (the Newsom Report) London: HMSO.

Dewdney, A. and Lister, M. (1988) *Youth, Culture and Photography* London: Macmillan.

Dickson, P. (1994) *A Survey of Media Education* London: National Foundation for Educational Research/British Film Institute.

Dimbleby, N., Dimbleby, R. and Whittington, K. (1994) *Practical Media: a Guide to Production Techniques* London: Hodder and Stoughton.

Dorr, A. (1983) 'No shortcuts to judging reality', in Bryant, J. and Anderson, D. (eds) *Children's Understanding of Television* New York: Academic Press.

Dorr, A. (1986) *Television and Children: A Special Medium for a Special Audience* Beverly Hills, CA: Sage.

Dowmunt, T. (1980) *Video with Young People* London: Interaction.

Dowmunt, T. (ed.) (1993) *Channels of Resistance* London: British Film Institute/Channel Four.

Doyle, B. (1986) *English and Englishness* London: Methuen.

Drotner, K. (1989) 'Girl meets boy: aesthetic production, reception and gender identity', *Cultural Studies* 3(2): 208–25.

Duncan, B., D'Ippolito, J., McPherson, C. and Wilson, C. (1996) *Mass Media and Popular Culture* Toronto: Harcourt Brace.

Dyson, A. H. (1997) *Writing Superheroes: Contemporary Childhood, Popular Culture and Classroom Literacy* New York: Teachers College Press.

Dyson, A. H. (1999) 'Coach Bombay's kids learn to write: children's appropriation of media material for school literacy', *Research in the Teaching of English* 33(4): 367–402.

Edwards, R. (1997) *Changing Places: Flexibility, Lifelong Learning and a Learning Society* London: Routledge.

Ellsworth, E. (1989) 'Why doesn't this feel empowering? Working through the repressive myths of critical pedagogy', *Harvard Educational Review* 59(3): 297–324.

Facer, K., Furlong, J., Furlong, R. and Sutherland, R. (forthcoming) *ScreenPlay: Children in 'Techno-Popular' Culture* London: Routledge.

Ferguson, B. (1981) 'Practical work and pedagogy', *Screen Education* 38: 42–55.

Film Education Working Group (1999) *Making Movies Matter* London: British Film Institute.

Freedman, A. (1990) 'Teaching the text: English and Media Studies', in Buckingham, D. (ed.) *Watching Media Learning: Making Sense of Media Education* London: Falmer.

French, D. and Richards, M. (1994) *Media Education across Europe* London: Routledge.

Fuenzalida, V. (1992) 'Media education in Latin America: developments 1970–1990', in Bazalgette, C., Bévort, E. and Saviano, J. (eds) *New Directions: Media Education Worldwide* London: British Film Institute.

Funge, E. (1998) 'Rethinking representation: Media studies and the postmodern teenager', *English and Media Magazine* 39: 33–6.

Gallimore, R. and Tharp, R. (1990) 'Teaching mind in society: teaching, schooling and literate discourse', in Moll, L. (ed.) *Vygotsky and Education* Cambridge: Cambridge University Press.

Gillespie, M. (1995) *Television, Ethnicity and Cultural Change* London: Routledge.

Gomery, D. (1994) 'Disney's business history: a reinterpretation', in Smoodin, E. (ed.) *Disney Discourse* London: British Film Institute.

Goodman, S. (1998) 'Interview', in Tyner, K. *Literacy in the Information Age* Mahwah, NJ: Erlbaum.

Goodwyn, A. (1992) *English Teaching and Media Education* Buckingham: Open University Press.

Gore, J. (1993) *The Struggle for Pedagogies: Critical and Feminist Discourses as Regimes of Truth* New York: Routledge.

Grace, D. and Tobin, J. (1998) 'Butt jokes and mean-teacher parodies: video production in the elementary classroom', in Buckingham, D. (ed.) *Teaching Popular Culture: Beyond Radical Pedagogy* London: UCL Press.

Grahame, J. (1990) 'Playtime: learning about media institutions through practical work', in Buckingham, D. (ed.) *Watching Media Learning: Making Sense of Media Education* London: Falmer.

Grahame, J. (ed.) (1991a) *The English Curriculum: Media 1* London: English and Media Centre.

Grahame, J. (1991b) 'The production process', in Lusted, D. (ed.) *The Media Studies Book: A Guide for Teachers* London: Routledge.

Grahame, J. (ed.) (1994) *Production Practices* London: English and Media Centre.

Grahame, J. with Domaille, K. (2001) *The Media Book* London: English and Media Centre.

Grossberg, L. (1987) 'Critical theory and the politics of empirical research', in Gurevitch, M. and Levy, M. (eds) *Mass Communication Review Yearbook 6* Beverly Hills, CA: Sage.

Hall, R. and Newbury, D. (1999) ' "What makes you switch on?" Young people, the internet and cultural participation', in Sefton-Green, J. (ed.) *Young People, Creativity and New Technologies* London: Routledge.

Hall, S. and Whannel, P. (1964) *The Popular Arts* London: Hutchinson.

Halloran, J. and Jones, M. (1968) *Learning about the Media: Communication and Society.* Paris: UNESCO.

Hart, A. (1992) 'Mis-reading English: Media, English and the secondary curriculum', *English and Media Magazine* 26: 43–6.

Hart, A. (ed.) (1998) *Teaching the Media: International Perspectives* Mahwah, NJ: Erlbaum.

Hart, A. and Hicks, A. (2001) *Teaching Media in the English Curriculum* Stoke-on-Trent: Trentham.

Harvey, I., Skinner, M. and Parker, D. (2002) *Being Seen, Being Heard: Young People and Moving Image Production* London: National Youth Agency/British Film Institute.

Hawkins, R. P. (1977) 'The dimensional structure of children's perceptions of television reality', *Communication Research* 4(3): 299–320.

Heath, S. B. (1983) *Ways with Words* Cambridge: Cambridge University Press.

Hebdige, D. (1979) *Subculture: The Meaning of Style* London: Methuen.

Heller, C. (1978) 'The resistible rise of video', *Educational Broadcasting International* 11(3): 133–5.

Hendershot, H. (1999) *Saturday Morning Censors* Durham, NC: Duke University Press.

Hodge, B. and Tripp, D. (1986) *Children and Television: A Semiotic Approach* Cambridge: Polity.

Hoggart, R. (1959) *The Uses of Literacy* London: Chatto and Windus.

Hurd, G. and Connell, I. (1989) 'Cultural education: a revised programme', *Media Information Australia* 53: 23–30.

Illich, I. (1973) *Deschooling Society* Harmondsworth: Penguin.

Jaglom, L. and Gardner, H. (1981) 'The preschool television viewer as anthropologist', in Kelly, H. and Gardner, H. (eds) *Viewing Children Through Television* San Francisco: Jossey-Bass.

Jenkins, H. (1992) *Textual Poachers: Television Fans and Participatory Culture* London: Routledge.

Jeong, H.-S. (2001) 'Theory, Practice and "Empowerment" in Media Education: A Case Study of Critical Pedagogy', PhD thesis, Institute of Education, University of London.

Jones, A. (1999) '*Translocations*: from media to multimedia education', in Sefton-Green, J. (ed.) *Young People, Creativity and New Technologies* London: Routledge.

Jones, K. and Davies, H. (2002) 'Keeping it real: *Grange Hill* and the representation of "the child's world" in children's television drama', in

Buckingham, D. (ed.) *Small Screens: Television for Children* Leicester: Leicester University Press.

Katz, J. (1997) *Virtuous Reality: How America Surrendered Discussion of Moral Values to Opportunists, Nitwits and Blockheads like William Bennett* New York: Random House.

Kenway, J. and Bullen, E. (2001) *Consuming Children: Education, Entertainment, Advertising* Buckingham: Open University Press.

Kinder, M. (1991) *Playing with Power in Movies, Television and Video Games: From Muppet Babies to Teenage Mutant Ninja Turtles* Berkeley: University of California Press.

Kinder, M. (ed.) (2000) *Kids' Media Culture* Durham, NC: Duke University Press.

Kress, G. (1997) *Before Writing: Rethinking the Paths to Literacy* London: Routledge.

Kress, G. and van Leeuwen, T. (1996) *Reading Images: The Grammar of Visual Design* London: Routledge.

Kubey, R. (ed.) (1997) *Media Literacy in the Information Age* New Brunswick, NJ: Transaction.

Lachs, V. (2000) *Making Multimedia in the Classroom: A Practical Guide* London: Routledge.

Lave, J. and Wenger, E. (1991) *Situated Learning: Legitimate Peripheral Participation* Cambridge: Cambridge University Press.

Laybourne, G. (1993) 'The Nickelodeon experience', in Berry, G. and Asamen, J. (eds) *Children and Television* London: Sage.

Leavis, F. and Thompson, D. (1933) *Culture and Environment: The Training of Critical Awareness* London: Chatto and Windus.

Livingstone, S. and Bovill, M. (1999) *Young People, New Media* London: London School of Economics and Political Science.

Livingstone, S. and Bovill, M. (eds) (2001) *Children and their Changing Media Environment* Mahwah, NJ: Erlbaum.

Lorac, C. and Weiss, M. (1981) *Communication and Social Skills* Exeter: Wheaton.

Lovell, T. (1983) 'Ideology and *Coronation Street*', in Kaplan, E. A. (ed.) *Regarding Television* Frederick, MD: American Film Institute.

Luke, C. (2000) 'Cyber-schooling and technological change: multiliteracies for new times', in Cope, B. and Kalantzis, M. (eds) *Multiliteracies: Literacy Learning and the Design of Social Futures* London: Routledge.

Luke, C. and Gore, J. (eds) (1992) *Feminisms and Critical Pedagogy* New York: Routledge.

Lusted, D. (1985) 'A history of suspicion', in Lusted, D. and Drummond, P. (eds) *TV and Schooling* London: British Film Institute.

Lusted, D. (1986) 'Why pedagogy?' *Screen* 27(5): 2–14.

Lusted, D. and Drummond, P. (eds) (1985) *TV and Schooling* London: British Film Institute.

McLaughlin, M. and Heath, S. (eds) (1993) *Identity and Inner-City Youth: Beyond Gender and Ethnicity* New York: Teachers College Press.

McRobbie, A. (1994) *Postmodernism and Popular Culture* London: Routledge.

Marsh, J. (1999) 'Batman and Batwoman go to school: popular culture in the literacy curriculum', *International Journal of Early Years Education* 7(2): 117–31.

Marsh, J. and Millard, E. (2000) *Literacy and Popular Culture* London: Paul Chapman.

Masterman, L. (1980) *Teaching about Television* London: Macmillan.

Masterman, L. (1985) *Teaching the Media* London: Comedia.

Masterman, L. (1989) 'Illumination', *Times Educational Supplement* 24 April.

Meek, M. (1988) *How Texts Teach What Readers Learn* Stroud, Gloucestershire: Thimble Press.

Melody, W. (1973) *Children's Television: The Economics of Exploitation* New Haven, CT: Yale University Press.

Messaris, P. (1986) 'Parents, children and television', in Gumpert, G. and Cathcart, R. (eds) *Inter Media: Interpersonal Communication in a Media World* New York: Oxford University Press.

Messaris, P. (1994) *Visual 'Literacy': Image, Mind and Reality* Boulder, CO: Westview.

Messaris, P. and Sarrett, C. (1981) 'On the consequences of TV-related parent–child interaction', *Human Communication Research* 7(3): 226–44.

Ministry of Education, Ontario (1989) *Media Literacy Resource Guide* Toronto, Ontario: Queen's Printer.

Morgan, R. (1996) 'Pantextualism, everyday life and media education', *Continuum* 9(2): 14–34.

Morgan, R. (1998a) 'Media education in Ontario: generational differences in approach', in Hart, A. (ed.) (1998) *Teaching the Media: International Perspectives* Mahwah, NJ: Erlbaum.

Morgan, R. (1998b) 'Provocations for a media education in small letters', in Buckingham, D. (ed.) *Teaching Popular Culture: Beyond Radical Pedagogy* London: UCL Press.

Moss, G. (1989) *Un/popular Fictions* London: Virago.

Mulhern, F. (1979) *The Moment of 'Scrutiny'* London: New Left Books.

Murdock, G. and Phelps, G. (1973) *Mass Media and the Secondary School* London: Macmillan/Schools Council.

Nava, M. (1984) 'Youth service provision, social order and the question of girls', in McRobbie, A. and Nava, M. (eds) *Gender and Generation* London: Macmillan.

Nixon, H. (1998) 'Fun and games are serious business', in Sefton-Green, J. (ed.) *Digital Diversions: Youth Culture in the Age of Multimedia* London: UCL Press.

Ohmae, K. (1995) *The End of the Nation State* New York: Harper Collins.

Ordidge, I. (1999) 'The NEMA experience', in Sefton-Green, J. (ed.) *Young People, Creativity and New Technologies* London: Routledge.

Orner, M. (1992) 'Interrupting the calls for student voice in liberatory education: a feminist poststructuralist perspective', in Luke, C. and Gore, J. (eds) *Feminisms and Critical Pedagogy* New York: Routledge.

Postman, N. (1983) *The Disappearance of Childhood* London: W. H. Allen.

Postman, N. (1992) *Technopoly: The Surrender of Culture to Technology* New York: Knopf.

Pungente, J. (1989) 'The second spring: media education in Canada', *Educational Media International* 26: 199–203.

Raney, K. and Hollands, H. (2000) 'Art education and talk: from modernist silence to postmodern chatter', in Sefton-Green, J. and Sinker, R. (eds) *Evaluating Creativity: Making and Learning by Young People* London: Routledge.

Richards, C. (1990) 'Intervening in popular pleasures: Media Studies and the politics of subjectivity', in Buckingham, D. (ed.) *Watching Media Learning: Making Sense of Media Education* London: Falmer.

Richards, C. (1998a) 'Teaching Media Studies: "the cool thing to do"?' *Changing English* 5(2): 175–88.

Richards, C. (1998b) *Teen Spirits: Music and Identity in Media Education* London: UCL Press.

Richards, C. (1998c) 'Beyond classroom culture', in Buckingham, D. (ed.) *Teaching Popular Culture: Beyond Radical Pedagogy* London: UCL Press.

Richmond, J. (1990) 'What do we mean by Knowledge about Language?' in Carter, R. (ed.) *Knowledge about Language and the Curriculum: The LINC Reader* London: Hodder and Stoughton.

Rideout, V. J., Foehr, U. G., Roberts, D. F. and Brodie, M. (1999) *Kids & Media @ the New Millennium* Menlo Park, CA: Henry J. Kaiser Family Foundation.

Robson, J., Simmons, J. and Sohn-Rethel, M. (1990) 'Implementing a media education policy across the curriculum', in Buckingham, D. (ed.) *Watching Media Learning: Making Sense of Media Education* London: Falmer.

Rosen, M. (1997) '*Junk* and other realities: the tough world of children's fiction', *English and Media Magazine* 37: 4–6.

Salomon, G. (1979) *Interaction of Media, Cognition and Learning* San Francisco: Jossey-Bass.

Scholle, D. and Denski, S. (1994) *Media Education and the (Re)production of Culture* Westport, CT: Bergin and Garvey.

Schwichtenberg, C. (ed.) (1993) *The Madonna Connection: Representational Politics, Subcultural Identities and Cultural Theory* Boulder, CO: Westview.

Scribner, S. and Cole, M. (1981) *The Psychology of Literacy* Cambridge, MA: Harvard University Press.

Sefton-Green, J. (1990) 'Teaching and learning about representation: culture and *The Cosby Show* in a north London comprehensive', in Buckingham, D. (ed.) *Watching Media Learning: Making Sense of Media Education* London: Falmer.

Sefton-Green, J. (1995) 'Neither reading nor writing: the history of practical work in media education', *Changing English* 2(2): 77–96.

Sefton-Green, J. (1999) 'Media education, but not as we know it: digital technology and the end of media studies?' *English and Media Magazine* 40: 28–34.

Sefton-Green, J. (2000) 'From creativity to cultural production: shared perspectives', in Sefton-Green, J. and Sinker, R. (eds) *Evaluating Creativity: Making and Learning by Young People* London: Routledge.

Sefton-Green, J. and Buckingham, D. (1996) 'Digital visions: young people's "creative" uses of multimedia technologies in the home', *Convergence* 2(2): 47–79.

Sefton-Green, J. and Sinker, R. (eds) (2000) *Evaluating Creativity: Making and Learning by Young People* London: Routledge.

Seiter, E. (1993) *Sold Separately: Parents and Children in Consumer Culture* Brunswick, NJ: Rutgers University Press.

Selfe, C. (2000) 'Digital divisions: cultural perspectives on information technology', *English and Media Magazine* 42–3: 12–17.

Selwood, S. (1997) 'Cultural policy and young people's participation in the visual arts', *Journal of Art and Design Education* 16(3): 333–40.

Shotter, J. (1993) *Cultural Politics of Everyday Life* Toronto: University of Toronto Press.

Silverstone, R. (1999) *Why Study the Media?* London: Sage.

Sinker, R. (1999) 'The Rosendale Odyssey: multimedia memoirs and digital journeys', in Sefton-Green, J. (ed.) *Young People, Creativity and New Technologies* London: Routledge.

Sinker, R. (2000) 'Making multimedia: evaluating young people's creative multimedia production', in Sefton-Green, J. and Sinker, R. (eds) *Evaluating Creativity: Making and Learning by Young People* London: Routledge.

Smith, R., Anderson, D. and Fisher, C. (1985) 'Young children's comprehension of montage', *Child Development* 56: 962–71.

Spence, J. (1986) *Putting Myself in the Picture* London: Camden Press.

Spencer, M. (1986) 'Emergent literacies: a site for analysis', *Language Arts* 63(5): 442–53.

Stafford, R. (1990) 'Redefining creativity: extended project work in GCSE Media Studies', in Buckingham, D. (ed.) *Watching Media Learning: Making Sense of Media Education* London: Falmer.

Stafford, R. (1994) *Hands On* London: British Film Institute.

Stern, S. (1999) 'Adolescent girls' expression on web home pages: spirited, sombre and self-conscious sites', *Convergence* 5(4): 22–41.

Street, B. (1984) *Literacy in Theory and Practice* Cambridge: Cambridge University Press.

Tapscott, D. (1998) *Growing Up Digital: The Rise of the Net Generation* New York: McGraw-Hill.

Turnbull, S. (1998) 'Dealing with feeling: why Girl Number Twenty still doesn't answer', in Buckingham, D. (ed.) *Teaching Popular Culture: Beyond Radical Pedagogy* London: UCL Press.

Tyner, K. (1998) *Literacy in a Digital World* Mahwah, NJ: Erlbaum.

Usher, R. and Edwards, R. (1994) *Postmodernism and Education* London: Routledge.

Van der Voort, T., Beentjes, J., Bovill, M., Gaskell, G., Koolstra, C., Livingstone, S. and Marseille, N. (1998) 'Young people's ownership of new and old forms of media in Britain and the Netherlands', *European Journal of Communication* 13(4): 457–77.

Von Feilitzen, C. and Carlsson, U. (1999) *Children and the Media: Image, Education, Participation* Göteborg, Sweden: UNESCO.

Vygotsky, L. (1962) *Thought and Language* Cambridge, MA: MIT Press.

Vygotsky, L. (1978) *Mind and Society* Cambridge, MA: Harvard University Press.

Waltermann, J. and Machill, M. (eds) (2000) *Protecting our Children on the Internet* Gütersloh, Germany: Bertelsmann Foundation.

Wartella, E., Heintz, K. E., Aidman, A. J. and Mazzarella, S. R. (1990) 'Television and beyond: children's video media in one community', *Communications Research* 17(1): 45–64.

Watts Pailliotet, A. and Mosenthal, P. (eds) (2000) *Reconceptualizing Literacy in the Media Age* Stamford, CT: JAI Press.

Wells, P. (2002) ' "Tell me about your Id, when you was a kid, yah?" Animation and children's television culture', in Buckingham, D. (ed.) *Small Screens: Television for Children* Leicester: Leicester University Press.

Wertsch, J. (1990) 'The voice of rationality in a sociocultural approach to mind', in Moll, L. (ed.) *Vygotsky and Education* Cambridge: Cambridge University Press.

Willener, A., Milliard, G. and Ganty, A. (1976) *Videology and Utopia* London: Routledge and Kegan Paul.

Willett, R. (2001) 'Children's Use of Popular Media in their Creative Writing', PhD thesis, Institute of Education, University of London.

Williams, R. (1958) *Culture and Society* London: Chatto and Windus.

Williams, R. (1961) *The Long Revolution* London: Chatto and Windus.

Williams, S. (1999) 'Roath village web: the Marlborough Road online school scrapbook', in Sefton-Green, J. (ed.) *Young People, Creativity and New Technologies* London: Routledge.

Williamson, J. (1981/2) 'How does Girl Number Twenty understand ideology?' *Screen Education* 40: 80–7.

Willis, P. (1990) *Common Culture: Symbolic Work at Play in the Everyday Cultures of the Young* Buckingham: Open University Press.

Worsnop, C. (1996) *Assessing Media Work: Authentic Assessment in Media Education* Mississauga, Ontario: Wright Communications.

Young, B. (1990) *Children and Television Advertising* Oxford: Oxford University Press.

Index

Action for Children's Television 100
activism 99–100
advertising 30, 63–5, 71–3, 109, 111–14
Alliance for Children and Television 100
Ally McBeal 118
art education 180, 183
assessment 47–8; *see also* evaluation
audiences 29–32, 59–61, 61–9, 73–7, 78–9, 94–5, 121, 146–9, 152–3, 166, 178, 187–8, 199

Bakhtin, M. 143, 164
Beach, R. 147
Beavis and Butthead 164
Bentley, T. 190
Big Brother 55, 76
Bragg, S. 148, 169–71
British Film Institute 40–2, 48, 70, 90
Buffy the Vampire Slayer 160
Burn, A. 185–6

chat rooms 175, 177
childhood, definitions of 19–22, 29, 31–2, 174, 176

children and media 5, 12, 15–16, 18–34, 42–7, 109–12
Children's Express 192
children's rights 31
churches 100
class, social 9–10, 46–7, 109–10, 113–14, 116–24, 157, 193–4, 195, 198
Cohen, P. 161, 194
Communications Studies 87
community media 99–100, 191–4, 195
conceptual learning 140–3, 145, 150–1, 158, 170, 184
consumer culture 26, 33, 159
content analysis 71
convergence 23, 27, 32
Cope, B. and Kalantzis, M. 134, 145–6
Cosby Show 117–18
creativity 127–9, 134, 137, 192; *see also* production, by students
critical pedagogy 108, 129
criticism, critical analysis 7, 33–4, 38, 42, 43–7, 83–4, 97, 102, 107–22, 125, 142–3, 145, 162, 171–2; *see also* textual analysis
Croft, Lara 160
cultural imperialism 10, 100

Cultural Studies 7
curriculum 68–9, 86–103

deconstruction 125, 127
demystification 8–9, 108
deschooling 201–3
development, child 40, 42–7, 139–40
Dewdney, A. and Lister, M. 194–6
Dickens, C. 114–15
digital divide 26–7, 181
digital media 23–4, 82–3, 95–7, 133, 173–88; *see also* internet; technology
discrimination 6–7
Disney 28–9
documentary 65–7
Dowmunt, T. 192
drama 135–6
Dyson, A. H. 128, 163–4

economics, of media 25–9, 54–5, 173–4
educational media 4–5, 90, 92, 179–80
educational policy 33, 87–8, 101–3, 202
Educational Video Center 192
English and Media Centre 61, 70, 90
English teaching 9, 49, 89, 93–6, 119–20, 121–2, 128–9, 184–5
ethnicity 116–17, 148–9, 161, 167, 169
evaluation 84, 128, 149–53, 166–8, 171–2, 199–201

fan culture 190
Ferguson, B. 124, 127
Film Education Working Group 40
Film Studies 87
Forum for Children's and Citizen's Television 100
Fraser, P. 112–14
Funge, E. 159–61

games 24, 174–5, 177, 181–2
gender 45, 112–14, 115–19, 130, 159–61, 166–8, 169, 176
genre 134–7, 169–70
globalization 25–6
Goodman, S. 200
Grace, D. and Tobin, J. 164, 168
Grahame, J. 61ff., 132–3, 135, 151–2
Grossberg, L. 107–8

Hall, R. and Newbury, D. 201
Hall, S. and Whannel, P. 7–8
Harvey, I. 153, 193–4
Hebdige, D. 194
Heller, C. 192
Hodge, B. and Tripp, D. 47
Hoggart, R. 7–8, 10

ICTs: *see* digital media
identity 15–17, 65–7, 129, 147, 159–61, 162, 167–8, 169
ideology 8, 72, 108, 114–19, 126, 134; *see also* representation
Illich, I. 201–3
imitation 124–5, 134, 136
informal learning 189–203
interactivity 27, 30
internet 20, 25, 95–7, 137, 176–9, 181–3, 187, 190, 193, 202–3
intertextuality 27–8, 135–6

Jeong, H.-S. 117–18, 130, 198–9
Jones, A. 182–3

Katz, J. 174
Kenway, J. and Bullen, E. 33
Kinder, M. 29
knowledge, definitions of 92, 142, 149
Kress, G. 36, 185

Lachs, V. 179
language, media 2, 36–7, 43, 55–7, 61–9, 71–3, 76, 77–9, 82, 112–14, 131–3, 134, 144–5, 150, 175–6, 178, 183–5, 186; *see also* literacy, media

Lave, J. and Wenger, E. 176
learning 14–15, 70–1, 84–5,
    119–21, 131–3, 138–54, 164,
    168, 175–6, 183–5, 188, 190,
    196–7, 201–2
Leavis, F. R. and Thompson, D.
    6–8, 10, 107, 124
literacy, media 4, 30, 35–50, 82, 97,
    131, 175–9, 181
literature: *see* English teaching
Livingstone, S. and Bovill, M. 181
Lorac, C. and Weiss, M. 89
Luhrmann, B. 79
Luke, C. 38–9

Madonna 161
Marsh, J. and Millard, E. 157–8
Masterman, L. 8, 71, 98, 107–8,
    121, 123–5, 191
Mayman, N. 112–14
McLaughlin, M. and Heath, S. 192
media, definition of 1–2
media education
    across curriculum 89–93
    aims 5–6, 13, 67–8
    definition of 4–5, 53, 84, 95, 97,
        179–81
    promotion of 87–8, 101–3
media effects 11, 31, 46, 109,
    111–12, 118–19; *see also*
    children and media
Media Studies 87, 89, 93, 119–20,
    127, 137, 167, 183, 195
Messaris, P. 36–7
metalanguage 73, 144–5, 185
Mighty Morphin' Power Rangers 28,
    163
Modern Review 110
morality 11
Morgan, R. 108, 191
multiliteracies 38, 145
Murdoch, R. 55
Murdock, G. and Phelps, G. 8,
    153, 191

National Curriculum (England)
    40, 88–9, 94

National Film Board of Canada 191
Newsom Report 8
Nickelodeon 31–2

parents 101
parody 134, 161, 165–8
personal response 118, 121, 148–9
photography 65–7, 129, 194–6
play 114, 122, 135–6, 137, 162–4,
    165, 168, 171
pleasure 110, 118–19, 162, 167–8
Pokemon 28, 33, 190
political correctness 116–17, 135,
    161, 164, 166–8, 198–9
popular music 80, 130, 135, 197–8
Popular Television and Schoolchildren
    89
Postman, N. 19–20, 29
postmodernity 16, 28, 158–61, 162,
    165–6, 171–2
privatization 25–7
production, of media 54–5, 61–9,
    73–7, 79–81, 94–5, 114, 121–2,
    135, 178; *see also* economics;
    technologies
production, by students 14, 49–50,
    55, 57, 59, 82–4, 89–90, 92, 96,
    98, 113–14, 122–38, 162,
    164–72, 179–88, 191–201
    and creativity 127–8
    and critical analysis 133, 153–4,
        184
    collaborative aspects of 128–31,
        137, 162, 187
    see also simulation; vocational
        training
protectionism 10–12, 33, 101, 126

quality: *see* value

race: *see* ethnicity
racism 10, 117, 161
Raney, K. and Hollands, H. 146
rationality 143, 170–1
reality, children's judgements
    of 42–8, 109, 141; *see also*
    representation

regulation, of media 11, 12–13, 24–5, 54, 60
representation 3, 40–2, 57–9, 61–9, 76, 112–14, 114–19, 129, 141, 159–61, 167–8, 178, 195
research, by students 60–1, 75–7, 146–9
Richards, C. 147, 191
Richmond, J. 150

Saussure, F. de 36
scheduling (TV) 80
schooling 189, 195–6
Screen, Screen Education 8, 10
Sefton-Green, J. 117, 119–20, 128–30, 135–7, 148–50, 167–8, 181–2, 184–6
self-evaluation: *see* evaluation
Selwood, S. 199–200
semiology, semiotics 8–9, 36, 56; *see also* textual analysis
Sesame Street 28
sexism 10
Shakespeare, W. 79
Shotter, J. 170
Silverstone, R. 5, 49, 162
Simpsons, The 28, 62–3, 68–9
simulation 79–81, 127, 135, 151–2, 167
Sinker, R. 180
SMTV Live 28
Spice Girls 160, 163
Springer, Jerry 190
stereotyping 44, 58–9, 141, 160–1, 163
storyboards 73, 133

Tapscott, D. 20, 27
teaching strategies 53–85

technology 23–5, 54, 56, 125–6, 186–7; *see also* digital media; internet
Teenage Mutant Ninja Turtles 28
Teletubbies 27
textual analysis 8–9, 49, 72–3, 113–14, 117, 120–1, 145; *see also* criticism
Three Ninjas 163
Titanic 163
training: *see* vocational training
'translation' 77–9, 150
Turnbull, S. 116, 121, 170

United Nations Convention on the Rights of the Child 22
Use of English 7
Usher, R. and Edwards, R. 16, 162

value 7–10, 72–3, 146–8, 200
vocational training 98–9, 124, 131, 193–4, 198
Vygotsky, L. 140–3

Wertsch, J. 142
Who Wants to be a Millionaire? 55
Willett, R. 136, 163–4
Williams, R. 7, 10
Williamson, J. 114–16, 160
Willis, P. 192
world wide web: *see* internet
writing 150–1, 163–4

Xena, Warrior Princess 160
X-Men 163

youth culture 160, 193–4, 196
youth work 130–1, 181–2, 191, 195–201

Lightning Source UK Ltd.
Milton Keynes UK
UKOW05f0103220217

295009UK00001B/109/P